Grace & Gumption

The Women of El Paso

edited by Marcia Hatfield Daudistel

TCU Press
Fort Worth, Texas

Library of Congress Cataloging-in-Publication Data

Grace and gumption : the women of El Paso / edited by
Marcia Hatfield Daudistel.
p. cm.
Includes bibliographical references and index.
ISBN 978-0-87565-430-0
1. Women--Texas--El Paso--History. 2. Women--Texas--El
Paso--Biography. 3. El Paso (Tex.)--History. 4. El Paso
(Tex.)--Biography. 5. El Paso (Tex.)--Social conditions. I.
Daudistel, Marcia Hatfield.
HQ1439.E4G73 2011
920.7209764'96--dc22
2011003035

TCU Press
P.O. Box 298300
Fort Worth, Texas 76129
817.257.7822
http://www.prs.tcu.edu
To order books: 800.826.8911

Book Design by Barbara Mathews Whitehead

For our mothers and grandmothers

Por nuestras madres y abuelas

Who led the way

Contents

Acknowledgments

GRACE AND GUMPTION: *The Women of El Paso* would not have been possible without the generosity of the families and friends of the women featured in the book. They shared their memories and photographs with us and we are grateful for their time and effort.

I was approached by TCU Press while I was working on *Literary El Paso,* part of their Literary Cities Series, to be the editor for this book. I happily agreed because the concept of gathering twelve El Paso women writers to each write a chapter on early El Paso women was an intriguing one. For the second book in the series, we followed the same guidelines as *Grace and Gumption: Stories of Fort Worth Women,* which were that the women in the book must be deceased and each chapter would be either written by a different contributor or jointly written. What we all had in common is our connection with The University of Texas at El Paso, either as faculty members, alumna, or as active members of the university community. We met every four to six weeks over late afternoon wine or tea and began to plan the book. Our group meetings were always lively, and information was shared about who should be included, and some swapping of names was negotiated.

Categorizing women is a difficult task; some women appear in more than one chapter because their accomplishments could not be limited to one category. The women in this book are not necessarily the most prominent women who lived in El Paso; by concentrating on a few women per chapter, we were able to provide more depth to the women chosen by each writer. We gave each other suggestions and leads for articles and photographs when there were no surviving family members of our selected subjects.

We also thank the staff of the Special Collections Department of The University of Texas at El Paso Library and Claudia Rivers, the Director of Special Collections, for her encyclopedic knowledge of El Paso and her assistance in locating images and resources for us.

Now that the project is finished, I thank the writers for their enthusiasm and fine work. The experience was a very pleasant one. We heard stories and discovered information that not only surprised us, but also gave us a new appreciation for the women who came before us. Their stories are inspiring, and in the hopes that these stories will go on to inspire the young women of El Paso, all royalties from *Grace and Gumption: the Women of El Paso* will be given to the Women's Studies Program at The University of Texas at El Paso.

Introduction

Words such as courage, pluck, grit, and forbearance are used to describe the women settlers of the United States. The word gumption is the one that most aptly describes the women of Texas. Gumption has the attributes of the other words, but has an added élan, a spirit, a sense of style that is particularly Texan. The experiences of early Texas women settlers are as varied as the landscape of Texas. These women made their homes in towns or on farms set in the lush, green, east Texas piney woods or in dusty, west Texas desert frontier towns or ranches surrounded by mountains. The vastness of Texas separated towns, ranches, and cities by many miles. The women of El Paso did not only come south and west from within the United States as citizens of this country or as immigrants from other countries, but north from Mexico. Many women and children boarded trains to flee from the Mexican Revolution and established homes in El Paso.

Writer George Covington, in an article for the *Alpine Avalanche* wrote: "I once said that our West Texas women were so tough they used tarantulas as powder puffs. Actually, they're tougher." This was certainly true of the women who followed husbands and fathers to El Paso, or even those who came alone. Women typically followed after the men set about establishing law and order on the frontier. El Paso, just across the Rio Grande from Ciudad Juárez, Mexico, had a colorful history of gunfighters, gamblers, confidence men, and brothels. It was in this atmosphere of lawlessness that sheriffs, deputies, politicians, attorneys, physicians, and journalists began to shape El Paso into a town that would be a safe home for their wives, daughters, and children.

Law and order could not be imposed overnight, so gunfighters and criminals such as John Wesley Hardin, Billy the Kid, and former criminal-turned-lawman John Selman fought with lawmen Pat Garrett, Bass Outlaw, and Dallas Stoudenmire. In the 1890s, El Paso became known, according to historian C. L. Sonnichsen, as the "six-shooter capital of the

West" and also earned the name "the Monte Carlo of the West" for the easy availability of saloons, gambling, and prostitution. When the railroad came to El Paso, the city became a hub for the dispatch of goods to people within hundreds of miles of surrounding territory in Texas and New Mexico, making El Paso less isolated.

The women who came to El Paso faced an unusual reality. In 1848 the Treaty of Guadalupe Hidalgo changed the border of the United States, and people who were previously citizens of Mexico—living in their native country, speaking their native language—were suddenly citizens of the United States, learning to speak a foreign language. So there was a language barrier for both the early citizens, the ones originally in Mexico, and for the newcomers. Later, the Mexican Revolution fought just across the Rio Grande was a backdrop to life in El Paso. Pancho Villa and his men and General "Black Jack" Pershing were familiar faces in El Paso, frequenting downtown hotels and bars. As a child, the artist and writer Tom Lea, whose father was mayor of El Paso, was threatened with kidnapping by Pancho Villa. With a revolution on their doorstep, the early women of El Paso had a very different experience in the development of this border city. They witnessed the Mexican Revolution from the rooftops of downtown buildings and even on the banks of the Rio Grande where families would bring picnics and watch the fighting across the river.

The landscape was also far from familiar to most of these women. It was difficult, if not impossible, to grow the familiar flowers and plants of their previous homes in this dry, arid climate. The Chihuahuan desert first appears brown and desolate. In time, the beautiful colors of the desert become evident to the eye: Desert Willows with their pink, purple, or white flowers; Texas Sage with its red, pink, or purple flowers; Chocolate Daisies; the Woolly Butterfly Bush with its silver leaves and orange ball flowers; the yellow trumpet flowers of the Yellow Bell and the Western Soapberry, with its creamy white blossoms, are only a few of the trees and plants that are part of the natural and vivid beauty of the desert.

The women came to a city of mountains. The Franklin Mountains at first glance are a looming, stark, rocky wall but in the light of sunrise or at sunset, the mountains catch fire in the intense orange light that contrasts with blue shadows. In time, they become a touchstone, a compass, and a soaring protective presence.

They came to a harsh climate. High desert winds caused spring windstorms of near biblical proportions; tumbleweeds flew through the air. Most of the annual rainfall came in middle to late summer during what is called the "monsoon season," a time of torrential rains. Intense summer heat combined with dry desert air was not kind to their skin. Scorpions, snakes, and lizards were also a fact of life.

The women who established homes on ranches and remote areas of Texas have left behind letters and journals, as well as the stories passed down from mothers and grandmothers to their daughters and granddaughters that have provided the information on their lives. Women who lived in more populated areas turned the small, dusty towns of west Texas into cities and left behind a more public record. The traditional wisdom is that women led obscure or hidden lives behind a wall of domesticity, but in fact they were hiding in plain sight. Their names did not appear on the front page of the newspaper, on political ballots, or on downtown buildings, but their names were well known throughout their communities from their work in establishing schools, libraries, medical facilities, and organizations that promoted art and culture to benefit the people of El Paso. Women were expected to be a civilizing influence on an emerging city, and that influence took hard, selfless work in addition to the responsibilities of home and family.

Among the women who have been influential in the history of El Paso are the orders of nuns, such as the Daughters of Charity, who came to El Paso in 1881 as nurses and hospital administrators and established Hotel Dieu Hospital; the Sisters of Loretto and the Sisters of Divine Providence, who were teachers and school administrators, and the Sisters of Charity, who acted as social workers and established St. Margaret's Orphanage. Answerable only to the hierarchy of their Mother Superior and the Roman Catholic Church, these women—already trained in their fields—were actively engaged in careers, particularly in administration, that lay women were discouraged from pursuing.

Long before women were considered capable of pursuing medical degrees, the *curanderas* were practicing the healing arts through the centuries-old tradition of herbalism. One of the most famous healers on the border was Teresita Urrea. Born in 1872 in Sinaloa, Mexico, she has been called "The Mexican Joan of Arc." Now, with the emphasis on holistic and natural approaches to health that has gained respect in traditional medical circles, the work of modern-day *curanderas* continues. As times changed in the early twentieth century, physicians Alice Blackadder Merchant and Ida Shope Bishop came to El Paso as trained medical professionals.

Women's voices were also heard through their writings in newspapers, books, and magazines. Journalist Peggy Hull, born in 1889, was the first woman from the *El Paso Morning Times* to be named a war correspondent in World War I by the State Department, and other women who wrote for El Paso newspapers found a way to work beyond their assigned society page beat. Clara Emily Guion Aguirre, while raising six children, wrote and published poetry until her nineties. Award-winning pioneer in Chicana literature, short story writer and playwright Estela Portillo Trambley also raised five children.

In addition, El Paso women expressed their creative talent through their art. They were not only artists, but also served as muses. Sarah Dighton Lea was the muse for her husband, artist Tom Lea. Sor Juana Inés de la Cruz was the muse for artist Martha Arat, and artist Gloria Osuna Perez was inspired by Coyolxauhqui, the Aztec goddess of the moon.

Equally inspiring was Maud Durlin Sullivan, who was instrumental in establishing the El Paso Public Library, and it was her influence on the budding artist Tom Lea that encouraged him to go to the Chicago Art Institute, where he studied and became an internationally known artist and writer. She also encouraged a young John Rechy, who wanted to be a writer and went on to be an award-winning, nationally prominent author.

It was Kathleen Lois Worrell, wife of the Dean of the Texas College of Mines, now The University of Texas at El Paso, who inspired the architects of the fledgling college to adopt the distinctive Bhutanese architecture that characterizes the now sprawling campus of over 22,000 students. Alzina Allis Orndorff DeGroff, a successful builder, left her mark on the architecture of downtown El Paso with the construction of the Cortez Building.

El Paso women were also successful businesswomen, parlaying their talents into commercial success. Mary Price and her sons ran Price's Dairy after she became a widow, and her perseverance and hard work made the business thrive. Hana Farah, an immigrant from Lebanon, founded Farah Shirt Manufacturing Company with her husband and sons. It grew to a multinational company with 9,500 employees at the height of its success. Effie Day, a proficient seamstress, became a successful dress designer after studying dressmaking in Paris and New York. Love of cooking earned Paula Rocha and Juanita Flores the reputation of legendary cooks at L & J Cafe. Paula's cooking methods, using less fat in traditional Mexican dishes, are particularly relevant today with the emphasis on healthy food preparation. Maria Vincenza Rosaria DiBonito married Joseph Ardovino and established Ardovino's Italian Gourmet Shop that became an El Paso tradition.

Attorney Ruth Kern, the only woman in her law school graduating class of 1946, left Chicago as a single mother and came to El Paso for her son's health. Unable to find work except as a legal secretary, she went on in later years to pass the State Bar of Texas and establish her own practice in El Paso, the only one headed by a woman in 1967. She was also politically active and involved in civic organizations, as was Maria del Socorro Ramirez, a resident of Sparks Colonia located in El Paso County, who worked tirelessly for improved living conditions, such as water availability at the city and state level.

Other civic and private organizations were founded with the goal of providing a better way of life for the citizens of El Paso. The Woman's Club of El Paso, one of the oldest of these organizations, not only sponsored cultural events, but supported many charitable projects. The local affiliate of the National Council of Jewish Women was formed to address border immigration problems. The YWCA continues the philanthropic work begun by the early women of El Paso. Olalee and Marshall McCall were active in the small African American community of El Paso. Their generous support ensured the establishment of a badly needed daycare center for African American children. Lucy Acosta, inducted into the Texas Women's Hall of Fame, founded the League of United Latin American Citizens' Project Amistad, a nonprofit agency that provides crucial services to the disabled and elderly citizens of El Paso.

The women of El Paso in this volume are just a few who left a living and enduring legacy in Texas. Their names live on, not only as part of the history of El Paso, but in the civic, political, and charitable organizations, and the schools and libraries of present day where their work continues. Their stories are kept alive through the memories of generations of their families, the oral history of *Las Comadres* and in the history books of El Paso. Their accomplishments were hard-won and required courage, persistence, and inspiration; but especially grace and gumption.

—Marcia Hatfield Daudistel

Chapter 1

THE ARTISTS AND THEIR MUSES

by Adair Margo

And now, O Muses, dwellers in the mansions of Olympus, tell me—
for you are goddesses and are in all places so that you see all
things, while we know nothing but by report. . .

Homer (c. 700 BC) Book II, *The Iliad*

THROUGHOUT THE HISTORY OF ART there have been stories of Muses—women who inspire artists to great literature and art. In medieval Florence, Beatrice awakened a vital spirit within Dante, who fell in love with her at first sight, borrowing Homer's words to describe her not as the daughter of a mortal man, but of a god. He carried an idealized image of Beatrice in his mind's eye throughout his life, though they met only twice and she died prematurely. Dante wrote that Love ruled his soul from the time he saw Beatrice, and that she removed all evil intentions from his being. It was Beatrice—her name implying beatific love—who inspired his literary masterpiece, *The Divine Comedy,* giving birth to the Italian language.

Another epic love story took place on the banks of the Rio Grande, where desert mountains rise above the cities of El Paso and Ciudad Juárez. It is a story about Sarah Dighton, who inspired artist Tom Lea to paint his magnum opus. Unlike Beatrice and Dante, whose love was distant and unrequited, Sarah and Tom knew each other completely as husband and wife, and were married for sixty-three years.

Twenty-four-year-old Sarah Dighton came into Tom Lea's life in 1938, traveling from Monticello, Illinois, to El Paso to visit a childhood friend. She had never been to the desert before, nor had she ever met an artist. She came from a green world of cornfields and shade trees where farms extended as far as the eye could see.

Sarah attended Monticello Academy near Godfrey before entering the University of Illinois. There she met a man, leaving school to marry him and give birth to a son she named James Dighton. When the marriage did not last, Sarah moved back home with her parents and her son, working as a bookkeeper at Monticello

National Bank. She had a precise and very sharp mind.

One of Sarah's friends named Catherine Hawbacker Pogson lived in El Paso, where her husband, Percy, worked for his father's accounting firm, Pogson Peloubet. In 1938, after they were settled, Catherine invited Sarah to visit the couple in El Paso. As an added inducement for the trip, Catherine described the loveliness of the desert vistas and mentioned that Percy had a childhood friend named Tom Lea whose wife had died two years before.

That first night Sarah met Tom Lea, sitting across the table from him in the Pogson's dining room. Immediately she noticed Tom's interest in her, his eyes brightening when he saw her face. The evening was too short for both of them, but the enlivening of their spirits had just begun. Sarah did not know that after his wife had died, Tom wondered if his heart could be filled again. Tom's mother and grandmother died that same year, leaving him bereft of the women he loved the most.

The two continued to see each other during Sarah's visit. One night, after viewing Tom's mural *Pass of the North* in the federal courthouse, they drove to McKelligon Canyon on the east side of Mount Franklin with the sloping windows of his Nash coupe partway down. With walls of rock narrowing their view of the sky, Tom asked Sarah to marry him. Looking at him, she said she would like to, but hesitated since it all seemed so fast. The next night after going to a club in Zaragoza, just across the wooden bridge below Ysleta, Tom stopped his Nash on Robinson Street near the Pogson's home, asking, "Will you, please?" Sarah responded, "Why yes, I want to—but Tom you need to meet my parents."

In early July 1938, Tom finished his mural on which he painted the words "Tom + Sarah" in small letters on the frontiersman's powder horn strap. Giving up his studio because he could no longer afford it, Tom drove to Monticello where Sarah was waiting for him. He was feeling flush with the four thousand dollars he had been paid for his mural of giants—the mural they had seen on Sarah's second night in El Paso.

The Dightons were delightful, Sarah's mother treating Tom with special consideration since he had lost his own mother. She did have concerns, though, asking her daughter in a private moment how she expected to live on an artist's income. "Watch me," is what Sarah said.

Sarah learned to cook and welcomed Tom's friends who would come over periodically in the evenings. Sometimes they would draw pictures about their conversations like the watercolors Sarah painted about the "artsy" world of Hollywood and the romantic novelist Ursula Parrott who was very much in the news. The lives of Picasso and the confused Mrs. Parrott were far removed from her own.

Tom's first portrait of Sarah was done on a sleeping porch of their third floor apartment where there was good light. It speaks of her living in the desert southwest and becoming a part of it. The folds of her tawny dress repeat those of the earth behind her. After painting it in 1939, Tom submitted the portrait to the All-Texas exhibition and it won a prize. At the time, IBM was buying paintings to represent each state in the union for a show that would travel the world. Sarah's portrait was chosen to represent Texas.

The couple spent the summer of 1939 in Monticello, a "wonderful summer of quietness." It was a land graced with green trees and softened

Above: Tom Lea. *Sarah (Portrait of the artist's wife)*, 1939. Oil on panel, 34 X 26-1/4". *Collection of the El Paso Museum of Art, gift of IBM.*

Right: Tom Lea. *Sarah in the Summertime*, 1947. Oil on canvas, 69 X 28". *Collection of Dr. James Dighton Lea, Houston, Texas.*

Sarah Lea. *Portrait of Ursula Parrott at Work,* 1939. Watercolor, 9-1/2 x 12-1/2".
Courtesy of Adair Margo Fine Art, El Paso, Texas.

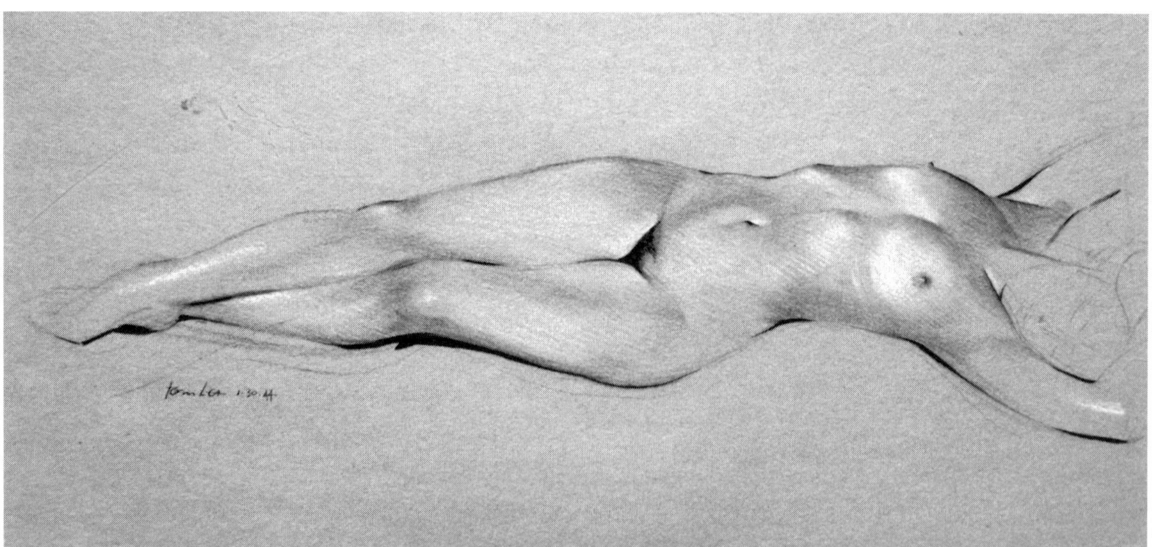

Tom Lea. *Reclining Nude,* 1944. Carbon pencil, India ink, and chalk, 18 x 12".
Collection of Mr. and Mrs. James H. Clement Jr., Dallas, Texas.

by rain, the opposite of the bare desert with its open space and sense of antiquity.

Sarah's son, Jim, came to live with Sarah and Tom a year after they were married, and Tom adopted him as his beloved son. The three temporarily moved into a one-room unfurnished apartment where they lived with a painting called *Lonely Town* on the wall. A Navajo blanket over a cardboard box was the coffee table, and Jim thought it the most beautiful place in the world.

Sarah felt settled after they found a white stucco house on Raynolds Boulevard with a view of the sunrise side of Mount Franklin. A studio for Tom was built in the back where he continued to work on his murals and make illustrations for J. Frank Dobie's books. Sarah stayed busy, volunteering in the community and raising money for worthy causes. She earned the name of a "gold dust girl" since no one could turn her down.

Tom and Sarah Lea, 1944.
Courtesy of C.L. Sonnichsen Special Collections Department, University of Texas at El Paso Library.

When Tom traveled as an artist correspondent during World War II, witnessing men waging war worldwide, he carried a snapshot of Sarah in his wallet, a picture of her standing in the light of their backyard at home. She wore a bodiced dress of pink and blue flowers on a field of white, and he looked at it, homesick, from a war-torn world.

Just as Dante carried "the glorious woman of my mind" with him long after Beatrice had died, Tom looked at Sarah's picture with a "distant kind of worship" when she was thousands of miles away. Sarah would pose for Tom when he returned home as a reprieve from his consuming work of painting war. On warm brown paper in 1944, Tom drew her nude form as if it were a desert landscape with light on bare mountains and the twisting line of a valley. Carl Sandburg's quote that "a mountain is something that's fastened down, something you can count on," applied to Sarah, too.

When he returned home for good, Tom had Sarah pose for him just as she was in the photograph so that he could capture the likeness he had gazed upon with so much longing. When immediate demands would pull him away, his interest in the painting would increase rather than diminish. He desired to get back to it, returning to the canvas each time with renewed devotion.

It took Tom two years to complete the paint-

Martha Arat. *Sor Juana Cuts Her Hair,* c. 1992. Oil on canvas. *Courtesy of Dr. Arsavir Arat, El Paso, Texas.*

ing, and when he did he signed it, framed it, and gave it to Sarah. It was placed on a wall in the living room of their home where he saw it every day. When asked to name his greatest work toward the end of his life, Tom said it was *Sarah in the Summertime,* and that the reason he loved it most was because he knew her. Before his death on January 29, 2001, the *El Paso Times* took a photo of Tom sitting in the living room of his home on the east side of Mount Franklin with *Sarah in the Summertime* hanging on the wall behind him.

Sor Juana Inés de la Cruz, "the Tenth Muse of Mexico," was the primary inspiration for El Paso painter Martha Arat. Born Juana Inés de Asbaje y Ramìrez de Santillana on November 12, 1648, she was a great intellectual, dramatist, and poet. Unlike the Muses—the nine mythical daughters of Zeus who ruled over the arts and sciences from Mount Olympus and never grew old—Sor Juana Inés was born of Spanish descent in a small village outside of Mexico City and died of the plague when she was forty-seven years old.

Registered a "daughter of the church" because she was illegitimate, Juana Inés was precocious and curious, studying the books in her grandfather's library. She was reading at the age of three and learning Latin by age nine. When long, beautiful hair on a young girl was esteemed, Juana Inés cut hers off when she didn't learn Latin in the time frame she had set, wondering why "hair should cover a head that was so bare of fact—the more desirable adornment." Juana Inés' remarkable knowledge earned her the reputation of a prodigy which brought her to the attention of the viceregal court. There she served as a lady-in-waiting. The Marquis de Mancera tested her knowledge against the most learned men visiting his court, and her brilliance amazed poets, theologians, and mathematicians. Court life, however, was unsatisfying for Juana Inés and with few options to pursue her love of learning, she entered the Convent of the Order of St. Jerome becoming Sor (meaning "Sister") Juana Inés de la Cruz when she was seventeen years old. There she was allowed to build her own library, hold intellectual court with her friends, and write poetry, plays, and letters. She became one of the greatest writers of the Spanish baroque period and an inspiration for the intellectual pursuits of Hispanic women.

Martha Arat studied the writings of Sor Juana Inés de la Cruz and dedicated over ten

Martha Arat. *Tarahumara Girl,* ca. 1980. Pastel on paper.
Courtesy of Dr. Arsavir Arat, El Paso, Texas.

years painting stories from her life. Martha felt a kinship with the Catholic nun whom Octavio Paz described as "curious about the world and about herself, about what happened in the world and what happened inside herself."

Born November 18, 1932, to Carmen and Enrique Amaya in Ciudad Juárez, Mexico, Martha loved to draw from the time she was a small girl. According to her family, she was attracted to the beautiful and the good, and that's what she aimed to record. Her mother was a housewife and her father helped farmers open water wells to irrigate their crops. Both were self-taught, her father a voracious reader of Mexican and world history who instilled a love of reading in his daughter.

Like many in El Paso/Juárez, Martha Amaya was educated on both sides of the border, attending elementary and secondary classes in Ciudad Juárez before going to El Paso for secretarial school. She learned the skill of bookkeeping and found a job at Hotel Dieu Hospital that was founded by the Daughters of Charity in 1892. While working as an assistant to the sister in charge of finance, Martha met a young intern of Armenian descent.

Arsavir Arat had studied medicine in Istanbul before coming to the United States. He was smitten by the beautiful Martha with her quiet elegance and her smooth white skin. They married and had a boy and a girl, Sarkis and Claudia, and built a home on the slopes of

Martha Arat. *Father Kino Visits Sor Juana and Her Friend, Siguenza y Gongora,* ca. 1992. Oil on canvas.
Courtesy of Dr. Arsavir Arat, El Paso, Texas.

Mount Franklin in an area named for the Spanish explorer Coronado. The elaborate stone molding carved for their front door evoked the baroque Mexico of Sor Juana Inés de la Cruz.

Following the example of her muse, Martha Arat lived a life of inquiry, continuing the drawing she began as a girl while she observed and recorded the world around her. Her drawing, she wrote, was "an attempt to capture the essence of life itself—the eternal seeking of mankind to find a place in the scheme of things."

Pushing herself to experiment, Martha attended The University of Texas at El Paso where she studied sculpture, printmaking, ceramics, and painting. The subject she loved most was the human figure that she created in oil and clay and bronze. Just as Sor Juana Inés' writings were layered with foreign accents and phrases including those of the indigenous Nahua, Martha Arat painted the native women of Mexico, including the Tarahumara of Chihuahua's Barrancas del Cobre. Though separated by centuries, both women found beauty in every strata of Mexican society and in the traditions of the native peoples.

When Sor Juana Inés was persecuted for her desire to learn and ordered by the bishop of Puebla to refrain from intellectual pursuits, she responded with a defense of women's God-given right to knowledge. Her writings became an

Martha Arat. *Calla Lillies*, 1991. Oil on canvas.
Courtesy of Dr. Arsavir Arat, El Paso, Texas.

important document in the emancipation of her sex. Martha Arat had the support of her husband who encouraged her to pursue her art; however, when she witnessed Hispanic men discouraging their wives from fulfilling themselves, she spoke out: "If the man tells his wife to not be creative, then that's it. But the woman has to learn to fight for her rights. She must struggle to express herself. . . ."

Arat's paintings were strong representations of women on the US/Mexico border as a source of life and change. She wrote, "My work presents images taken from the beauty and diversity of my people, their hopes, aspirations, and dreams." Remaining a classicist, her paintings never devolved into a purely personal language but spoke universally.

Many were drawn to Martha Arat's work and asked to use her paintings to communicate their messages. Always willing to share, she allowed the use of her images for invitations, posters, and books. Her *El Paso Mona Lisa* became the logo of the El Paso Arts Resources Department and *Calla Lillies* was used by the Mexican American Legal Defense and Eduational Fund (MALDEF).

La Perla—in which a pearl rests on the upturned palm of a woman who offers it to another woman—graces the cover of *Desert Echo: Women Illuminate the Sacred,* a book of

Left: Martha Arat. *La Perla,* 1992. Oil on canvas, 33 x 29". *Collection of Juan A. Sandoval.*

Below Left: Martha Arat. *Oyeme con los ojos,* 1992. Oil on canvas. *Courtesy of Dr. Arsavir Arat, El Paso, Texas.*

Below Right: Martha Arat, c. 2000. *Courtesy of Dr. Arsavir Arat, El Paso, Texas.*

poetry and paintings that benefitted the Women's Museum in Dallas. It was enlarged into banners for the opening and came to represent the best of a woman's character—her helpfulness towards others and her willingness to share.

During the quincentenary of the "Tenth Muse of Mexico" in 1992, Ciudad Juárez and El Paso hosted a celebration titled *Oyeme con los ojos, Sor Juana Inés de la Cruz.* The program announcing the scholarly panels, comic operas, and poetry readings had a beautiful portrait of Sor Juana Inés on its cover, her skin smooth and white, her inquisitive eyes looking out. It was a painting in the exhibition of work by Martha Arat organized as part of the celebration and entitled *Sor Juana Inés de la Cruz: Mujer de todos los tiempos.*

Martha Arat died on April 23, 2002, five years after being diagnosed with a cancerous tumor on her kidney. The cities of El Paso and Ciudad Juárez mourned her passing. Like the muse who inspired her, she had become a woman for all times. The story of her life and the testimony of her paintings will speak to the eyes, hearts and minds of generations to come.

Coyolxauhqui, the Aztec goddess of the moon, was the muse of Gloria Osuna Perez who first saw her in Mexico City. A monolithic stone bearing her image was unearthed in 1978 on the precise site of the Templo Mayor, one of the main Aztec temples in their capital city of Tenochtitlan. Osuna Perez saw "a woman lying on the ground who had been dismembered into five sections with serpent knots on various parts of her body. The life-blood is flowing from her and mixing with the earth to give life to mankind," she wrote. She found the expression on her face so beautiful that she could not get it out of her mind.

A woman of intellectual curiosity and commitment to hard work, Gloria Osuna Perez began a quest for the meaning of *Coyolxauhqui,* her name derived from the Nahuatl—"she who paints rattles on her face." The goddess was the moon who struggled against Huitzilopochti, her brother the sun. When she fell to earth, she created life through her own death and a harmony between the earth and the sky. Like other pre-Columbian stone monuments, Coyolxauhqui was an astrological map, although Osuna Perez was most interested in personifying her as a woman.

The idea of an installation made up of a stylized facsimile of the monolith discovered in 1978, juxtaposed with five portraits of accomplished women from Mexico and five from the southwestern United States took hold of her. "What I tried to do was tie in the pre-Columbian image of the nurturing woman to women I would like to learn more about because of the important things that they did," Osuna Perez wrote.

The project took twenty months to research and the installation of *Coyolxauhqui, Madre Cósmica* was displayed at the El Paso Museum of Art in 1996. Osuna Perez's facsimile was six feet in diameter, a mosaic of individual tiles fired in her kiln by moonlight. The dignified portraits of women were painted in her distinctive style using acrylics, although their strong faces looked as if formed of dark clay.

The Mexican women chosen were Leona Vicario, who facilitated communications through the wives of Mexican patriots fighting for independence from Spain; Dolores Jiménez y Muro, a colonel in Zapata's revolutionary army; Nahui Olin, a poet, artist, and model for Diego Rivera; Rosaura Revueltas, the actress in *Salt of the Earth,*

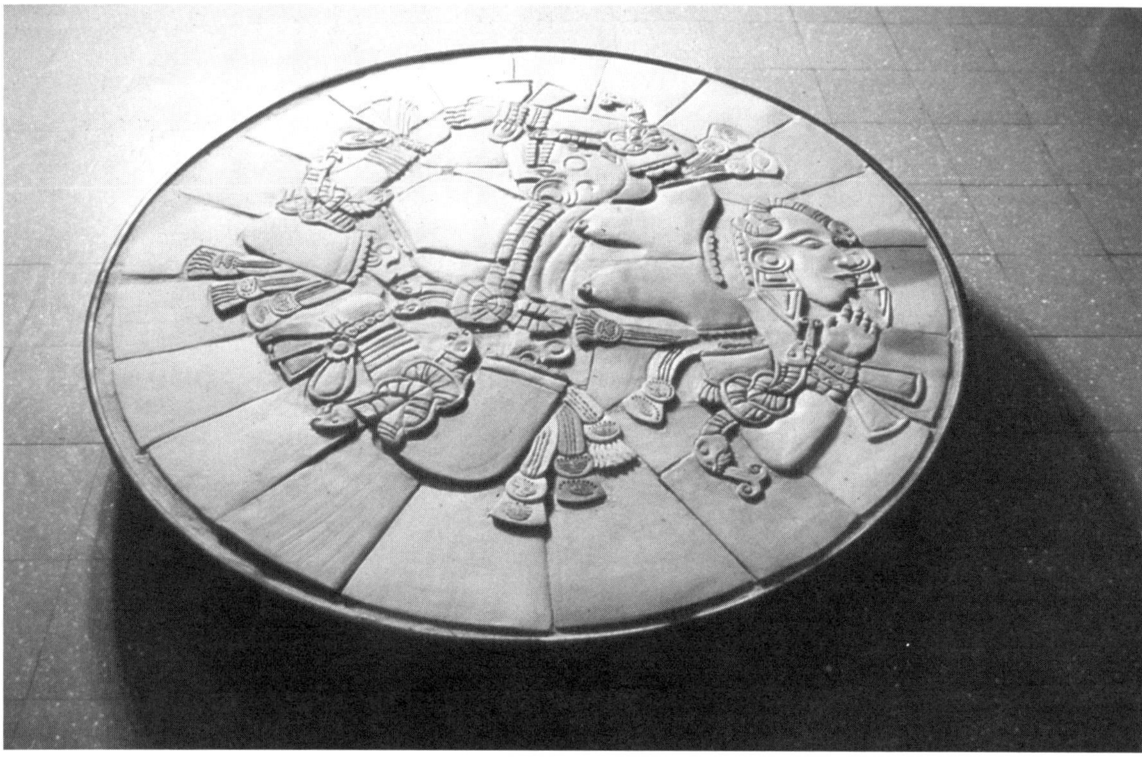

Gloria Osuna Perez. *Coyolxauhqui, Madre Cosmica*, 1996. Fired clay, 6' diameter.
Courtesy of Roberto Perez-Diaz.

Gloria Osuna Perez. Installation of *Coyolxauhqui, Madre Cosmica*, 1996.
Courtesy of Roberto Perez-Diaz..

Above Left: Gloria Osuna Perez. *Maria Hernandez,* 1995. Acrylic on canvas, 30 x 30". *Collection of Roberto Perez-Diaz.*
Above Right: Gloria Osuna Perez. *Vessel with the Sacred Heart of Jesus,* 1998. Glazed and fired clay.
Courtesy of Roberto Perez-Diaz.

a movie about the struggle of Mexican American miners for equality; and, Rosario Ibarra de Piedra, a human rights activist and member of the Mexican House of Representatives.

The women from the Southwest were Eulalia Arrila de Perez, the holder of the keys at the San Gabriel Mission; Jovita Idar, a journalist, educator, and founder of La Cruz Blanca; María Hernández, a Chicana orator and author; Virginia Chacón, who worked for wage equality for Latino workers; and Dolores Huerta, who helped César Chávez organize the United Farm Workers Union.

In sharing the portraits and stories of strong Latina women, Gloria Osuna Perez became a woman others wanted to learn about too. Born in Madera, California, to a migrant farming family, Osuna Perez worked alongside her parents in the fields of the San Joaquin Valley picking peaches and grapes. Her experience encouraged her to support the work of César Chávez years later, and she became the official artist for the Teatro Campesino, painting and designing sets and posters under the leadership of Luis Valdez.

She was first introduced to clay at Fresno City College and loved it. After meeting her husband, Roberto Perez-Diaz in 1970, she devoted herself to the medium, trying to understand everything about using a potter's wheel and getting the temperatures just right. While raising four children—Xoilo, Lucia, Migdalia, and Elida—she began making functional kitchenware and selling the items at craft fairs. She learned the techniques she later applied to *Madre Cósmica*, her most ambitious work.

After moving to El Paso in 1985, she began

Gaspar Enriquez. *Gloria Osuna Perez,* 1998.
Acrylic and airbrush on paper,
22-1/2 x 29-1/2".
Courtesy of Roberto Perez-Diaz.

painting portraits of people in her neighborhood and members of her family. There was a universal quality about the faces, although she found a way to capture each person's uniqueness and personality—manicured fingernails, a farmworker's straw hat, a gold cross necklace. In *Mi Chulita,* a woman with braids and clip-on earrings communicates an individual still clinging to Mexican traditions while embracing life in the United States. It appeared on the book cover for the Hispanic Journalists Conference that was held in El Paso in 1995. The next year at the conference in Chicago, Osuna Perez presented a painting titled *Ana* to First Lady Hillary Rodham Clinton.

When Gloria Osuna Perez found out she had ovarian cancer in 1996, she began to think of designing her own urn. She started a series of fired clay pieces she called "spiritual vessels" after being told that she had only six months to live. Facing her own death seemed more like an end at first, but led her to a new form of expression, renewing her strength as she worked.

She called these designs her Aztlánware Series, since they were vessels made from her cultural background, incorporating both Spanish and indigenous cultures. Some represented religious beings like the Virgen de Guadalupe and the Sacred Heart of Jesus. One of them contained a deep indentation like a niche in the shape of a cross that was inlaid with milagros, small votive ornaments, and a top in the shape of flames. She saw the vessels as symbols of faith—and the womb in indigenous cultures—pointing to the continuation of life.

In an act of solidarity, Roberto Perez-Diaz shaved his head when his wife lost her hair from chemotherapy. One of her last projects was to illustrate a children's book published by Cinco Puntos Press called *Little Goldstar/Estrellita de Oro,* a Cinderella story told by Joe Hayes. Although she sketched all fifteen images for the book, she completed only three before her condition worsened and she could not finish. Asking her daughter Lucia if she might finish the paintings, she shared the colors she was using and her thoughts about the remaining illustrations.

After Gloria Osuna Perez died on June 25, 1999, at the age of fifty-one, Lucia Perez painted the remaining scenes for the book with her eye on her mother's example. Lucia continued to paint, becoming an artist, and when her first child was born, she named her Gloria.

Bibliographic Essay

Knowing Sarah Lea, Martha Arat, and Gloria Osuna Perez enriched my life. It has been a privilege to ponder their lives over the past months in order to put down in words a short record of what each of them left behind.

I am grateful to their families for their help in answering questions and gathering research materials, especially Jim Lea, Arsavir Arat, and Roberto Perez-Diaz. Their generous spirits reflect the love Jim has for his mother, and that Arsavir and Roberto have for their wives. Juan Sandoval, a collector of Martha Arat's work, generously provided his archive of articles, artist's statements, and invitations. The staff at the El Paso Public Library was also helpful with their El Paso Artists files. Photographs were gathered with the help of Michele Villa of the El Paso Museum of Art; Arturo Flores of Adair Margo Fine Art; Jamey and Judy Clement of Dallas, Texas; Chris Lopez, editor of the *El Paso Times;* and Laura Hollingshead of the C.L. Sonnichsen Special Collections Department at The University of Texas at El Paso Library.

I consulted numerous books, articles, and papers during the course of preparing this chapter. The most significant are listed below.

Arocha, Zita. *Gloria Osuna Perez, Coyolxauhqui, Madre Cósmica.* El Paso Museum of Art, 1996.

Byrd, Lee and Roberto Perez. *Gloria Osuna Perez: Portrait of a Madre Cósmica.* El Paso: Bridge Center for Contemporary Art Publication, Summer, 2000.

Craver, Rebecca and Adair Margo. *Tom Lea, An Oral History.* El Paso: Texas Western Press, 1995.

Hampton, Elaine and Meredith Abarca. *Sor Juana: Woman of Inquiry.* El Paso: University of Texas at El Paso, 2002.

Lea, Tom. *A Picture Gallery.* Boston: Little Brown and Company, 1968.

Perez, Gloria. *Coyolxauhqui, Madre Cósmica, The History of an Installation* (unpublished). El Paso, 1996.

Chapter 2

MORE THAN GOOD WORKS

by Mimi Reisel Gladstein

"A BURNING BICULTURAL HEART" is the expression *Dallas Morning News* reviewer Jane Sumner uses to describe the singular appeal of *Literary El Paso,* an anthology of El Paso's varied and talented writers. Sumner's description is a good launching point for recounting the good hearts and resultant beneficial works of not just the bicultural, but the rich multicultural nature of the charitable activities of El Paso women. In the brief but philanthropically bountiful time since women have been in El Paso, their contributions can be seen to have influenced both individuals and the community at large, a history that chronicles their more-than-good works. This frontier city is home not only to the Anglo and Mexican cultures, but to a variety of ethnic and religious groups. An amusing example of El Paso's openness to various immigrant groups is the mayor's race of 1889. Adolph Krakauer, a Jewish German immigrant, won the vote, but had to be disqualified because it was revealed that he had not yet completed his citizenship papers. In the chaos that followed, one Irish-born Richard Caples was chosen and sworn in just minutes after he became a United States citizen.

But let's start at the beginning. Early El Paso had a rough founding. In the late nineteenth century it was a lawless, wide-open frontier town. It awaited the firm hand of the legendary sheriff Dallas Stoudenmire to slowly reduce lawlessness; that done, a school system and cultural life followed. The first public school opened in March of 1883 and Mary Stanton created what later developed into a public library when she started a reading club for boys. Mary Stanton, whose family name distinguishes one of the major streets in our community, allowed some twenty boys to help themselves from her library of five hundred to eight hundred books. The library was kept in a room in the Sheldon Building; the elevator operator kept the key. When many El Paso women asked to be able to use the books also, a public library was born. Open to the public, the small book collection was maintained in the Sheldon Building until 1904 when a new building for the library was made possible through the Andrew Carnegie Foundation.

Once an official public library was established, Stanton's good work was further enhanced by the energies of Maud Durlin Sullivan. Maud Durlin was born in Wisconsin in 1872. She studied library science at the Pratt Institute and left her job with the Oshkosh Public Library when she moved to El Paso to become its librarian in 1908. When she married John Kevin Sullivan, a Harvard-educated mining engineer, they moved to New Mexico's Mogollon Mountains. After she returned to El Paso and her library position in 1917, she began a stewardship that would bring her national and international acclaim. In his memoir, Tom Lea calls Sullivan's effects on the community "one of the richest contributions a good citizen ever brought to West Texas." It was, he states, "a gift imponderable and impossible to accurately measure and survey." Among the contributions that can be quantified is her building the content of the library. In 1919 it housed some 17,453 volumes that more than doubled in a decade to 36,842.

Maud Sullivan understood her context and developed the library holdings to reflect that. She wanted resources available for the various populations of the city. Sullivan built a sound mining reference section, widely used by engineers from the area. She also taught herself Spanish in order to choose wisely for a Spanish-language section. Her development of the significant Southwest Collection inspired the donation of original manuscripts, among them J. Frank Dobie's *Apache Gold and Yaqui Silver.* Her capabilities did not go unnoticed. From 1923-1925 she was president of the Texas Library Association and founded and edited its bulletin. In 1935 the Carnegie Corporation named her to its International Relations Committee and sent her to the International Congress of Libraries and Bibliography in Spain. Because of her efforts, El Paso was one of only two libraries in Texas to receive the Carnegie Art Reference Set.

In addition to Maud Sullivan's quantifiable contributions is her role as El Paso's unofficial patroness of local artists. She maintained a sizable collection of art books and prints. Tom Lea remembers: "Only when I went to art school and met students from other parts of the country did I realize how good and how wide a selection of books on painting Mrs. Sullivan had already put before me." Besides Lea, Carl Hertzog, Peter Hurd, José Cisneros, and John Rechy have all spoken of her support and encouragement.

Always generous with help, her quiet and well-ordered office, merry eyes, and smile reminded Tom Lea of the title page of a book—a balanced and immaculate preview of what to expect. Hertzog and Lea were pallbearers at her funeral in 1943.

The first significant women's group in town was The Woman's Club of El Paso, originally called the Current Topics Club. C. L. Sonnichsen, in his ground-breaking history *Pass of the North,* credits it with being a key force in the movement that brought El Paso from a wild border city to its current status as the Sun City. Though there was resistance from some sources, voices that questioned the appropriateness of women being out of their homes, the club, started in 1894, flourished and is still an active group in the community; it has long maintained its own building. Many El Paso women remember playing their first music recitals in that building when it was one of the few venues in town that could house such events.

Woman's Club of El Paso, shortly after its construction in 1916.
Otto H. Thorman architectural records, MS147, Special Collections Department, University of Texas at El Paso Library. Courtesy of the University of Texas at El Paso Library.

Mrs. W. W. Mills was the founder and her friends Mrs. T. J. Beall, Mrs. Leigh Clark, Mrs. W. M. Jones, Mrs. Ernst Kohlberg, Mrs. E. R. Neff, Mrs. J. C. Townsend, Mrs. W. S. Tilton, Mrs. J. C. Voss, and Misses Mary Stanton and Thirza Westcott were the original members. Although the purpose of the club was more geared to the intellectual culture of the members, its yearbook also states that assisting the "betterment of physical, intellectual and moral conditions in the community" is part of the club's mission.

Texas Women: A Celebration of History lists Olga Bernstein Kohlberg (Mrs. Ernst Kohlberg) as noteworthy for her work in establishing the first public kindergarten in the state of Texas. This project developed out of a study of child training that was one of the Woman's Club's projects. Much work and some lobbying of the Board of Education ensued, but in September 1893 that first public kindergarten in the state of Texas opened in Central School in El Paso with Miss Lucretia Jones in charge. Kohlberg was a pioneer in the introduction of early childhood education and understood its importance more than most. "There are many who will never go beyond the lower grades, who cannot afford to," she explained. "What you learn in childhood will have a lasting effect on your whole life."

Kohlberg was not a native El Pasoan; she was born and raised in Central Europe. Once in El Paso, she threw herself into the betterment of her community. She served as Woman's Club president for two terms, and then remained on the board until her death in 1935. In addition, for thirty years she was chair of the finance committee, and it was under her careful stewardship and guidance that a clubhouse was built after years of having to count on temporary locations. Kohlberg was also one of the three directors of the first El Paso Library Association, having been quite active in the establishment of the public library.

A most unusual, perhaps unique, project that Mrs. Kohlberg, Mrs. Winchester Cooley, and Mrs. S. Tilton helped establish, circa 1916-1917, was the Cloudcroft Baby Sanatorium. The sanatorium was a dream of Dr. H. E. Stevenson, whose concern was that babies had a difficult time surviving the extreme summer heat in El Paso in those pre-air conditioning days. With the generous contributions of some interested El Pasoans, Stevenson was able to build his sanatorium in Cloudcroft, New Mexico, a small mountain community not far from Alamogordo. The path between the two communities was difficult and so the Sacramento Mountain Railroad ran a daily excursion line, dubbed the "Cloud Climbing Route." That train, once the world's highest standard gauge line, operated from 1899 until the last excursion on February 12, 1938. In the meantime, the advent of the automobile and trucks made the necessity of a railroad for lumber hauling and personal convenience unnecessary. Doctors going to Cloudcroft for the weekend would sometimes take sick babies with them. The Baby San, as it was called, had a very positive effect on the babies sent there. The women who worked in the sanatorium reported that the cool pine-scented air worked wonders, and that quite quickly the babies began gaining weight and color returned to their cheeks. Woman's Club members were active in raising funds for the Baby San. When conditions in El Paso no longer necessitated the trip for purposes of health, the Baby San was then converted to a recreation camp for underprivileged children.

Not quite as old as the Woman's Club of El Paso, but still one of the oldest philanthropic associations in town is the Young Women's Christian Association, or YWCA, which recently celebrated its 100-year anniversary. El Paso's YWCA is a point of pride for the community as it is the largest YW in the country, a singular accomplishment for a city that is not even one of the four largest urban centers in the state of Texas, much less the country. The creation and development of the YWCA is a paradigm for the inclusive nature of many community associations in El Paso. Though it began with a group of women from Protestant churches, its founding members represented a variety of religions. The first meeting was held on April 8, 1909, at the First Christian Church, and the initial mission was to open a lunchroom and provide a residence for women, many of whom came to this area to seek a healthy climate or who came to find work. A building campaign was launched with plans donated by Trost & Trost Architects and Engineers. When the community could only raise half of the $20,000 needed, a letter was written to Mrs. Russell Sage, a wealthy New Yorker who was involved with the national YWCA. The letter must have been persuasive because Mrs. Sage provided a check to cover the balance and a boarding house opened in October of 1910.

That same year, a gymnasium was rented to provide for the fitness needs of the young women. As time passed and the programs grew, it became obvious that a building in which to combine all

Hospitality House, ca. 1920s. *Courtesy of YWCA El Paso del Norte Region.*

Early YWCA Home on Missouri Street, ca. 1920s. *Courtesy of YWCA El Paso del Norte Region.*

the programs was needed. A fundraising campaign was initiated. That campaign was the first of its kind in El Paso and some 2,287 subscribers raised more than $120,000. Among its numerous early supporters was Adolph Schwartz, owner of the Popular Dry Goods Company, for many years El Paso's leading department store. Mr. Schwartz said: "I regard this subscription as an investment which will yield returns through the girls employed in my store who are members or may become members of the YWCA." Involved since the founding, female members of the Schwartz family have served in various positions with the YW: Ann Schwartz Schaechner, Susan Amstater Schwartz, and Tania Schwartz are featured in the centennial book *100 Years: 100 Women.*

The Racial Justice Imperative is a current YWCA initiative, but the foundations for the YW's inclusiveness were present from its inception. In 1919 the national board organized the Hospitality House at the International Bridge; its purpose was to aid Mexican immigrants. Also in 1919, the War Work Council of the YWCA formed the International Institutes to teach Spanish-speaking women cooking, sewing, and English. The World Fellowship Committee was formed in 1922 to promote better understanding among girls of all races and creeds, with programs designed to help members learn about and appreciate other cultures. In the 1930s an African American woman was appointed to the Girls Reserves Committee to represent the African American girls' clubs. The Girls Reserves changed its name to Y-Teens in 1946. Then, in 1951, Drusilla Nixon, who had begun her association with the YWCA by serving on the Girls Reserves Committee, was nominated to serve a three-year term on the El Paso YWCA Board of Directors. Nixon, who worked on the board until 1954, was the wife of Dr. Lawrence A. Nixon, who in the 1920s and 1930s successfully challenged Texas voting rights laws that did not allow African Americans to vote in the state primaries. Mrs. Nixon worked side-by-side with her husband in the efforts to win voting rights.

Diversity was promoted further when Myrna Deckert became executive director of the YWCA in 1969 and appointed the first Hispanic women, Rosa Guerrero, Leticia Paez, and Rosa Gonzalez, to the board. The amalgamation and spirited activity of all members of the YW family, so representative of the multicultural spirit of El Paso, is illustrated by the success of these women. New members of the board, regardless of their race, religion, or ethnic background were mentored and integrated into the multiple programs of the group. Letty Paez, one of the original Hispanic members became president of the El Paso YWCA and went on to be president of the National YWCA. The yearly fundraising luncheons have featured such speakers as Barbara Bush, Cokie Roberts, and Jackie Joyner-Kersee. Today, table captains include Catholic, Greek Orthodox, Jewish, and atheist women.

Another of the rich traditions of the YWCA is the faithfulness and dedication of generations. Serving the community through working for the YW is a commitment that is handed down from grandmother, to mother, to daughter. Lily Cowden Staten was born in Midland; her parents were ranchers. Lily graduated from Baylor University, an unusual accomplishment for a woman of her generation. When she married Dr. Burleson Staten, she moved to El Paso, where she was one of the founders of the Woman's Department of the Chamber of Commerce and also a president of the YWCA. Following in her footsteps, her granddaughter Betty Ruth Wakefield Haley also served as president of the local YW and was on the national YWCA board. Continuing the family tradition, great granddaughter Adair Wakefield Margo is currently a board member. One of Lily's daughters, Ruth Staten, was the first Sun Queen of El Paso's yearly Sun Carnival festivities.

Katherine White Harvey is another member of a prominent El Paso family who followed in her family's philanthropic footsteps. Zach T. White, her father, was a pioneer and a generous donor. He built the Paso del Norte Hotel, now the Camino Real, and donated the land on which the first bridge to Ciudad Juárez, Mexico, was built. Land he contributed to the Girls Scouts and Boy Scouts, later acquired by the YWCA, now houses the Mary Ann Dodson summer camp. Following in her father's footsteps, Katherine White Harvey donated land to be used for a West Side YWCA facility, which now bears her name; Zach White Elementary School is named for her father. The West Side YW has both an indoor and an outdoor pool. It offers a variety of activities related to health and maintains a full service child development center. Further evidence of her charitable spirit are her 1933 contributions to the founding of the Junior League and her volunteer work during World War II for the Red Cross and the Family Welfare Service.

Over the years, the growth of the YWCA has been phenomenal—from a small boarding house on West Missouri Street to buildings and programs spread throughout the city. There is an administrative building, five branch buildings, plus a camp, a transitional living center, and Independence House, a living center for women and children who are fleeing domestic violence. Twelve apartments, built by the Community Development Corporation, are available for low-income seniors. From twenty-seven employees in the early days, the staff has grown to some 600.

El Paso's Jewish community has been a small but active component of the city's economic and cultural growth. Prior to the advent of saturation by national chains, many downtown retail stores were owned by Jewish merchants. They often helped to advance the cultural climate of the town. Sam Schutz, one of those retailers and also an immigrant, built the first opera house in 1883, followed by the Myar Opera House in 1886. While their husbands contributed to the economy, Jewish women were involved in philanthropic work from the early days of their arrival in the small western town. They worked for diverse charitable organizations and were particularly active with the YWCA; they also worked in women's organizations that were based in religion. Philanthropy, *tzedakah,* meaning "righteousness" in Hebrew, is a key tenet of the faith. Among the earliest Jewish women's organizations was the Ladies Aid Society, which was organized to provide assistance to the poor and the sick. Then in 1917, in response to immigration problems along the border, seventy-eight women formed the National Council of Jewish Women (NCJW), a local affiliate of the national organization, which was founded in 1893. Their many projects in El Paso included a soup kitchen at Franklin and Lincoln schools that eventually evolved into a free lunch program for children who could not afford the price of a school meal. The NCJW was also instrumental in establishing the Lighthouse for the Blind program, which helps train the blind and visually impaired in job as well as life skills

The Lower Valley YWCA, one of a number of branch locations, ca. 1990s. *Courtesy of YWCA El Paso del Norte Region.*

management. It later became an agency of the United Way. NCJW members like Sally Rosen and Ida Bendalin helped transcribe books into Braille. In 1934 the first Braille training workshop in the state was opened in El Paso. When the El Paso Council for Retarded Children began its efforts to establish a school, an NCJW member served as a teacher and NCJW women provided the transportation. Regina Reisel enlisted the aid of her daughters, Miriam and Harriet, in this project because it was necessary for someone to monitor the children during the drive. It was quite a harrowing experience for the girls as sometimes their young charges attempted to exit the car while en route. Fights, hair pulling, and screaming were not unusual.

While the El Paso community has benefited from all of the National Council of Jewish Women's projects, perhaps none is more crucial to an ever-growing population's health care needs than the Visiting Nurses Association (VNA). The association began as a project spearheaded by Beatrice "Bitty" Gladstone. Bitty, originally from Dallas, would often accompany her husband, Dr. Larry Gladstone, as he made house calls. During those times she came to recognize the dire need for supportive home health care services.

As her husband remembers it, it was Bitty's experiences with another NCJW project, Drive-a-Meal, a project that provided meals for shut-ins, that confirmed her resolve that something needed to be done to address the situation for people who could not leave their homes for reasons of health or limited mobility. At that time, in the 1960s, there was no home health care agency in El Paso. When Bitty became president of the

Dr. Larry and Bitty Gladstone, founder of the Visiting Nurses Association, ca. 1990s.
Courtesy of Dr. Larry Gladstone.

National Council of Jewish Women she won approval from the board of directors to initiate the project. Brenda Ehrlich, who succeeded Bitty as a president of NCJW, recalls: "Bitty not only had a sense of vision, but she had an inner strength that took her from the inception of a concept to the fruition of the project." Those who remember Bitty recall her wonderful imperturbable manner; she never raised her voice in frustration or anger, but one look at the steely resolve in her bluish-gray eyes was enough to set offending parties straight. "Bitty started caring for others as a youngster—and made it a lifelong career," wrote Ruth Taber.

Sister Teresa persuaded the Daughters of Charity to assign Sister Marcelline, a public health nurse, as the first director of the VNA. Cliff Haggerty of the Medical Society contacted the State Department of Health for funds to hire three nurses. Vera Zablovsky was a key figure in the initial organization. Brenda Ehrlich volunteered her husband Herbert to be president of the board of directors and legal advisor. The project had a smooth beginning. NCJW put up the seed money, and, in 1967, VNA began its service to El Paso. Thomason Hospital provided the office space, while United Way certified the program as one of its agencies. The summer 2004 issue of *Health Beat,* the VNA newsletter, was dedicated to the "Memory, Courage and Legacy of Beatrice 'Bitty' Gladstone." A Resolution of Tribute printed in *Health Beat* cites her efforts as the "guiding force" in shaping the first and only not-for-profit home health agency in El Paso. Noting Bitty Gladstone's work with the Volunteer Bureau of the United Way, the Child Treatment Center, and Hospice of El Paso, among others, the resolution goes on to express the "sincere and enduring grief" caused by her loss to the nursing profession.

Today, the VNA has a budget of $16,000,000 and 950 employees. Hospice, Home Health, Private Duty Home Service, and Primary Home Care are all parts of this program. The manner in which the various agencies and entities worked together to create and fund this much-needed service to the community is paradigmatic of the El Paso way.

The methodology of the National Council of Jewish Women is to search for a need in the community, and then to initiate a project to meet that need. Once the project is established, and a funding source is found, it is turned over to the community. Among the other projects that Bitty Gladstone worked on was a school for emotionally disturbed children that opened at the First Presbyterian Church with Dr. Richard Walker as its medical director. When Mr. and Mrs. Luis Zork donated their family home as a site for the Child Guidance Center, Bitty and many other NCJW women worked on that. Concern for people, a concern that transcends cultural and economic lines, is the driving force of this organization. Unfortunately, the El Paso chapter of the National Council of Jewish Women, which was so instrumental in establishing a number of significant service institutions for the city, is no longer in existence. Fortunately, the schools, public television station, and many good works of the NCJW continue to survive.

In keeping with its historic hospitality and open acceptance, it is probably not surprising that it was an El Paso coach and multi-cultural team that in 1966 were credited with breaking the color barrier in college basketball. That team went on to be the only Texas team to date to win the NCAA tournament, beating an all-white Kentucky team in the championship game. Though, like all cities in Texas, El Paso has a segregated past, and the discrimination that African Americans endured should not be diminished, it has also marked up many "firsts" in Texas in the area of civil rights. Currently it has what statisticians call an "atypical" African American community. One late twentieth-century study noted that the African American community in El Paso had a higher income average and a higher education average than either the Mexican American or Anglo American communities. That may be unique in Texas and probably in the country. So, it is not surprising that a 1949 *School Board Journal* article concluded: "McCall Nursery School is the only one of its type known to exist in Texas or the South, and is a good example of 'the Lord helping those who help themselves!'"

The McCall Day Nursery was founded in the 1940s when Olalee McCall and her husband Marshall gave a generous donation toward providing a safe place for little black children to stay while their parents worked.

It was an outgrowth of the Roosevelt Day Nursery that had been established when a fire

Above: McCall Day Nursery. Mrs. Crumady teaching a group that included L. C. Cox, Bertsie Vanduvall, Dot Miller, ca. 1940s. *Courtesy of McCall Neighborhood Center.*
Below: Olalee McCall, educator and philanthropist, ca. 1930s. *Courtesy of The University of Texas at El Paso Library.*

claimed the lives of three black children who had been left at home while their mother worked. In those days, Douglass School was the only school for blacks in El Paso and served grades one through twelve. Emmanuel Campbell, the principal of Douglass, is credited with initiating the idea for providing a professional day care service for black parents that, at the same time, would be used as a training lab for black homemaking students from Douglass High School. Olalee, besides being a generous benefactress, was also an English teacher and then principal of Douglass School. The McCall Day Nursery provided a full day's care, operating six days a week from seven AM to six PM. The services included breakfast, lunch, morning and afternoon snacks, and materials for arts and crafts and music. Payment was made on the basis of ability as determined by the nursery school's caseworker. In the 1940s this meant that the maximum tuition fee was $4.50 per week; some children were admitted free of charge. Funding was also provided by the El Paso Community Chest and donations. The El Paso Public School system contributed to the maintenance of the building and grounds, as well as the salaries of the teachers. McCall Day Nursery served the black children of El Paso for over a decade, until the end of segregation in Texas. Then it continued to serve all until it finally closed its doors in May of 1986. At that time, only two percent of the children enrolled were black.

Frances Hills, who was a student at Douglass School, remembers Olalee McCall as "demanding" and "very intelligent." "She handed me my high school diploma," Hills recalls. McCall was the first woman in the El Paso Independent School District to be a high school principal. Frances Hills' mother taught Spanish at Douglass High School and later in Fabens. She had known Olalee before she married Marshall McCall, when she was still Olalee Fowler. Summing up her character, Hills remembers: "If she was asked to do something, she got it done." The family name is also associated with a cultural center and museum devoted to the black community in El Paso. The McCall Neighborhood Center is housed in the home in central El Paso that was once owned by Marshall and Olalee McCall.

If ever there was an exemplification of the word "dynamo," that person would be Lucy Acosta. Her many honors include being selected Outstanding League of United Latin American Citizens (LULAC) National Woman of the Year in 1973, the Texas Women's Hall of Fame, and receiving the city's highest honor, the Conquistador Award.

Image from 2009 Project Amistad Annual Report. *Courtesy of the Acosta Family.*

Among Lucy's many accomplishments is the establishment of LULAC Project Amistad, which she served as executive director for twenty-five years.

Project Amistad, a nonprofit agency, has as its main goal to provide services to many of El Paso's elderly and disabled adults. It sends workers into homes to help the aged with information about Social Security benefits and other services. Transportation, such as for appointments to doctor's offices, is also provided when needed. In addition, members sponsor hot lunch programs, shoe buying projects for needy children, and aid to handicapped and retarded children as well as the aged at the country general hospital. Its most recent annual report touts the accomplished goal of finally moving its three different locations and a sixty-two-bus fleet to one large facility. In 2009, the Project Amistad Transportation programs included Job Access though which individuals from rural areas were transported to job sites, interviews, school, and similar destinations. The Medical Transportation Program drove Medicaid and eligible persons to and from their medical appointments, the pharmacy, therapy, or for other approved medical procedures. New Freedom is a program created to transport people with disabilities to medical appointments, social visits, entertainment, or other destinations. It works in conjunction with Volar, the Center for Independent Living. Other transportation programs include Job Access, Susan G. Komen for the Cure, the Area Agency on Aging, and the Housing Authority of the City of El Paso. Alejandro Acosta, Jr. (Alex), remembering his mother, marvels that what began as a discussion at their kitchen table became an organization with an annual budget of over six million dollars. The growth and success are indeed objects of wonder. When first formed, Project Amistad employed four people with a budget of whatever donations Lucy Acosta could accumulate; today there are some one hundred employees. Originally it served El Paso County only; today it serves six counties. In keeping with the tradition of charitable works being handed down from generation to generation, the Acosta family is still involved with Project Amistad. Lucy's granddaughter, Andrea Acosta, Director of the Pediatric Residency Program at Texas Tech Medical School, currently serves on the board. Though not a member of the family, Xavier Banales, the current director of Project Amistad, was a protégé of Lucy's who he met when he was a teenager in a junior LULAC group.

Community service was stressed in the Acosta family. Alex, one of two sons, expresses amazement that his mother was able to do as much as she did. He observes that she may have been an icon to others, but to him and his brother, she was an "ordinary mom." She attended PTA meetings, organized after-season athletic parties, and was there for them when they needed her. Philanthropy was not the word used in the household, but the idea was expressed as a way of giving back to the community. Granddaughter Andrea remembers her grandmother repeatedly telling her that community service is not a responsibility, it is a privilege. Lucy always had the backing and support of her husband, Alejandro. As high-school sweethearts, they shared goals and values—they were a team for many years. Alex Acosta emphasizes the fact that while he learned passion from his mother, it was his father who taught him strength and confidence.

Begun in 1992, the Lucy G. Acosta Humanitarian Award is presented most years to recognize

Team Acosta: Lucy and Alejandro Sr., ca. 1990s.
Courtesy of the Acosta Family.

those individuals who actively work to make positive change in the community. It follows that among those honored over the years are people like Myrna Deckert, whose positive contributions through the YWCA are mentioned earlier in this chapter, and Bitty Gladstone, the driving force behind the Visiting Nurses Association.

Besides being a humanitarian, Lucy Acosta was active in politics. During the campaign to elect Raymond Telles the first Mexican American mayor of El Paso, Lucy Acosta was an active participant in the program to register voters before the poll tax deadline. In her oral history recording, she recalls how she and other women stationed themselves in front of the local Sears and JCPenney stores as well as the Popular Dry Goods Company, and the White House, locally owned department stores. The result was a significant increase in Mexican American registration; Acosta recalls that it was not difficult to convince them to pay their poll tax when they knew they would have a chance to vote for Telles. During the Telles administration (1957-1961), Acosta served on various committees and continued to serve subsequent mayors. In 1972, she became the first woman in the history of El Paso to be appointed civil service commissioner. Subsequently, Telles was appointed ambassador to Costa Rica. As the ambassador's wife, Delfina Telles began a long career of charity work and community service. In particular, she was very active leading fundraising drives for a children's hospital and a rehabilitation center for children with disabilities in Costa Rica. On her return to El Paso, she was the co-chair for the annual Easter Seal Drive for El Paso's Cerebral Palsy Treatment Center. After her death on May 6, 2010, the Honorable Dennis A. Cardoza read into the Congressional Record an account of her tireless work on behalf of the March of Dimes, the American Red Cross, the American Cancer Society, and the Women's Auxiliary of Providence Memorial Hospital. Hers was a deep commitment to making a difference in her community.

Lucy Acosta, Bitty Gladstone, Olalee McCall, and Lily Cowden Staten are but four women who, along with many others of their friends and family members, serve to represent the multicultural warmth and hospitality that permeates El Paso. This multicultural ambience and openness is not restricted to the past or to El Paso women. Even today, as Fort Bliss, El Paso's military base that once stood on the banks of the Rio Grande, is about to lose its commander, Major General Howard Bromberg, he will be replaced by Major General Dana Pittard, an African American who grew up in El Paso. The president and chief executive officer of the Greater El Paso Chamber of Commerce is Richard Dayoub, an Arab American. Throughout its history and even today El Paso has benefited and will continue to benefit from a diverse and multicultural population. And women have been key in developing its rich philanthropic resources.

Bibliographic Essay

Whenever one writes about El Paso history, it goes without saying that the first volume to consult is Charles Leland Sonnichsen's *Pass of the North,* published by Texas Western Press in 1968. It was a primary source for information about not only the early days of city development, but also the role of women in nineteenth- and early twentieth-century El Paso. In 1990 Texas Western Press published W. H. Timmons' *El Paso: A Borderlands History,* which was also helpful. In addition, Mary S. Cunningham's *The Woman's Club of El Paso* was a significant resource. In conjunction with its centennial celebration, the YWCA published *100 Years, 100 Women: Profiles of a Century of Leaders and Visionaries.* It was a primary source for information about the women who were instrumental in the establishment and early growth of the YWCA. Susan Goodman Novick allowed me to use her script for the YWCA exhibit at the El Paso Museum of History. Cynthia Farah Haines shared with me "An Historical Portrait of the El Paso Section of the National Council of Jewish Women," a paper she had written some years ago. Claudia Rivers and the staff of Special Collections at The University of Texas at El Paso Library were also helpful. Maceo Dailey, Director of the African American Studies Program at The University of Texas at El Paso provided names and telephone numbers for possible sources. Barbara Byrd, Director of the McCall Neighborhood Center, met with me on August 5, 2010, and provided the picture of the schoolroom at McCall Day Nursery as well as the names of the students she recognized, including her sister. Frances Hills was kind enough to speak to me on the telephone and recall her time as a student at Douglass High School where Olalee McCall was principal. Alejandro (Alex) Acosta Jr. was most generous with both time and resources, making sure that I got information I needed to flesh out my essay about both his mother and Project Amistad. He also put me in touch with his daughter Andrea Acosta, who provided the pictures of her grandmother and the Project Amistad building and bus. I was fortunate enough to get to speak with Dr. Larry Gladstone shortly before his death, and he provided me with both the picture of him and his wife Bitty, and with material about the Visiting Nurses Association, including their *Health Beat* newsletter, which was dedicated to his wife. Brenda Ehrlich was kind enough to share her remembrances about the foundation and early days of the project.

Chapter 3

HEALING THE BORDERLANDS ACROSS THE CENTURIES

by Yolanda Chávez Leyva

She wakes early, lights candles before
her sacred statues, brews tea of hierbabuena.
She moves down her porch steps, rubs
cool morning sand into her hands, into her arms.
Like large black bird, she feeds on
the desert, gathering herbs for her basket.

Her days are slow, days of grinding
dried snake into power, of crushing
wild bees to mix with white wine.
And the townspeople come, hoping
to be touched by her ointments,
her hands, her prayers, her eyes.
She listens to their stories, and she listens
to the desert, always the desert.

From *Curandera* by El Paso poet Pat Mora

THE DESERT IS A BEAUTIFUL PLACE if you listen to its wisdom. Each plant, cactus, every "weed" holds its own healing properties. For many who grew up on the border, in the midst of the Chihuahua Desert, there are memories of *abuelitas* who put a sprig of *gobernadora* (creosote) in their water overnight, turning it into an earthy pungent liquid that strengthened them as they started a new day. Before corporations began to mass market prickly pear cactus as a supplement to fight diabetes, there were the recollections of harvesting *nopalitos* in the spring when the new cactus pads were just beginning to grow and their thorns were still soft and their flesh tender. For desert peoples, these plants held promises of health. Later, other herbs made their way into this body of knowledge–*manzanilla* (chamomile) and *hierbabuena* (mint) for stomachaches and cramps, oregano for the lungs, and *sábila* (aloe vera) for skin problems. The women who sustained this knowledge from generation to generation were the *curanderas*, the traditional healers.

"Curandera," renowned author Pat Mora's ode to traditional healers in Mexican-origin communities, evocatively highlights the importance of these skilled women, historically and in contemporary times. As Mora writes, people seek out *curanderas* as they have for centuries, hoping to receive healing through herbs, hands, and prayers. A profound understanding of plants, prayers, anatomy, illness, health, and community life provides the basis for the *curanderas'* relationships with others. Historically, *curanderismo* has been rooted in "a community's shared values, beliefs, and symbols," helping to make it an effective system.

Along the US-Mexico border, there survives a vital and intriguing history of women healers whose therapeutic techniques go back centuries to indigenous communities in what are now Mexico and the southwestern United States. Activist and community scholar Elizabeth Martinez has written about the ways in which "the timeless *curandera* or healer [demonstrates] the power of women's historical presence." Indeed, from the centuries-old Mesoamerican codices and their drawings of indigenous women using herbs to heal to the modern website of one of the most well-known current day *curanderas,* Elena Avila, who hails from El Segundo Barrio in El Paso, traditional healers have proven critical to the survival of Mexican origin communities, physically, psychologically, emotionally, and spiritually. This has been true in El Paso-Ciudad Juárez as in other border communities.

Traditional healers, both historically and in contemporary times, base their work on the fundamental concepts that there exists no separation between mind, body, spirit, and soul and that healing must address all four aspects of the individual. Healing implies restoring a balance among the four components. While understanding these connections, *curanderas* often specialize in a particular type of healing modality. *Yerberas* use medicinal plants in their work. *Sobadoras* and *hueseras* work on the muscles and bones of their clients, akin to modern-day massage therapists. *Parteras,* or midwives, often deliver thousands of babies in their lifetimes.

Prior to the twentieth century, *curanderas* were often the principal medical care for people. Their importance cannot be overstated. Even today, along the US-Mexico border, significant numbers of people turn to *curanderas* for their medical needs. A recent study showed that almost half of the respondents in an El Paso survey used "complementary or alternative medicine." Of this group, the majority employed the services of *yerberas, yerberos,* and *sobadores.* In addition to providing critical medical care and counseling in communities with few resources, *curanderas* have helped foster community and identity. They have kept alive centuries-old knowledge about plants and healing modalities. In addition, they have played a crucial role in maintaining cultural mores and values. During times that Mexican communities and cultures have come under attack, *curanderas* and the mothers and grandmothers who embody the ancient ways have helped the culture survive.

Despite the vital role *curanderas* have played in border communities, they and their histories of healing are often invisible, absent from documented history. In part, this is because *curanderas'* knowledge has been passed on orally from generation to generation within a family. Although in recent years, universities have offered classes on *curanderismo* and *curanderas* have authored some books, traditional knowledge about plants, prayers, and healing is frequently taught at the kitchen table, on walks in the desert while harvesting plants, and in other intimate settings. Such an approach to passing on knowledge leaves little written record.

The persistence of such traditional knowledge is impressive, given the obstacles that healers have confronted over the past five hundred years. For example, following the creation of the Holy Office of the Inquisition in colonial Mexico (which included the El Paso region) in the sixteenth century, *curanderos* and *curanderas* faced charges of sorcery, witchcraft, and being superstitious. The Inquisition brought charges against individuals for being a "*curandera adivina*" (a healer who told fortunes), a *partera*, a *sobadora* or *yerbera*. The records document punishment for *curanderas* and *curanderos* ranging from reprimands and prohibition of their healing practices to public humiliation or exile.

Without oversimplifying the matter, it is difficult to ignore this history of persecution when in 1896 the priest of the "Mexican Catholic Church" in El Paso denounced the work of internationally known Mexican *curandera* Teresita Urrea, saying her powers came "from the devil." Negative attitudes towards traditional healing persisted throughout the twentieth century. A 1973 article in the *El Paso Herald-Post* echoed centuries-old warnings that healers were now operating "openly" in El Paso. Reporter Ray Chavez also reminded readers that in the recent past, "faith healers, readers and fortune tellers in El Paso were arrested under the catch-all statute known as the vagrancy laws." He also warned of the charlatans who took advantage of the "ignorance or blind faith of believers," charging large sums for their services. While frauds have existed over the centuries, categorizing *curanderas* as "superstitious" or linked to the devil has created an atmosphere of fear, meaning many traditional healers have kept their work limited to family and close friends.

Women from the *Florentine Codex, General History of the Things of New Spain,* vol. 12. *Public domain.*

Outsiders have long denigrated the age-old practices of traditional healers. Spanish chroniclers, for example, characterized indigenous healing practices as simple "superstition" in the colonial period. Centuries later, Mexican American healers in El Paso faced a similar depiction. A

1971 article in the *El Paso Herald-Post,* for example, described the 1917 problem with smallpox in Stormsville, a Mexican American community located on what is now Rim Road. Describing the appointment of Dr. Hugh S. White as city health officer, the newspaper characterized the situation as a "problem." "Superstition compounded the difficulties but, with the aid of a priest, Dr. White's little ivory lancets stopped the threat of a major smallpox [epidemic] in El Paso for all time."

This chapter tells the stories of women who have healed using herbs, hands, and prayers over the centuries in the El Paso-Ciudad Juárez area. First, Juana María Apodaca of San Elizario faced the Spanish Inquisition in 1800 for her work as a healer. Then, one of the city's most well-known *curanderas,* Teresita Urrea, who came to El Paso in 1896, brought with her the healing knowledge she had learned in Sonora, and attracted reporters, spies, and thousands of Paseños seeking help. Finally, we'll examine stories of healers in the twentieth century like Doña Pabla Juárez, whose knowledge is still remembered and honored today by her children, grandchildren, and those who knew her.

In March of 1800, Juana María Venegas of the Presidio of San Elizario was brought before Fray Diego Muñoz Jurado, an authority of the Santo Oficio, more commonly known as the Spanish Inquisition. The priest accused her of healing her neighbor María Filara de los Dolores González. Numerous witnesses testified about her work as a "*curandera supersticiosa,*" a superstitious healer. Although we don't know the ultimate outcome of the investigation, we do know that Venegas was one of the last *curanderas* taken before the Inquisition in Mexico before its dissolution in 1820. The testimony given by witnesses is important in the telling of the histories of *curanderas* in the El Paso region. It reveals that *curanderismo* is deeply rooted in the area, that historically women have been the keepers of the traditional ways of healing, and that many of the ways of healing used in centuries past continue to be used in contemporary times.

When she was brought before Fray Muñoz Jurado, Venegas (also called Apodaca in the Inquisition records) was a resident of the relatively new settlement of San Elizario. The presidial settlement of San Elizario and the church, Nuestra Señora del Pilar y el Glorioso San José, had been completed in 1794, only six years earlier. Unlike other forts in the borderlands, Spanish officials built the presidio not to "protect" the El Paso region, but rather to help administer the "peace" program initiated by the Spanish government in 1786 where government officials provided supplies to native peoples, including alcohol and firearms in order to create a dependent Apache population. The presidio was built on the site of a previous hacienda, Los Tiburcios, which had been abandoned earlier because of a declining population resulting from smallpox epidemics and Indian resistance to colonial rule.

Los Tiburcios had, at one time, been a vibrant community producing grapes, beans, chile, cotton, and maize, among other crops. Founded in the 1720s, the hacienda thrived for a time because of the rich soil and access to water for crops. In fact, in 1779 it was second in the production of maize in the El Paso area. Populated in large part by the extended family of the Tiburcio de Ortegas, the hacienda also included citizens and *genízaros*—detribalized indigenous people. The transition from Los Tiburcios to San Elizario was so recent that the Inquisition documents continually referred to the settlement by both names. The final decades of Los Tiburcios and the first decades of San Elizario saw difficulties as government policies shifted alliances, war with native groups changed, and indigenous people, mestizos, and people who identified as Spaniards worked side by side in the community by the Rio Grande.

Indigenous resistance to colonial rule resulted in a number of successful rebellions throughout the history of Los Tiburcios. The Sumas and Mansos, for example, rebelled against exploitative treatment numerous times in the eighteenth century. In the fall of 1798, Apaches from Magdalena and the San Mateo Mountains gathered and headed for the presidio. The commanding officer of the presidio asked for 150 men. By the summer of 1800, as various *españoles* were appearing before the Spanish Inquisition, pledging that they understood the purpose for which they had been called before the tribunal, military officials from San Elizario began monthly campaigns intended to capture Apaches in order to jail them at the presidio.

Within this atmosphere of constant change, warfare, and uncertainly, Fray Muñoz Jurado began summoning witnesses against the *curandera* Juana María Apodaca. The documents point out that she was also known by the *"mal nombre,"* or bad name, of *La Chalis*. Fray Muñoz Jurado declared that he had attempted to gain information on *"la vida y costumbres de* [the life and customs of] *Juana Venegas,"* although he had learned little. The priest had been born in Santa Eugenia, Córdoba, Spain, in 1749 and was well-known, and sometimes controversial, in New Mexico for decades prior to his coming to El Paso del Norte where he was appointed *vicecustodio* of El Paso in 1798. He carefully took testimony over the course of several months about the healing activities of *La Chalis*. Among the witnesses was María de los Dolores González, who had been treated by Juana María for her severe health problems. Other witnesses included María Elena Olguin, the sixteen-year-old wife of presidial soldier Bernardo Bustillos and daughter of María de Dolores who had also been treated by *La Chalis;* Bustillos himself; María Garcia, who was married to the *alférez* (second lieutenant) of the Presidio of San Gerónimo, Don Juan Olguin, and who was the sister-in-law of María de los Dolores; and Manuel Olguin, the husband of the afflicted woman. All the witnesses were classified as *"españoles,"* a sign of status more than nativity in colonial-era Paso del Norte. Few details are described but the testimony revealed that *La Chalis* was a widow who supported herself through her healing work.

Significant testimony was provided by thirty-year old Bernardo Bustillos of the presidio who told the priest that *La Chalis* has worked on both his mother-in-law and his wife, Elena Olguin. He was also listed as a *"natural"* of the presidio, or a native of San Elizario, which may have meant he was from Los Tiburcios. Bustillos testified that *La Chalis* had cured his wife of tumors that had appeared on her knee and breasts. The healing had occurred while he was out of town, in the Villa of Chihuahua. When he returned, *La Chalis* approached him, asking for payment for the treatment. *La Chalis* told María Elena that she suffered from the same disease as her mother, María Filara de los Dolores González.

The women suffered from a series of debilitating symptoms in addition to the tumors, including headaches and joint and muscle pains.

According to Bustillos, *La Chalis* told them they suffered from a *"maleficio,"* a curse. His wife, María Elena Olguin, testified that *La Chalis,* after taking her mother's pulse, told her that she had the thorns of the nopal, the prickly pear, stuck in her breasts and legs. María Filara testified before the Inquisition that her illness had begun six years earlier when her right arm began to hurt with a terrible pain that ran from her shoulders to the tips of her fingers. Her fingers would become stiff. As time passed, the pain spread to her joints and her legs. In 1799, *La Chalis* arrived at her house and asked if she had suffered an accident. The *curandera* told María Filara to drink an herbal tea each morning.

The remedies described in the Inquisition records included using smoke, herbs such as rosemary and rue, saliva and prayer. Olguin, for example, testified that *La Chalis* had put an herb in her mother's mouth and then her saliva on María Filara's face. The swelling began to subside. She then asked for lamp oil, wet some cotton with it, and put it in the afflicted woman's nostrils. Olguin described a terrifying scene as worms began to come out of her mother. María Elena's testimony echoed her husband's. María Filara's forty-six-year-old husband, Manuel Olguin, told the priest that *La Chalis* had sent them to find herbs, including rosemary and rue, that María Filara would carry in a bag, along with the Apostle's Creed. According to Olguin, *La Chalis* stated that it was with "this that she cured." Olguin told the inquisitor that he had responded to this request by telling *La Chalis* that he believed that only God gave life and because of this, he reported *La Chalis* to his lieutenant.

Like Pat Mora's twentieth-century *curanderas, La Chalis* used prayers and herbs to heal. The herbs used in *La Chalis'* healing practice, rosemary and rue, continue to be employed by *curanderas* today. While the herbs are European in origin, their use by indigenous people is believed to reflect much more ancient beliefs. During the early colonial period the two herbs, which are mentioned in western traditions as far back as Hippocrates, replaced the indigenous plants, *iztauyatl* (wormwood) and *yauhtli* (sweet marigold), which had been used to treat illnesses in Mesoamerican culture for centuries. *La Chalis'* healing of María Filara hearkens to a more ancient time when indigenous people in Central Mexico associated certain diseases and certain healing herbs with specific deities. The pre-invasion use of *iztauyatl* and *yauhtli* was associated with Tlaloc, a Mesoamerican deity connected to diseases such as rheumatism and parasites. The use of rue and rosemary by *La Chalis* for María Filara's symptoms of joint pain and worms reflects the survival of ancient healing methods.

The charges against Juana María Venegas came to an end somewhat abruptly five months after Fray Muñoz Jurado began his investigation. On October 8, 1800, Fray Muñoz Jurado's superior wrote that the *calidad,* or ethnicity, of *La Chalis* had to be clarified because there was evidence that she was an Indian woman and therefore, outside of the jurisdiction of the Inquisition. We do not know what happened to Juana María Venegas nor do we know many details about her life. What she represents is part of a long history of traditional healing going back to pre-contact societies and moving forward to the twenty-first century in the El Paso region.

On June 19, 1896, the *Galveston Daily News* reported on the arrival of Teresita Urrea to El Paso. The reporter noted that she had "generated little attention" when she arrived in El Paso sever-

Teresita Urrea, ca. 1897. *Courtesy of Southwest Collection, Texas Tech University.*

al days earlier, "[b]ut today her name is on everybody's lips." Perhaps it had taken time for word to spread of her healing abilities. "According to report[s] she has made a number of miraculous cures and to-day the modest little home in which she is stopping was besieged by thousands of people . . . all anxious to have the living saint of the Mayo tribe place her hand upon them and heal them." Reporting that many Mexicans had come from the "mountains and valleys," the thousands of people gave the scene "the appearance of a vast army in camp." Newspaper reporter George Speck shared that Teresita's touch had healed him of the long-time rheumatism in his ankles. The same day Teresita announced that there would be rain within four hours although the skies were clear. Despite initial laughter from the crowd, three hours later the clouds gathered and the rains came.

A September 1896 newspaper article with an El Paso byline painted Teresita in a much less favorable light. "For seven years, ever since she was sixteen years old, she has been a veritable firebrand, inciting her fanatic followers to crazy deeds of violence." Labeling her followers "ignorant" and "superstitious," the article told readers they would do anything she asked of them. The reporter cited the numerous rebellions by indigenous peoples in northern Mexico carried out in her name, claiming that Teresita had secretly gone into Mexico following her exile to cause trouble. The article described her as possessing a "squatty figure and a round, fat face just as hundreds of ordinary Mexican women have." Characterizing her followers in equally negative terms, the article asserted that the Yaquis, indigenous people who had rebelled against the Mexican government in a raid on Nogales, Sonora, just three weeks earlier, "were not really Indians" but descendants of Aztecs "who had inherited few of [their] meritorious qualities. . . ." During Teresita's time in El Paso, and throughout her short life, opinions of her varied widely.

The impression she made upon El Pasoans was powerful. When Teresita Urrea came to El Paso in 1896, thousands who had heard about her healing powers waited for her near her home-to-be on Overland and Campbell Streets. During her time in El Paso she lived in three different places, two locations connected to healing in the years following her residence there: her home on Campbell Street eventually became the Tillman Health Center, and the corner of Third and S. Oregon, where she lived later, became the Ladies Hospital, "It's as if the spirit of Teresita left her mark on the urban landscape of our city where history keeps repeating itself," writes historian David Romo.

Teresita was a powerful woman, despite her youth. People said that she smelled of roses when she healed. Skeptics believed in her work after they saw her, and her followers carried her photo and cried out her name as they entered battles against the dictatorship of Porfirio Díaz. Today, people still visit her gravesite in Clifton, Arizona, and scholars continue to write about her. As her great nephew, acclaimed writer Luis Alberto Urrea says of her: "Her presence and her medicine are still powerful."

Teresita Urrea, ca. 1897.
Courtesy of Southwest Collection, Texas Tech University.

Teresita Urrea was many things to many people—a *curandera*, a poor *mestiza* brought into her *hacendado* father's house at the age of fifteen, a revolutionary or at the very least an inspiration for revolutionaries, a Mexican Joan of Arc, a saint, a journalist, and even a beauty queen. She was full of contradictions. Nevertheless, one thing remained consistent throughout her short life: she believed in truth and justice for the poor on both sides of the border. During a period when employers and governments exploited the poor in the harshest of ways, she brought them hope and, often, healing. Teresita spoke out frequently, particularly as she matured. "Truth is everything. Of truth I have no fear. In truth I see no shame," she said. She spoke on behalf of the poor and disenfranchised. She healed with her hands and with herbs and asked for no money. Like generations of *curanderas* before her, she worked for her people. Even though all social classes, races, and ethnicities came to her door for help, "her people" were especially the poor workers and the indigenous peoples of the Mexican North and the US Southwest. Family friend, journalist, and revolutionary Lauro Aguirre, who also made his home in El Paso, believed that she could change their beloved Mexico because of her deep love and ability to speak the truth.

Teresita was born on October 15, 1873, in Rancho de Santana, Ocoroni, Sinaloa, Mexico, in the territories where the Rio Yaqui and the Rio Mayo come together. Over the course of her life, and often fearing for her life, she and her family lived in various locations: Sinaloa, Sonora, Arizona, and for a time, in El Paso, Texas. In a 1900 interview, Teresita told the *San Francisco Examiner* reporter, Helen Dare, that her mother was a very poor Mexican girl. Her name was Cayetana Chávez.

> My father was well-to-do. His name is Tomás Urrea. I am not a legitimate child. My mother was only fourteen when I was born. My father has eighteen children and my mother four, and not one of them is my own brother or sister. I went to school when I was nine years old, but I did not want to study; but later I felt I wanted to know how to read, and I learned my alphabet from a very, very old lady. My writing came to me of itself. I wanted to write, and I wrote, but how I learned I don't know, for I was not taught. On the floor of my mother's house I first wrote with my little finger in the dust.

Teresita's mother, Cayetana Chávez, a Tehueco Indian, lived a difficult life, giving birth at fourteen. Although her child's father, Tomás Urrea, owned a fine home, she gave birth, as had generations of indigenous women before her, under a *ramada,* on a *petate,* on the edge of an *arroyo.* Her first child, baptized Niña Garcia Nona María Rebecca Chávez, would be later called "Teresita, la Santa de Cabora."

When Teresita was three years old, Porfirio Díaz, a hero in Mexico's fight against the French occupation in the 1860s, took power. From 1876 until his exile in 1911, Díaz ruled Mexico with a heavy hand. He and his advisors intended to "modernize" Mexico, and the Mexican government invited foreign investors and many American businesses began to buy property in Mexico. The government took land from small farmers in order to turn it over to large landowners. Rather than growing the staples that could feed the nation—corn and beans—commercial agriculture began to turn to exportable crops like rubber and coffee. The government deported thousands of Yaquis and other native people to the Yucatán as slaves. Increasingly landless, with the price of food increasing and wages decreasing, or facing a quick death in concentration camps, tropical plantations, or mines, Mexico's desperate poor began preparing for revolution.

However, it was not only the poor who opposed Díaz. Many middle-class landowners also went again him. Díaz responded with threats of arrest, imprisonment, and sometimes execution. When Tomás Urrea found himself a target of the *Porfirian* government for supporting the wrong political candidate, he moved his household, including Cayetana and her family to Cabora,

Sonora. Teresita grew up nearby, at the rancho of Aquihuiquichi, in a mesquite hut, with her mother and her aunt's family. Sometime before Teresita's fifteenth birthday, her mother left the family, and Teresita was left alone to deal with her abusive aunt. In 1888, Don Tomás sent for Teresita to come to his *hacienda* in Cabora, some say at her request.

In Cabora, Huila, a *curandera* who helped run the Urrea household, took Teresita under her wing. She was a midwife and a healer who attended the poor and the native peoples of the area. She taught Teresita how to heal with herbs, although by then it was clear that Teresita already had a *don*, a gift for healing. Teresita's life changed. She began to join her father and his friends as they discussed philosophy, politics, and history. Her work as a healer truly began after a violent incident in Teresita's life. When she was sixteen years old, she went into a coma. There are different stories to explain the coma. Some say that a man named Millan raped her after she rejected him. Others attribute the coma to an overdose of the medicinal plants she worked with, or perhaps epilepsy. After days of attending her as she lay comatose, Huila and the others, including her father and a physician, saw that she had no pulse and that she felt cold to the touch, so they prepared her body for burial. Laying her in the casket they had built for her, her body bathed and dressed in white, the people of the rancho entered, mourning. She unexpectedly woke up and announced that someone would die within three days. When her teacher Huila died three days later, she was buried in the casket built for Teresita.

Her time in El Paso made a profound difference for many people. The story of the Vargas family is but one example.

> In 1915 or 1916, Anita [Urrea Treviño] went to the house of Manuel and Liberata Vargas in El Paso. In this house was a wax statue of Teresa, dressed in beautiful garments, and under glass. The Vargas had made the statue, took it to the Exposition in St. Louis where it won first prize. . . . The reason for making the statue was that Mrs. Vargas lost her son in the river and asked Teresa what had happened to her son, Teresa told them where to find the body in the river. They were so grateful they made a life-sized statue of Teresita.

Teresita, la Santa de Cabora, represents a complex historical figure whose healing work changed people everywhere she lived.

In his study of Mexicans in El Paso, historian Mario T. Garcia points to the presence of *curanderas* in Mexican communities at the turn of the twentieth century. Garcia writes that "in their transition to a new American setting," Mexican families preserved many "native cultural traditions." These traditions included songs, religious ceremonies, and food. They also included the use of medicinal herbs. Quoting Mexican anthropologist Manuel Gamio, who conducted extensive interviews in Southwest immigrant communities, Garcia points to the fact that, "In almost all parts of America where there are Mexicans and Mexican Americans, there are Mexican drug stories in which there is a great sale of every sort of medicinal plant."

While Esperanza Estevis may not have called herself a *curandera,* the owner of El Paje Botiquín carried out the ancient healing tradition of using herbs to heal. Mrs. Estevis and her husband opened the *yerbería* at 702 S. Oregon Street in South El Paso in 1927. At the time, she was a twenty-nine-year-old mother of five children. She had come to the United States as a teenager in 1917. According to their son, Rodolfo, the store allowed the Estevises to support their seven children. In a 1960 article in the *El Paso Herald-Post*, Mrs. Estevis related that her herbs, which came from all over Mexico and the United States, were good for many things, ranging from stomachaches to *mal de ojo*, an illness caused by envy or admiration and to which babies were particularly susceptible. Popular herbs included *manzanilla*, *yerba buena*, and *Té Malabar*, a tea that cost a dollar a box. In addition, Mrs. Estevis sold a variety of herbs used for cooking, including laurel (bay leaf), star anise, sassafras, and *popotillo* (Mormon Tea). Finally, El Paje also sold incense and items like *ojo de venado*, which the reporter Ken Flynn wrote could "ward off a curse." Flynn described this as a "superstition among rural Mexicans." In the early 1970s, Mrs. Estevis's son Rodolfo reopened the store at 515 S. Oregon. Rodolfo told reporter Robert Seltzer that his customers came from southern New Mexico as well as El Paso, and that he purchased herbs from Mexico City, Monterrey, and San Antonio as well as harvesting herbs from the desert.

Grandmothers and mothers in Mexican com-

El Paje Hierberia—Inside View, 1960s. *Courtesy of Clark S. Knowlton Collection, Special Collections Department, The University of Texas at El Paso Library.*

Nazaria Hernández de Yáñez.
Courtesy of Alvaro Yáñez.

Filomena Herrera de Rodríguez.
Courtesy of Jaime Ruiz.

munities in both Mexico and the United States have maintained traditional ways of healing through the present day, particularly within their families and among their close neighbors. Alvaro Yáñez remembers his mother Nazaria Hernández de Yáñez's abilities to use herbs to cure ailments such as *"mal de ojo," "empacho,"* cough, sore throat, stomachaches, and fever.

Nazaria was born in Camargo, Chihuahua, in February 1935 where she attended school through fourth grade. After her marriage, she and her family moved to Ciudad Juárez and then to El Paso. Like Estevis, she did not call herself a *curandera,* yet she maintained knowledge of plants and prayers, using this expertise for the benefit of her children and grandchildren. She employed *manzanilla, estafiate, yerba buena,* and *gordolobo,* herbs which she would purchase from Tarahumara vendors in Chihuahua. Throughout cities in Chihuahua, it is a common sight to see Tarahumara women, dressed in brightly colored floral skirts and tops, selling their handmade, fragrant pine needle baskets and small packages of herbs.

Her daughter-in-law Edith Yáñez remembers Nazaria's knowledge of traditional healing that became apparent when her daughter was born. She was the first granddaughter on her husband's side of the family and therefore received a great deal of attention. The baby "would cry incessantly and we'd try soothing her with no relief." It was during one of these times that Nazaria took an egg and rubbed it on her new granddaughter while saying prayers. The tradition of healing with an egg is a timeless practice in Mexican communities. The egg absorbs the negativity from an individual's body. Although Edith was skeptical at first, she soon saw that her daughter stopped crying. When her mother-in-law broke the egg, they discovered that it had cooked during the healing. The memory of Nazaria's traditional knowledge lives on in the memories of her son and daughter-in-law.

Within some border families, the knowledge of traditional herbs has been passed down from generation to generation to the present. Rosa Maria Rodríguez, born in Parral, Chihuahua, a piano teacher for over forty years, still retains the extensive herbal knowledge of her mother, Filomena Herrera de Rodríguez, and her grandmother, Ramona Poblano de Herrera Yáñez. Ramona was born at the Hacienda de Santa Rosa, near Parral, around 1888. She was widowed at thirty-three when her husband died during the Spanish Flu epidemic of 1918. Her daughter Filomena was born in 1914 during the Mexican Revolution. When Filomena moved to Ciudad Juárez in 1937 as a newlywed, her husband suggested they bring her mother, and Filomena moved in 1941. The two women laid a strong foundation for their family, turning to the use of herbs for common ailments. Because it was not customary for people to visit doctors when Ramona and Filomena were raising their families, the knowledge of herbs was vital to the health of their children. The women obtained herbs from the *yerberias,* herbs shops, in downtown Cuidad Juárez, as well as from Tarahumara women who sold them to make a living. Rosa remembers the extensive number of herbs utilized by her mother and grandmother for common ailments. Some ailments are culturally specific to Mexican communities. *Empacho,* for example, refers to food sticking to either the stomach or the intestine, causing great discomfort. Filomena and Ramona, like other women, turned to a tea of *estafiate* along with massaging the back of the legs. Another culturally defined ailment is *aire* or air, whose symptoms include experiencing pain when breathing, which can occur when a person is exposed to cold air. A tea of laurel (bay leaf) and cinnamon was used. In addition, the practice of *ventosas* was used to pull the air out of the person's body. A copper coin was placed on the area exhibiting *aire,* a small candle and a glass were placed on top. This caused a vacuum that pulled the *aire* out. Other traditional remedies, such as lemon, water, and salt for dehydration or *nopales* for diabetes have been appropriated by commercial interests in contemporary times. Today, the family of Filomena and Ramona continue to use traditional remedies, honoring the knowledge of their mother and grandmother.

Paola L. Juárez provided a precious gift to all the people who knew her—the unconditional love of her "healing way." Pabla, as her family called her, was an *abuela,* a grandmother of the healing way whose knowledge was rooted in the ways of native peoples of this area. She was born somewhere between Zuni Pueblo in New Mexico and the Huichol region of the Mexican state of Zacatecas as her family traveled, visiting relatives. For generations her family had journeyed back and forth between what is now the US southwest and the Mexican north. Pabla was born on one of those travels, and she grew up knowing the region on both sides of the river intimately—the land,

Ventura and Pabla in the 1920s in Zuni.
Courtesy of Andres Juárez & family.

the plants, and the people. She was a "child of *los llanos,*" relates her son Andres Juárez. Pabla and generations of her family followed the practice of indigenous peoples who have traveled across the continent for millennia, sharing knowledge, goods, and technology with relatives and other communities.

Pabla and her family's history was truly what her son called "a back and forth story." Her brother, Marcelino, for example, fought both in the Mexican Revolution and in the US military during World War I. Her uncle was born in the United States yet experienced being "returned" to Mexico during the tragic repatriations of the Great Depression. Pabla also experienced the harshness of the artificial border and remembered being deloused at the border when she was a child entering the United States on her family's travels. At El Paso, then the most significant port of entry from Mexico into the United States, government officials built a disinfection plant in 1917 where thousands of Mexicans entering the country were fumigated and exposed to hazardous chemicals. Such disinfections went on for decades as the US government attempted to stop the spread of infectious diseases that officials claimed Mexicans brought. She attended the school at Zuni as a young child until her mother withdrew her because of the activities of the Bureau of Indian Affairs. This going back and forth, as a child and an adult, created challenges that Pabla navigated throughout her life. Although the political dividing line played a role in Pabla's day-to-day life and that of her family, in many ways, the border was "really an abstraction."

Like the generations of women before her, Pabla was "embedded in an ancient way," says her son. She learned the healing way from her mother Ventura, who was born in the 1860s. Ventura, in turn, had learned from her mother, Eustaquia who was probably born in the 1840s. Pabla's children can still name at least seven generations of grandmothers who healed their families and their communities: Pabla, Ventura, Eustaquia, Braulia, and three or four Juanas. One Juana was from Zuni, another from the Tarahumara country in Chihuahua. The family stories of the grandmothers, the generations, go back to pre-Colombian times.

The women's histories and their knowledge

of healing crisscross the modern-day border. The facts of Pabla's life reflect this. She spent her childhood in Valparaiso, Zacatecas, and Zuni Pueblo; her young adulthood was spent in Boquillas, Chihuahua, and her adult years in Ciudad Juárez and El Paso. There was no "conception of European boundaries. It was all about the familial ties."

Her son believes that there are "plenty of Pablas in the world." Her life, like those of so many other women, was filled with joys and sorrows. Pabla gave birth to thirteen children, nine of whom still live. She was known for her generosity and hospitality. All were welcomed, and she kept a pot of beans cooking on the stove to feed the steady stream of people who came to see her. Her sense of dignity was steadfast in the face of racial slurs and insults. Her husband, Marcelino M. Juárez, worked as a migrant worker and was a noted Matachin teacher and dancer. He was also of an ancient family with roots in the medicine ways. Marcelino could build anything he envisioned and for years kept traditional ceremonies alive. Abuela Pabla, Andres, and Juan Francisco Juárez, MD, another of Doña Pabla and Don Marcelino's children, were pivotal to the founding of the Traditional Circle in El Paso, which maintains traditional ceremonies and practices.

Doña Pabla at age eighty.
Courtesy of Andres Juárez & family.

Pabla's "healing way," the way of the generations of healers in her family, included the use of herbs. She knew the plants and their uses, as well as where they grew in the region from Zacatecas to Zuni to the Mimbres Mountains. Andres remembers the days spent with his mother and siblings harvesting the many medicinal plants that grow in the Chihuahua desert. It is said that every plant in the desert has a healing property that has developed as a response to living and often thriving in the arid and hot environment. Their father, Marcelino, would drive them to Hueco Tanks, supplied with water and lemons to quench their thirst during the hot desert day, returning for them at the end of the day. Hueco Tanks, now a state park, has been home to indigenous peoples for over 11,000 years. Its presence as a natural concentration of water, plants, and animals has drawn people to it for thousands of years. Pabla's gathering plants on that ancient land is part of a long tradition. She recalled making similar journeys to Hueco with her mother during her days in Zuni. During those visits they would stay at the home of her mother's first cousin, also a healer who lived in San Elizario.

Abuela Pabla's healing ways worked miracles for those in need. A woman in Casas Grandes with rheumatoid arthritis experienced a miracle, for example, when Pabla used lard, tobacco, and other herbs to make an ointment which she rubbed on the affected hand. Following the treatment, the gnarled hand straightened out. She used *saguaro,* the Sonoran Desert's stately cactus with its thick column arms reaching out to the sky and its creamy white flowers, to heal a woman's breast that had turned black. "It was magical to a child," says her son. He witnessed many other such healings conducted by his mother. Although he never saw it happen, his mother told him that Abuela Ventura could perform surgeries.

Pabla did not call herself a *curandera,* which she viewed as a too narrow a term. The healing way involved not only the physical, but also the emotional and the spiritual. "What others did was of no matter to her," remembers Andres. "She was there to fix that broken arm . . ." and to be of service. Pabla believed that judgment of others or what she thought about an individual was of no use in her role as a healer. This lack of judging others, along with her sense of giving, enabled her to help many. From the example of his mother, Andres believes that the healing way is "not an assembly line" medical model. It is intimate and based on unconditional love. "Her touch and her embrace helped us belong." Raised with a world view that placed her as part of a long line of grandmothers with relations to families and communities that could not be partitioned by an artificial border, Pabla imparted a fundamental sense of belonging. Her son stated that his mother's lesson was the "miracle of just being. That's the biggest story and it's not unique to my mother. We are in relationship to each other." Doña Pabla's healing ways continue to serve the community through the work of her apprentice, Carlos Aceves, and through the lives of her children and grandchildren.

For generations, women have healed their families and their communities, keeping ancient traditions alive. Through their knowledge and love, they have created stronger community bonds and ensured the physical, spiritual, emotional, and intellectual survival of their children and grandchildren. Despite their invisibility in the historical record, their memories and their wisdom remain present in the family stories handed down through the generations. This wisdom, with its roots in the ancient cultures of Mexico and the Southwestern United States, ties the generations together in the most profound of ways.

Bibliographic Essay

This chapter would not have been possible without the assistance of several individuals who generously shared the stories of their mothers and grandmothers with me: Alvaro and Edith Yáñez, Andres Juárez, Jaime Ruiz, and Rosa Maria Rodríguez. Cynthia Renteria provided the initial information on the Spanish Inquisition trial of Juana María Venegas from the Spanish Archives of New Mexico. Jessica Ruizquez researched contemporary *curanderas* with great enthusiasm. Thank you all for your kindness. Secondary sources on traditional healing include psychiatric nurse/*curandera* Elena Avila's *Woman Who Glows in the Dark: A Curandera Reveals Traditional Aztec Secrets* and several books by Eliseo "Cheo" Torres, including *Curandero: A Life in Mexican Folk Healing. They All Want Magic: Curanderas and Folk Healing* by sociologist

Elizabeth de la Portilla also provided important information. To learn more about the life of Teresita Urrea, see William Curry Holden's *Teresita,* Luis Alberto Urrea's novel *The Hummingbird's Daughter,* and David Dorado Romo's *A Ringside Seat to a Revolution: An Underground Cultural History of El Paso and Ciudad Juárez, 1892-1923. Cultural Encounters: The Impact of the Inquisition in Spain and the New World,* edited by Mary Elizabeth Perry and Anne J. Cruz, as well as Rick Hendrick's *San Elizario: Spanish Presidio to Texas County Seat* helped me contextualize the life of *curandera* Juana María Venegas. Newspapers such as the *El Paso Herald-Post,* the *Galveston Daily News,* and the *San Francisco Examiner* provided significant information on societal views of traditional healing. Finally, The University of Texas at El Paso has created a website to provide information on the safety of herbal remedies and Mexican Traditional Medicine (MTM), which can be accessed at www.herbalsafety.utep.edu.

I would also like to thank Pat Mora and Arte Público Press for permission to use an excerpt from the poem *Curandera.*

Finally, this chapter is dedicated to Elena Avila, a *curandera* and author born in El Paso, who passed away in March 2011.

Chapter 4

THEY MARCHED TO A DIFFERENT DRUMMER

by Nancy Miller Hamilton

SINCE EL PASO'S EARLIEST DAYS, outstanding women have drawn on courage and ingenuity in moving the community forward. For some, their focus was on family, but others explored businesses and unusual careers. One woman built a million-dollar hotel; another pursued the rare vocation of bullfighting.

An enterprising newcomer to the El Paso valley in 1860 said she was the first to make butter and sell it in town, making her perhaps the first female entrepreneur in the area. Despite her success in small business, she reacted to the combination of Indian raids on livestock, her husband's call to arms as a Confederate soldier, and the influx of "northern troops" and moved eastward with her small children by 1863.

Susan Dowell Shacklett churned milk at her brother Ben Dowell's ranch upriver from El Paso in 1860 and sold butter in El Paso for a dollar a pound. *Courtesy of Robert Poppenhusen.*

Susan Dowell Shacklett and her husband, Burnis B. Shacklett, were living happily in Kentucky when her brother, Benjamin S. Dowell, returned there with his Tigua Indian wife, Juana, and their six-year-old daughter Mary, to visit family. He had become a successful businessman and rancher in El Paso and persuaded his kinfolk to join him in his ventures out west. His brother

Nehemiah (Nim), who had been there a while, was tending to Ben's affairs in his absence.

Susan's memoir recalled that after ten years of marriage, she and Burnis had four children when they "left our native land" of Kentucky. On the way west, they had to camp at Turkey Creek for a month awaiting a wagon train. "We could not travel any further alone, on account of danger of Indians," she explained. "We traveled mostly at night because the Indians were so hostile and water was so scarce from [one] watering place to another. We carried water in kegs for the family, but the mules had to do without."

They reached El Paso about August 15, 1860, and lived on a ranch owned by Ben in the area formerly called White's Rancho or Frontera. (A current landmark in the vicinity is the State Line Restaurant.) Ben had acquired hundreds of acres of land in the Upper Valley eight miles up the Rio Grande from the town, as well as business properties in the town itself. His claim to fame would become his election in 1873 as El Paso's first mayor.

Susan said they spent a year at the ranch, with Mexicans to herd and milk the thirty-five milk cows. "I made fifteen pounds of butter a week," she recalled, "the first butter made in that country, sold it for one dollar per pound."

But the hostile Indians (unlike her sister-in-law's Tiguas, who were scouts for the US Army) came around the house at night. "We could not see them, only their tracks. At last they killed the man that carried milk and butter to town. So we thought it time for us to leave. So we went to El Paso and kept a hotel until the northern troops came in on the north and cut our soldiers off from their supplies and they had to retreat and come south."

The Shacklett family joined the Confederates for part of their march from New Mexico back into Texas, going as far as San Antonio. Then they went to Sherman, where her brother James was living. Burnis entered the army about that time, and Susan's brood had grown from four to six children, the oldest aged ten. After the war, they lived on a farm near Sherman for twenty-five years, then moved to Gainesville in 1881, where Burnis died seven years later. Susan penned her memoir in 1915 at age eighty-five. She never went back to El Paso.

Susan Shacklett's husband and her brother Ben were both veterans of the War with Mexico. While it would be pleasant to think of Susan Shacklett as the example of El Paso's first businesswoman, actually that role was taken by another veteran of that war whose *nom de guerre* was The Great Western. Her first name was Sarah, but over the years her surname had variations related to her several marriages, among them Borginnis, Davis, and finally Bowman, the name on her tombstone at the National Cemetery Presidio at San Francisco. But it was as The Great Western—likening her imposing stature to that of the largest ship afloat (when it was built in 1838)—that she was remembered by most who encountered her.

Early in the war, Sarah was dubbed the Heroine of Fort Brown for her bravery in feeding the troops during a bombardment by the Mexicans. As the wife of a soldier, she was allowed to travel with the troops as laundress and cook, and continued her adventures in Mexico. In Monterrey, she set up the American House with all the comforts of home for the soldiers. Moving on to Saltillo in early 1847, she set up another American House, described as "a sort of headquarters for everybody." The Battle of Buena Vista erupted in February near Saltillo. Sarah's long red hair and six-foot height drew attention as she nursed the wounded of Zachary Taylor's army and carried them to safety.

The widowed Sarah remained in Mexico several months after the close of the war. She tried to join a departing military column but was told she had to be the wife of a soldier in order to do so. She found a willing subject and signed on as a laundress. At Chihuahua, the troops split, one group heading north to Santa Fe and the other to California. When Sarah chose to go north, she ended up in El Paso to become the one historians recognize as the town's first hotelier and businesswoman.

The historical record finds her noticed by Lt. Henry Chase Whiting of the US Corps of Topographical Engineers, rowing a canoe from El Paso del Norte, Mexico, across the Rio Grande to what would become El Paso, in February 1849. When she met Whiting and his soldiers on the shore, she was so excited, he said she "lifted us one after another off our feet." She wanted to wait in Texas for the army to arrive. The military was not only leaving Mexico; the US Army planned to establish the Post of El Paso (later to become Fort Bliss), with six companies of soldiers headed that way in June of 1849. For a hotel keeper, there was also the prospect of business from gold-seekers heading for California. Thousands were camping in the river valley at the time Sarah settled there.

Travelers did not soon forget her or her hospitality. One of them wrote in a July 1849 letter: "We found the far-famed Great Western at this place on our side of the river. She was celebrated in the Mexican War and did good service in a number of battles. She is six feet one inch in height, and well proportioned. She treated us with much kindness." Another man heading westward that same month kept a diary in which he entered: "Among the residents of the place is numbered 'The Great Western,' a female notorious in the late war."

Sarah left the valley for Socorro, New Mexico, site of another army post. Sometime in 1850, she was counted in the census there as Sarah Bourjette, age thirty-three, born in Tennessee. She was known as the wife of a sergeant, Albert Bowman, and went by that name the rest of her life, spent mainly in Yuma, Arizona.

Francisca (Doña Paca) Alarcón vda. de Faudoa, a pioneer landowner and political activist, came to El Paso in 1856 as a young widow with three small children. They traveled by oxcart from Chihuahua City, through territory subject to Indian raids.

Born in Chihuahua in 1838, she married the president of Banco Minero, Luis Faudoa. She was in her twenties when he died, leaving her well off, and she decided to move to El Paso, where she began acquiring property in what became the downtown district. As opportunities arose, she made money from her properties, renting apartments and providing room and board to prominent businessmen such as Anson Mills. When Benito Juárez was in exile in the 1860s across the river in Paso del Norte, which was later renamed after him, Doña Paca carried secret messages to him from the US Army officers of Fort Bliss.

She married her second husband, William (Bill) Conklin, not long after he moved to town in about 1858. Anson Mills drew the first plat of El Paso in 1859 and labeled Lots 83 and 86 on El

Mrs. Francisca Alarcón, affectionately known as Doña Paca, was a political activist in El Paso many years before women were allowed to vote. Francisca Alarcón moved to El Paso in 1856 from Chihuahua City and acquired land holdings in what became the downtown area. *Photo from family scrapbook of her granddaughter, the late Rita Faudoa. Author's files.*

Paso Street as owned by Conklin. Lot 86 became part of Sonora Street when Hotel Paso del Norte was built in 1912 immediately to the north.

Bill Conklin was described by Rex Strickland, editor of W. W. Mills' memoir, as "a merchant, gambler, adventurer of parts, and occasional driver for the Butterfield Overland Mail." The circumstances of his death a few years later were unknown, according to the historian. Doña Paca's granddaughter, Rita Faudoa, told an interviewer in 1961 that she thought Conklin had been assassinated by a prominent El Pasoan but she gave no further information about the incident.

Rita Faudoa also recalled that Doña Paca's home had a large living room where the first Jesuit mass was held in El Paso. It had a ballroom for social gatherings for Fort Bliss officers and friends from the community.

Long before women were allowed to vote in Texas, Doña Paca became a political activist. Anglos dubbed her Grandma Parker, as they heard "Paca" as the more familiar English surname. Her daughter Ysabel married George Look, who campaigned successfully for a city council position, which he held from 1894 to 1895 and from 1901 to 1907. She would ride a mule sidesaddle through town, doling out silver coins to potential voters at a rate of about three dollars a vote.

George Look had business enterprises in Ciudad Juárez with Park Pitman, but was best known as a partner in one of the town's most popular saloons, the Gem, at 127 South El Paso Street, from 1898 to 1906.

Doña Paca's son, Francisco (Don Pancho) Faudoa, built a brick house in the Cape Cod architectural style at 416 West Overland Street. In her later years, she lived there, as did her granddaughter, Rita.

One of her favorite memories was of the day the Southern Pacific Railroad came to El Paso in 1881. In a 1923 interview, she said the arrival of the railroad was undoubtedly the biggest local event she ever witnessed. It forever changed the nature of the community, linking it with the rest of the world in all directions.

Strickland said Mrs. Alarcón was the last of pre-Civil War residents of El Paso at the time of her death at ninety-seven on November 6, 1925. She had twenty-one grandchildren and fourteen great-grandchildren. Rita remembered her grandmother as a woman of great generosity who helped many of her tenants and others in need.

Edith Phelan Lane covered the Mexican Revolution for American magazines and spent her later years in El Paso. The man at her right is Francisco Madero, who would shortly become president of Mexico. *Author's files.*

El Paso historian Cleofas Calleros described Edith Phelan Lane as "one of the most interesting of the people brought to El Paso by the [Mexican] Revolution. . . . She was a fine reporter and gave the world firsthand, accurate news of the revolution, often traveling with Villa's army to get her stories." She gave Calleros Pancho Villa's saddle blanket, which he used to bind a set of books.

Edith was assigned by *Harper's Weekly* to cover the Revolution in 1910, with her mother going along as chaperone. Francisco Madero, who was to successfully unseat Porfirio Díaz as president, granted her an interview when his revolutionary troops were camped along the Rio Grande opposite the El Paso smelter. She wrote "Campaigning with Mr. Madero" for *Collier's* (October 28, 1911) and "Situation in Mexico" for *Harper's* (August 8, 1912). She also did pieces for *Literary Digest* and *Outlook* during this period.

In January 1914, she produced "American Woman's Letters from Mexico" for *World's Work* and a description of the Fort Bliss army camp for *Outlook*. Under the pseudonym McGregor, she did a *Harper's* piece on "The Mexican Revolution and the Character of Its Leaders" (December 20, 1913).

Also for *Harper's*, she wrote in 1914 of revolutionary leaders Pancho Villa, Venustiano Carranza, and Victoriano Huerta, the last again as McGregor. For *Outlook* she described "Fighting on the Mexican Border" (September 15, 1915), and for *Nation* wrote of the current news coverage of events in Mexico.

Through all this, she spent some time riding with Villa's troops and was briefly his publicity agent, helping him maintain an acceptable appearance with American readers whose funds and arms were important to his cause.

After the revolution, Edith traveled widely in Europe and other parts of the world and chose to live her last forty-nine years in El Paso. During the 1950s, she enjoyed visiting the newsroom of the *El Paso Times,* reminiscing with fellow journalists about her adventures as a reporter. She died September 15, 1959, at her home, 817 Myrtle Avenue, and had no known survivors.

Thanks to a woman's influence, the campus of The University of Texas at El Paso is unique in its adoption of the architectural style of the tiny Himalayan kingdom of Bhutan.

Kathleen Lois Worrell came to El Paso in 1914 when her husband, Stephen H. Worrell, was placed in charge of the new School of Mines and Metallurgy, which was administered under The University of Texas Board of Regents. He was both dean and professor of mining and metallurgy, having gained his professional experience in Mexico and the United States. Community leaders had purchased a former military academy's campus for the school east of Fort Bliss (now part of the main post).

An artist and writer, Mrs. Worrell quickly adapted to the role of hostess for social events and mother hen to the twenty-seven students.

Tragedy struck early in the morning of October 29, 1916, when fire destroyed the Main Building, despite the efforts of a bucket brigade of soldiers. Dean Worrell was away in Arizona, so his wife telegraphed news of the fire to Robert E. Vinson, president of The University of Texas in Austin. He passed the word to Governor James E. Ferguson and advised that a new site would be needed for the school, along with funding from the legislature. That possibility had already loomed, as there was a military buildup due to Pancho Villa's raid of Columbus, New Mexico, in March 1916, and a water shortage on La Noria Mesa, site of the school and the fort.

The governor at that time had stormy relations with the legislature and the board of regents; appointments to fill vacancies on the board were stalled in the senate. By August 1917, the house of representatives brought articles of impeachment against the governor, and after charges were sustained by the senate, he was deposed. These actions delayed progress on the new school.

Meanwhile, Kathleen Worrell was busy with suggestions for a new campus for her husband's school. A group of El Paso businessmen had donated a new site in the Franklin Mountains foothills north of Sunset Heights. She noted the resemblance of the rugged andesite hills to the Himalayan vistas pictured in the April 1914 issue of *The National Geographic* magazine. John Claude White, a British engineer and political officer, had written "Castles in the Air" about Bhutan, illustrated with seventy-four photographs.

She won her husband's approval for the proposal and he wrote to Vinson on December 14, 1916:

> We have selected as a tentative plan a type of architecture suited to mountainous country known as the Bhutanese, which is a type of architecture peculiar to Bhutan country in the Himalayas about 250 miles north of Calcutta.

Tom Lea Sr., El Paso attorney and a member of the site committee appointed by Governor Ferguson, had just had a house designed by El Paso's most prominent architect, Henry Trost, and recommended him for the design of the new school. Charles M. Gibson of another architectural firm was engaged to execute preliminary sketches. Trost, who had designed the buildings for the military academy which was the first home of the mining school, then was assigned the project of doing a new school in Bhutanese style, relying on Mrs. Worrell's magazine pictures as guidelines. Features of the style, which is also found in neighboring Tibet, were a low-hipped roof with wide, overhanging cornices, and battened outside walls which increase in thickness toward the bottom. An ornamental frieze of brick and tile extended parallel to the roofline, technically signifying to the Bhutanese that the building was used for religious purposes.

The first group of buildings was ready for occupancy in January 1918 for an enrollment increase to sixty-one students. Dean and Mrs. Worrell built a bungalow adjacent to the campus in 1921 and lived there until he decided to return to the engineering profession in 1923. Worrell's successor as dean, John W. Kidd, and his wife resided there until his death in 1941. The house had various other uses until 1990 when UTEP President Diana Natalicio assigned it to the Heritage Commission. It houses displays and research materials about the history of the university.

The Worrells moved to Hawaii where Kathleen continued to pursue her interests in art and writing. She became active in the National League of American Pen Women and served as president of the Honolulu Branch from 1928 to 1931. The organization's national magazine, *The Bulletin*, reported in June 1931 that she had published a short story and a poem in issues of the *Honolulu Mercury*. According to the May 1932 issue, more of her poems had been published in *Woman's Magazine* of London and an article drawing on her experiences as an engineer's wife, "Women in the Mexican Hills," in the *Mexico Mining Journal*. She also had to her credit a book of poetry, *Hawaiian Moods*.

SUNDAY MORNING, SEPTEMBER 9, 1928.

To Visit on Mainland

Mrs. S. H. Worrell will sail on the City of Honolulu on the twenty-second of the month for a visit of several months on the mainland.—Post Photo.

Newspaper clipping announcing the arrival of Kathleen Worrell in Hawaii. *Courtesy of the Honolulu Branch of the National League of American Pen Women, Hamilton Library, University of Hawaii at Manoa.*

Dean Worrell died in 1938 in Hawaii. His

widow moved to Fresno, California, in 1942. She died in Riverside County on December 17, 1951, at age sixty-eight. They had no children.

Her heritage lives on at UTEP where there are not only buildings related stylistically to Bhutan, but relics of connections between that nation's government and the school in the form of embroidered banners and an ornate inlaid wood altar. An annual celebration of Bhutan Days has been established, and in recent years the university has accepted a number of Bhutanese graduate and undergraduate students.

A remarkable woman left as a monument to her business acumen the Hotel Cortez Building, facing San Jacinto Plaza downtown. Alzina Allis Orndorff De Groff was the spirit behind one of the most successful hotels in the history of the community, briefly operated another one as well, and even found time for the women's suffrage movement.

Originally from Louisiana, she had married Lee H. Orndorff from Missouri at seventeen and they soon moved to Tucson. Their three sons—Burtram, Seth, and Lee—were small boys when their father was killed in a railway accident. Alzina supported her family by renting an eight-room hotel that she named the Orndorff.

Part of her legendary history has to do with the famed Apache leader Geronimo who spent much of his time in Arizona. While she was operating the small hotel, word went out that Geronimo was leading a raid on the town. Instead of fleeing from him, however, Mrs. Orndorff prepared a large meal and when he came to the door, invited him and his friends in to eat. "*Mi casa es su casa* (my house is your house)," she said in the Southwestern tradition. They thanked her and left, committing no thievery or abuse. A few days later, a young Apache came to the hotel and presented her three baskets as gifts from Geronimo, who continued to send her gifts over a period of time.

The young widow quickly demonstrated her innate understanding of the hotel business. She educated her three boys in her skills and during the 1880s and 1890s the Orndorff prospered, eventually becoming a sixty-room enterprise. When she married Tucson's postmaster, Charles De Groff, he joined her in the hotel operation but was lukewarm when she proposed moving to El Paso in 1898. He gave in to her wishes, even though the sale of the Tucson business did not come close to covering the cost of their new one. Its success enabled them to repay a loan in good time.

Alzina De Groff and her second husband, Charles, moved to El Paso in 1899 to assume ownership of the city's oldest hotel, the Vendome. They bought it from Joshua Raynolds and Charles Reeves for $41,000 and renamed it the Orndorff, honoring her first husband. She added a fourth floor and verandas around the lower three floors.

The formal opening of the refurbished hotel was on June 24, 1899, complete with a grand ballroom and dining hall. An El Paso newspaper reporter said the building had undergone a complete transformation, with walls repapered, floors covered with Brussels carpets, and elegant new furniture. Every room had hot and cold water, with public baths on each floor. Glass chandeliers burned gas. Room rates were fifty cents single, one dollar double, with three meals a day for thirty dollars a month.

The three Orndorff sons also moved to El Paso with their families. Burt continued in the hotel business and Seth and Lee entered real estate. Seth also spent several years in public service as a county commissioner and sheriff. A distinction for Burt was his election in 1916 as a delegate to the League of Nations meeting in Washington, DC.

In 1907, the family purchased the Sheldon Hotel opposite the southwest corner of the plaza, the site where the present Plaza Hotel stands (the Sheldon having burned in 1929). Burt managed it for several years. The De Groffs sold their interest in 1916.

Texas Street (now Avenue) starts in mid-downtown and extends east, but had few buildings beyond downtown when Mrs. De Groff came to El Paso. She anticipated that it would attract businesses in the near future and bought acreage along it, including the site for a family home, The Ranchita, at 2301 Texas. The family also bought extensive acreage below Ysleta for The Big Ranch.

Besides her business interests, "Mama Dee," as she was known to family and friends, was involved in her community. She was the first president of the El Paso Equal Franchise League, advocating women's right to vote, and also headed the El Paso Civic League. In 1923, Texas Governor Pat Neff named her to the first board of directors of the new Texas Technological College in Lubbock, which boasted 2,000 students.

Her vision for improving the Orndorff Hotel continued to fascinate her, and in 1925 she had the building razed in order to replace it with a million-dollar edifice. She saved the bricks and used them to build a block of stores fronting on Texas Street and her Ranchita there.

Henry Trost, El Paso's premier architect, was engaged to design the eleven-story building, whose total cost ran to $1.5 million. Trost's biographers describe the style as Spanish Colonial

Alzina Allie Orndorff DeGroff, a dynamic civic leader and businesswoman, built the Orndorff Hotel, now the Cortez Building, a landmark in downtown El Paso. *Courtesy of her family.*

Revival, based on traditions of Renaissance and baroque buildings of Central Mexico and Spain, featuring ornament concentrated on select areas such as entrances and decorative wrought iron balcony railings, window grilles, and gates.

Mama Dee was a perfectionist in all her undertakings, and especially for this hotel. As the building neared completion, she visited it one day to check out the progress on each floor. The steam heating system was being tested and she became quite warm, then, to cool off, stepped outside into a rainstorm. She became ill with pneumonia and died very quickly on August 6, 1926. Her magnificent hotel opened on September 11 under Burt's management, but the family sold it in 1927 to local businessman Harry Hussman, who changed the name from Orndorff to his own. It was purchased in 1935 by the West Texas Hotel Corporation, which held a contest to rename it, and "Hotel Cortez" won, recognizing a conquistador such as those whose sculpted heads are above the entrance. The building has undergone various incarnations since then—as hotel, office building, and other uses—but it continues to be a point of beauty and a tribute to the vision of Mrs. De Groff.

Callie Fairley was the first female vice detective in El Paso, retiring in 1952 with twenty-seven years' service. *Police Department photo courtesy of UTEP Library Special Collections.*

She wasn't any bigger than a minute, Callie Fairley, but "she had a constitution like a crosscut saw," according to a newspaperman who wrote of her detective work in 1943. At four-foot-nine, she weighed in at 146 pounds and looked every inch the grandmother she was.

By the time she retired at age seventy in 1952, she was the oldest member of the El Paso Police Department with twenty-seven years of service. She had arrested many thousands of prostitutes as the city's first female vice detective—and had put comparable numbers of girls on buses back home to find better ways of life.

The girls came from all over the country, hoping to make their fortunes in an army town with a long history of leniency toward their brand of hospitality. As early as 1882, the El Paso City Council had taken a long look at the practice of arresting prostitutes, charging a fine, perhaps jailing them overnight, and turning them loose to start the process over again. It seemed to be more practical—and easier on the paperwork—just to charge them a monthly fee about equal to the fines they had been paying, and in the meantime requiring them to have regular health checkups. Over the years, groups such as the Law and Order League, often headed by prominent ministers, would pressure the city fathers to close the red light district, which was centered on Utah (now South Mesa) Street. Sometimes they succeeded, but the girls only moved across the river to Ciudad Juárez or west to Tucson. Unfortunately, this brought disastrous decreases in the Police Department's operating funds and escalating incidences of venereal diseases.

The Zone of Tolerance continued to operate, its boundaries changing from time to time, until World War II when pressure from the federal government and the army was unavoidable. While Callie Fairley had originally worked on rounding up the girls in their territory and checking their health records, she adapted to the greater challenge of raiding hotels that had become brothels after the change in rules. She carried a "heavy purse," pointing out that it wouldn't have been necessary to have a pistol but for "the gentlemen friends on the street that wanted to take the girls' part and the girls didn't even know them." She worked solo.

Callie's greatest concern was for runaways who "were not the type of girls that you would lock up." She looked for ways to help them, leading to her self-described talent as a "moocher." In 1931 the department set up a Welfare Bureau to look after prostitutes. At the end of the year, a report showed 331 hotels and houses had been inspected, 999 girls interviewed, and 507 VD cases found. Ninety percent of the work had been done by Callie.

She found an ally in "Mother Warren" of the Salvation Army, who provided a hotel room where Callie could take a girl she felt was worthy. "I could put her in that hotel room and she would have a meal ticket till we could raise enough money to send her home." Callie did not hesitate to ask the most modest to the most prominent of businessmen for funds, although they often preferred to take their donations to her superior officers.

Despite the long hours and working with some rough criminal types, Callie found her greatest reward in turning girls around. "We had right here in this city young ladies—they are grandmothers now—that changed through our efforts. They have lovely homes, girls, and college, and they are doing fine," she recalled at age eighty-three as participant in a panel on law enforcement for the El Paso County Historical Society in 1963. "You feel like you have had some reward out of smoothing the rough edges of El Paso's rough times," she concluded.

Callie Fairley died in May of 1965 at age eighty-four.

At the opposite end of the spectrum is an El Paso woman whose career as a piano teacher was seldom boring, due to the unusual interests of her second husband, Roscoe P. Conkling. Margaret B. Vear had come to El Paso in the late 1920s with an ailing husband, during a time when the area was a refuge for people with sicknesses that might be helped by the mild climate. Following his death, she became active in the musical community and met Conkling, who was a cellist as well as a mining engineer and statistician for American Smelting & Refining Corp. He had studied with Antonin Dvorak at the National Conservatory in New York.

Margaret's credentials were also impressive. She had received her bachelor of music degree in 1923 from the American Conservatory of Music in Chicago, where she studied with the Polish virtuoso Heniot Levy, followed by graduate studies at Columbia University and the University of California.

Roscoe organized the El Paso Chamber Music Society in 1930 with Margaret as pianist. The Chamber Music Society gave four programs a year at Radford School for Girls until World War II. One of Roscoe Conkling's major achievements was a concert he conducted May 6, 1933, eight hundred feet underground in Carlsbad Caverns, with members of the El Paso Symphony performing Haydn's *The Creation*.

But Roscoe's interests were not limited to musical endeavors, and Margaret soon joined in his explorations of nature and history. They were married in June 1930 in a cave in the Organ Mountains just north of El Paso. He had explored the cave and stirred the interest of the

Margaret Conkling in her traveling costume for tracing the Butterfield Overland Mail route in the early 1930s. Dressed for the road, she accompanied her husband in retracing the Butterfield Trail from Missouri to California.
Author's files.

scientific community when he reported finding the bones of ancient animals there.

The newspaper account of their wedding, dated June 17, said: "Yucca blossoms and other desert flowers decorated the 'bridal chamber' in the Bishop's Cap caverns." The participants in the ceremony—a minister, the bride and groom, and two witnesses—were steadied by ropes as they descended into the cave. One of the witnesses was Judge Albert Fountain of Mesilla, who had shared with Roscoe the discovery of the cave, which became the subject of articles in scientific journals.

The Conklings' home at 4507 Pershing Drive soon began reflecting not only their musical interests but also their new research project: the Butterfield Overland Mail. Amid busts and portraits of Brahms and Bach, rare violins, and a fine piano, they displayed maps of the American West and models of buildings along the trail, which they set out to explore from start to finish. Together they traveled more than 65,000 miles tracing the mail route from Tipton, Missouri—160 miles west of St. Louis—all the way to San Francisco.

They told a newspaper reporter:

> At times we made no more than 20 miles a day, although we had a splendid car which gave us no trouble even in the most difficult country. Farmers were kind, even taking down their fences to allow us to follow the old trail. In many places the ruts are still visible, worn six to eight inches deep in the stony hillsides.
>
> The Butterfield Trail took no account of hills. In order to save mileage, it went over them rather than around them, if pos-

> sible. Some of the hills over which the half-wild teams dragged the stages at breakneck speed are quite steep, but the trail is right there today, plainly showing the route.
>
> It was not unusual for us, since we persisted in following the trail exactly, to be obliged to cut through the brush in order to make passageway for our car. Somehow we always got through. It was a thrilling experience to trace out the old trail of the pioneers. It was exhilarating, all in all. Through Missouri, Arkansas, and Oklahoma, the Butterfield Trail traversed a country of which much is very beautiful. It was a delightful trip.
>
> All the way, we found people in thorough sympathy with our undertaking. Citizens of towns, chambers of commerce, automobile clubs and others were most kind in offering us any facilities we needed.

They visited 175 stage station sites, built in 1857 and 1858. A few buildings had been put to use after the demise of the mail route, and some were occupied by descendants of the mail station operators.

Margaret was the notetaker for the adventure, typically wearing khaki pants, a heavy sweater, high-top boots, and a slouch hat. When they got hungry, they stopped the car, built a fire, and set up a table with white cloth and napkins for their meal.

The fruit of their research was a three-volume set of books published by Arthur H. Clark Co. of Glendale, California, in 1947—*The Butterfield Overland Mail, 1857-1869,* a classic in historic writings about the American West. It is subtitled: *Its organization and operation over the Southern Route to 1861; subsequently over the Central Route to 1866; and under Wells, Fargo and Company in 1869.* The venture, which had started with great promise, was discontinued because of the Civil War.

Roscoe Conkling retired from AS&R at the end of World War II and the couple moved to Los Angeles. He died in 1971 at the age of ninety-four and Margaret died three years later. They stayed in touch with several El Paso friends over the years, and he was honored by the El Paso Archaeological Society posthumously in 1980, having served as president in 1942 and 1943.

During the more than thirty years that Mabel Welch was a professional woman and civic leader, hat and gloves were required before she stepped out the front door of her home on Wheeling Street.

Born in Mississippi on November 8, 1890, she had become a Texan when her family moved three hundred miles west to De Kalb in 1899. It was there that Mabel Clair Vanderburg grew up, completed high school, and met Malcolm Hiram Welch, whom she married in 1915 after a five-year courtship. She took up work available to women at the time, millinery and interior decorating. When Malcolm was examined in 1916 prior to enlisting in military service for World War I, he was found to have tuberculosis, and he and Mabel followed a physician's recommendation to move to El Paso, whose climate was favored for that disease. Their son, Elvin, was born there on December 17, 1919.

As Malcolm's health improved, he began building houses in 1920 for which Mabel provided the drafting. They were typically of dark brick with white eaves and trim and black outlines around windows and doors. Among the neigh-

Mabel Welch was El Paso's first woman architect.
Courtesy of UTEP Library Special Collections and El Paso County Historical Society.

borhoods where he built were Manhattan Heights, Government Hill, Alta Vista, Highland Park, and the Lower Valley. As he completed a house, she would decorate it and they would move in until it sold.

Their enterprise suffered a setback when Malcolm's health deteriorated in 1924, but Mabel continued their work, despite objections by some male crew members who didn't like taking orders from a woman. As she explained in her memoir, she had to show them who was boss. While Malcolm was bedfast, she completed their home at 3131 Wheeling and built fifteen houses on that street.

Before her husband's death in 1927, Mabel had visited California where she was impressed by the Spanish-influenced architecture. She felt that El Paso should reflect this regional heritage in its buildings and set out to make an impact on the city.

"Until I began building such homes," she recalled in her memoir, "there was hardly a house in El Paso built in Spanish style with red tile roofs, wrought iron balconies, and similar touches. . . . In 1935 Mayor Ray E. Sherman and the entire City Council gave me a commendation for being responsible for changing El Paso's architecture from American bungalow to the charming Spanish-Mediterranean style that had done so much to make El Paso a unique city."

Despite the economic impact of the Great Depression, Mabel continued to design and build homes, several of them on upper-income Rim Road. Her only commercial building was for the A. B. Poe Motor Co. at 601 Texas Avenue in 1935. The most expensive home was for a family in Chihuahua City, at a cost of over two hundred fifty thousand dollars.

When Mabel was honored in 1939 by being admitted to the Society of American Registered Architects, the printed certificate referred to her as "he," as women were scarce in that professional field. The organization granted her fellowship status in 1956. She was pleased to be recognized as her city's first woman builder, first woman registered architect, and first to earn the society's fellowship rank.

Over several years, she devoted considerable time to the Women's Division of the Chamber of Commerce, which during the 1930s took up several projects related to architecture and beautification. She served as chairman-director in 1943 to 1944.

By the 1940s she was designing houses for cities elsewhere in Texas, but had to take time out during World War II when construction on the homefront stopped. She worked with Coles Brothers Realty. After the war, she resumed home building until 1952 when her focus was on remodeling existing homes.

Characteristically, she enjoyed finding unusual decorative items, such as marble mantles and stair treads salvaged from the old Federal Building at Mills and Oregon, which were used in the Schuster home on Rim Road, and a grill from an ancient bus used in the home of another physician. For the Zeta Tau Alpha lodge at then College of Mines (now The University of Texas at El Paso), she used telephone poles as pillars for the back patio. It is now the De Wetter Center for alumni.

During the 1950s, the immaculately dressed Mabel Welch, hat and gloves of course, haunted the offices of the *El Paso Times* and *El Paso Herald-Post* to drum up interest in a cause dear to the Chamber of Commerce women's group—saving the classical pillars on the front of the county courthouse. They also opposed the painting of high school letters on the Franklin Mountains, succeeding in the campaign to remove them but losing on the courthouse project. She founded the Beautify El Paso Association in 1966, and its influence is still felt in a big way.

Mabel Welch died in 1981 and was honored posthumously by the El Paso County Historical Society when it named her to its Hall of Honor in 2008. Her memoir was published in the society's journal, *Password* (Vol. 53 No. 4, Winter 2008). Her son, Elvin, followed her wishes by burning her papers, including architectural drawings, after her death.

During the 1950s, when Patricia Hayes spent some time in El Paso, she pursued an unlikely career for a woman: bullfighting. Born in Des Moines, she had grown up in San Angelo, and was majoring in music at North Texas State University, hoping for a position as bassoonist in a symphony orchestra. Then in 1953 while visiting relatives in Del Rio, she attended a bullfight across the Rio Grande in Villa Acuña. She changed her goals and arranged to study the art of *tauromaquia* in Mexico City.

Although some of her family and friends were less than enthusiastic about her choice, her father, John H. Hayes, was supportive and encouraged her to pursue her dream. In an interview sometime later her brother, Bill C. Hayes of El Paso, recalled that family members (there were five sisters besides Bill and Patricia) lived in different parts of Texas, and "no one wanted her to do it. . . . When she was in Mexico, the family tried everything, even not sending her money, to get her to quit."

Her first trainer in Mexico City was Carlos

Patricia Hayes spent some time in El Paso in the 1950s as she pursued a career as a bullfighter, which took her throughout Mexico and to Portugal where she was dubbed "the Grace Kelly of the bullring." Patricia Hayes in a publicity photo attired for the bullring. She was among several American young women who became bullfighters in the 1950s. *Author's files.*

Suárez, associate of Dr. Alonso Gaona, *impresario* of the Plaza México. Then Raul Muñoz, sword handler for Luis Procuna—who had performed in Villa Acuña at her first bullfight—became her manager and trainer.

Pat's command of the Spanish language was limited and her early education in the *fiesta brava* had been the books of Ernest Hemingway, Barnaby Conrad, and El Pasoan Tom Lea Jr., along with movies such as *The Brave Bulls* and *Blood and Sand*. She discovered that the field was ancient, governed by rituals, required great athleticism, and threatened physical harm to those who faced the bulls. Yet she persisted.

She made a dozen appearances and killed fifteen bulls in her first year as a professional. Her bookings included Acapulco, Irapuesto near Mexico City, and Jalisco. On the first Sunday of April in 1954, she returned to Villa Acuña on the bill with two matadors, and was awarded an ear of the bull for her performance. The bullring judge may grant one ear, two ears, or both ears and tail of the bull for outstanding achievement on the part of a *torero*.

Patricia Hayes had been drawn to her new profession in a time when young men and women from all over the United States were moving to El Paso and other border cities in order to attend and, hopefully, apprentice in bullfights. The Alberto Balderas bullring in Ciudad Juárez was accessible from the streetcar that connected Ciudad Juárez to El Paso. Among these aspirants were several women who would achieve some fame, notably Patricia McCormick, who was an art student at Texas Western College (now UTEP), Bette Ford, a model from New York City, who became the first woman to perform in the Plaza México, and Georgiana Knowles, who grew up in El Paso and became a *rejoneadora,* fighting bulls from horseback. Prominent Mexican *toreras* of that time included Juanita Aparicio, Rosa Berta Martínez, and María "La Serranita" Cobian. Pat Hayes was acquainted with McCormick and Ford, and studied briefly with Juanita Aparicio and her father.

The women dressed more modestly than their male counterparts, who wore heavily embroidered "suits of lights." Women's garb included tight-fitting Spanish-style pants, short, buttoned jackets, and frilled blouses. Their hats were wide-brimmed, flat-topped Cordoban, although Conchita Cintrón, the celebrated Peruvian *rejoneadora*, also wore a higher-crowned Andalusian model.

While some of the Americans performed mainly along the border, Pat Hayes found bookings in other parts of Mexico and ultimately made it to Mexico City's Plaza de Toros. She also performed in Ecuador and spent two years in Portugal, where the press dubbed her "La Grace Kelly del Toreo" for her resemblance to the blonde film star.

In 1957 she returned to El Paso, where earlier she had briefly played bassoon with the symphony orchestra. She was the houseguest of Mr. and Mrs. Abraham Chávez on Corto Street in Sunset Heights. She would strike out daily on a fairly long walk to the Alberto Balderas bullring as part of her training regimen. Chávez was at that time the symphony's concertmaster, later to become the conductor/music director.

By that time, Pat had made twenty-five professional appearances and was planning a tour of South America. She was the only American woman bullfighter who placed her own *banderillas,* barbed sticks demanding great skill on the part of the bullfighter who placed them in the bull's neck, and the only one who had been appearing in Portugal's arenas. Diamantino Viseu, major Portuguese matador, took an interest in her work and taught her in his spare time.

Pat told an *El Paso Times* reporter (August 27, 1957): "A woman can show that it is not necessarily strength, but intelligence and delicate control of the cloth that means success for a bullfighter. The size of the bull does not make too much difference once the bullfighter has gained that control and judgment. And Patricia McCormick has proved that a woman can take gorings as well as a man."

Patricia Hayes retired from her career in the mid-1960s, having had her share of bumps and bruises, but no serious gorings. She was married for a while, with the new surname Franklin, and devoted her time to art, working in oils, acrylics, pastels, charcoal, and ink drawings. She was in an Odessa, Texas, hospice at the time of her death on January 14, 2010. Her niece, Adele Waring, described her as "a petite and soft-spoken beauty with amazing courage and artistic gifts, living ahead of her time in Western culture through exercising meditation and practicing yoga, while sharing her faith and offering kindness to all in her life."

Bibliographic Essay

Susan Dowell Shacklett's handwritten memoir was made available to genealogy researchers by her great-granddaughter, Edde [*sic*] M. Baucum, in 1978. Her photo was provided to the author by Bob Poppenhusen, a Dowell descendant. Susan's brother's biography is *Ben Dowell, El Paso's First Mayor* by Nancy Hamilton (El Paso: Texas Western Press, 1976). The Great Western is described in Brian Sandwich, *The Great Western, Legendary Lady of the Southwest* (El Paso: Texas Western Press, 1991) and Nancy Hamilton, "The Great Western," in *The Women Who Made the West* (Garden City, NY: Doubleday, 1980). Paca Alarcón's history was related by her granddaughter, Rita Faudoa, to Marshall Hail of the *El Paso Herald-Post* (August 15, 1961). She is also mentioned in *Password* 1:2 May 1956, and W. W. Mills' *Forty Years at El Paso, 1858-1898* edited by Rex Strickland (El Paso: Carl Hertzog, 1962). Alzina Allis Orndorff De Groff was described by two granddaughters, Burtram Pierce and Alzina Gay, in "'Mama Dee': Tower Builder" in *Password* 18:1 Spring 1973. Betty Hagans wrote about Hotel Cortez in "Mama Dee's Vision" (*Password* 28:3 Fall 1983) and "Cortez Renovation" in *Cactus Points,* El Paso Electric Co. publication (Summer 1983). She was named to the El Paso Women's Hall of Fame in 2010. Edith Phelan Lane was described by Cleofas Calleros in *Pancho Villa: Intimate Recollections by People Who Knew Him* edited by Jessie Peterson and Thelma Cox Knoles (New York: Hastings House, 1977). Kathleen Worrell remained a little-known figure until recently when William F. Quinn, research chairman for the UTEP Heritage Commission, was able to learn about her years after leaving El Paso and found newspaper photos of her. An excellent account of the decision to use Bhutanese architecture is found in *Henry Trost, Architect of the Southwest* by Lloyd C. and June-Marie F. Engelbrecht (El Paso: El Paso Public Library Assn., 1981). The Trost book also describes the architectural design of Hotel Cortez. Dale L. Walker, former director of the UTEP News Service, has written extensively about Bhutanese architecture, including a booklet, *Shangri-La on the Border,* published by UTEP. Old Main was featured in *Portals at the Pass: El Paso Architecture,* published by El Paso Chapter, American Institute of Architects, in 1984. Margaret Conkling and her husband Roscoe, who bore the name of a more famous kinsman, were interviewed by a reporter in the *El Paso Herald* (December 5, 1930). In preparing the El Paso Archaeological Society's tribute to Roscoe, Helen Davis interviewed many of their El Paso friends and made her notes available to the author. Margaret's life is reviewed in Robert M. Stevenson's *Music in El Paso 1919-1939* (El Paso: Texas Western Press, 1970) and Janet Y. Brockmoller's article, "A Music of Two Spheres" in *Password* 30:3 Fall 1985.

Callie Fairley's work was described by Gordon Frost in *The Gentlemen's Club: The Story of Prostitution in El Paso* (El Paso: Mangan Books, 1983). Rachel Murphree wrote about her for El Paso Community College's *Borderlands* 27:10, 2009-2010, and she is quoted in "Oral History: Law Enforcement in El Paso" in *Password* 22:1 Spring 1977. Mabel Welch's memoir was published in *Password* 53:4 Winter 2008, with the tribute given by Troy Ainsworth when she was inducted posthumously into the El Paso County Historical Society Hall of Honor. Patricia Hayes was interviewed by the author for the *El Paso Times* (August 27, 1957). A *Herald-Post* interview (August 4, 1954) and an article by Haldeen Braddy on women bullfighters in his *Mexico and the Old Southwest* (Port Washington, NY: Kennikat Press, 1971) were also resources as well as Internet sites including a tribute in *The Mex Files* of January 9, 2010, [http://mexfiles.net/].

Chapter 5

PARA LA COMUNIDAD: FOR THE COMMUNITY

by Irasema Coronado

THE WOMEN DISCUSSED in this chapter share an amazing capacity of sacrifice for the benefit of their community. Whether building architectural splendors that grace the community at large, or securing basic rights for the residents of the Sparks Colonia, or challenging entrenched customs that prevented women from achievement in the legal profession, these women evidence what it means to have grace and gumption.

For her role in constructing the Cortez Building, Alzina Allis Orndorff De Groff, affectionately nicknamed Mama Dee, was posthumously honored at the Twenty-first Annual El Paso Commission for Women Hall of Fame Induction Ceremony on March 26, 2010. The Cortez Building, once a hotel, is now a landmark in El Paso. At the induction ceremony, her granddaughter, Gloria Basden, spoke to the audience about the accomplishments of this woman who broke barriers and challenged stereotypes. During Basden's speech, it also became clear that Mama Dee was not only a successful builder, she was also the foundation and the cement that held a family together, and her lasting influence still serves to unite the family.

Mama Dee was born in Washington, Louisiana, in 1859. It is interesting to note that Washington is the third oldest settlement in that state. Over 80 percent of the buildings in the town have historic or architectural significance.

In 1876, at the age of seventeen, Mama Dee moved to Mountsville, Missouri, where she met and married Lee Orndorff. They had three sons—Lee, Seth, and Burt. Mama Dee had a lung condition that forced the family to move to the dryer climate of Tucson, Arizona, in 1886. Not long after the family's move, Lee Orndorff, then employed by Southern Pacific Railroad, was killed in railroad accident.

As sole provider for her family, Mama Dee began leasing out rooms. While tales vary whether she started with just one room or as many as eight rooms, the fact remains that she used the situation not only to support her family, but to teach her sons the hotel management

Mama Dee presented at the Twenty-first Annual El Paso Commission for Women Hall of Fame Induction Ceremony, March 26, 2010. *Courtesy of the Orndorff Family Archives.*

business. With the proceeds from her rooming house, she managed to purchase a sixty-room hotel, which she named The Orndorff. In 1890, she met and married Charles De Groff, who worked as the United States Postmaster in Tucson. Soon after the marriage to De Groff (who was nicknamed Papa Sox) Alzina developed the nickname "Mama Dee."

Despite her success with the Orndorff Hotel in Tucson, Mama Dee was not fond of the location. The hotel was near a red-light district, and she was concerned about her three sons' exposure to that kind of environment. Sometime in the 1890s, Mama Dee heard about the Hotel Vendome in El Paso, Texas, on the corner of what we know today as Mills and Mesa Streets. The hotel was failing, and Mama Dee took advantage of the opportunity to buy the building in 1899. She sold all their possessions in Tucson and moved her family to El Paso. They redecorated the entire hotel, added a fourth story to the building, and renamed it Hotel Orndorff. In 1924, she followed her ultimate dream of creating a deluxe hotel. Mama Dee sold her investments and borrowed one million dollars to tear down the Hotel Orndorff and reconstruct an eleven-story building, known in El Paso as "The Castle of Old Spain on the Plaza." Today this old hotel is the Cortez Building.

With great foresight Mama Dee was able to see El Paso's expansion and bought several other plots of land. These included an acre of land at 2103 Texas Street where she had her home and thousands of acres east of Ysleta where she had the Big Ranch. Along with her purchases, Mama Dee also bought and ran the Sheldon Hotel. Around 1912, Mama Dee revitalized and operated The Lodge in Cloudcroft, New Mexico.

In 1926, Mama Dee developed pneumonia after she inspected a hotel steam heater and was exposed to a wet environment. An unfortunate turn of events claimed her life one month prior to the grand opening of her dream hotel. Mama Dee died August 11, 1926. Her son, Burt, ran the hotel for about a year, but by then the economic downturn that lead to the Great Depression had begun.

Not only did Mama Dee leave behind a beautiful and revered building for future generations to enjoy, she also contributed greatly to the civic and political life of this community. In her spare time, Mama Dee organized and became the first president of the Equal Franchise League, an organization that heavily promoted women's suffrage. She served as president of the El Paso Civic League and was involved in the beautification of Houston Square. In 1923, Governor Pat Neff appointed Mama Dee to serve on the first board of directors of Texas Technological College, a clear indication that she was well connected politically in Texas. One of the most famous guests ever to stay in what is now the Cortez Building was President John F. Kennedy, who spent the night there in 1963.

Socorro Ramirez emerged as a community leader in Sparks Colonia, a one square mile area that was home to 6,000 people, located on the far east side of El Paso. Lack of affordable housing in the larger community led many residents to seek alternative housing in the region. *Colonias,* unincorporated housing developments where predominately Mexican American families built their dwellings, evolved from the combination of unscrupulous land owners selling land that was no longer commercially viable or fertile for agricultural purposes and the lax county and state laws, codes, and regulations that allowed sales of land on a contract-for-deed basis with no requirements to provide services. Lack of credit and low wages led people to build their homes without regard to building codes with the help of their relatives, friends, and neighbors. In some cases, these homes lack adequate plumbing and electrical systems. *Colonias* also lack basic infrastructure such as water and sewer systems, sidewalks, and other urban amenities. Socorro Ramirez's mission became the improvement of the quality of life for her neighbors and making life better and easier for her community. She worked tirelessly to increase awareness of the conditions in the *colonia* and the plight of its residents and lobbied elected officials for legislation to improve the quality of life in *colonias*. One of Socorro Ramirez's major accomplishments was bringing water and sewer infrastructure to Sparks Colonia.

Born in Mexico, Ramirez found herself living in Sparks Colonia with her children after her marriage dissolved. Approximately 500 to 600 families lived in the *colonia* and life was difficult for everyone because there was no water and no sewer. Some septic tanks were leaking and when it rained the area flooded. Health conditions were certainly not optimal and Ramirez was anxious that the situation was having a detrimental effect on children. Deeply disturbed, she started going door-to-door and asking people what they should do in order to obtain basic services for their *colonia.*

Socorro Ramirez worked very closely with Cecilia Rodriguez, a self-taught real estate and contract law expert, who learned her skills in order to find ways to challenge developers and make demands of politicians and elected officials. House Bill 001 was passed in 1999 by the Texas Legislature to impose platting and service requirements on persons selling property in economically distressed subdivisions, and to impose civil and criminal penalties for failure to comply. While this legislation in theory was to address the plight of *colonia* residents, it did not necessarily yield immediate results.

Ramirez attended a water district meeting at which people were discussing the wastewater treatment plant in Horizon City and how the overflow of that plant during the period from 1985 to 1989 was finding its way into Sparks Colonia. The population of Horizon City is predominately Anglo, with many who are US military retirees. The community has a golf course and other urban amenities. Horizon City abuts Sparks, and, because it is located on higher ground, water and wastewater easily flow towards the *colonia.* During the course of the meeting, derogatory statements were made about the residents in Sparks Colonia. They were called wetbacks, and people laughed when someone correlated the floodwaters from the overflow "wetting" the wetbacks even more. Outraged, Ramirez pointed out that some residents of Sparks Colonia were US citizens and legal residents.

After that meeting, Socorro decided to go commissioners court and request a remedy to the flooding situation and request water and sewer services for Sparks Colonia. She started to learn about Texas real estate laws and the rights, or lack thereof, that property owners had; she started asking questions about the water code and open meeting laws. This is even more remarkable considering the fact that Socorro had limited English-speaking skills and was teaching herself the language. Several friends helped her understand the complexities of the laws and codes and served as an interpreter at many meetings.

Cecilia Rodriguez felt that as she taught Socorro English and law, she also learned a lot about human dignity and commitment to one's community. She described Socorro as "caring about what was fair." People were beginning to lose their land because under contract-for-deed, if they missed payments, the land, along with the improvements that had been made would revert back to its original owner. This kind of injustice is what motivated Socorro to work to bring justice and dignity to the community.

Another remarkable aspect of Ramirez's life is that she did not drive, yet found her way to commissioners court in central El Paso on a regular basis. She would ask family and friends to join her as she lobbied elected officials for services. Children were dying in Sparks Colonia, one in a tragic flood and others because of poor sanitary conditions. Socorro's mobile home became a meeting place, the food bank for the community, and a drop-off point for donations. She invited public officials to visit Sparks and see for themselves the issues that the community was dealing with; she had a modicum of success when county commissioners Rogelio Sanchez and Miguel Teran came to visit Sparks Colonia.

Socorro served as a member of the board for *La Fe Centro de Salud Familiar,* (known as La Fe Clinic, a community health center). At one point, there was an attempt to build a satellite office for La Fe Clinic out in Sparks so that people could have access to health care. Unfortunately, due to politics this never came to fruition.

Socorro's leadership qualities and expertise did not go unnoticed, however. She was invited to speak in Washington, DC, and in New Orleans, Louisiana, to share the plight of Sparks Colonia. When she was in Washington, she met Senator Ted Kennedy, a meeting that had a profound impact.

She became a health advocate and in that role became more politically aware. Commissioner's court was growing weary of her. At one point when she was begging for water services, one of the commissioners told her that he was "getting tired of her" and that she had to keep in mind that there were only fifteen people who voted in Sparks Colonia and "Why should I care about them?" Socorro wanted to keep elected officials informed, and in many ways she served as their conscience because she made them feel guilty.

This event only motivated her to learn more about Texas Water Development Board policies, to engage the Lower Valley Water District, and to find funding sources for water infrastructure. Along with Trini Lopez and Suki Ramos she started a committee, "*Agua para los Niños del Lower Valley*" (Water for the Children of the Lower Valley), to raise awareness about the negative health outcomes when people do not have a basic right—access to water. Senator Eliot Shapleigh and many others in the community including El Paso Interreligious Sponsoring Organization (EPISO) were able to find funding mechanisms so that Sparks Colonia would have a water infrastructure set in place.

On May 5 and 6 of 1995, Socorro attended a conference sponsored by the Mexican Center of the Institute of Latin American Studies at The University of Texas at Austin. By this time, she had founded Sparks Community Housing Development Corporation, a 501(c)3 organization.

An online transcript of the conference proceedings helps to capture the issues that were important to Socorro. One was the fact that thirteen women were working with the Sparks Community Housing Development Corporation, and no men offered to help. Socorro also felt that they were not activists but that "they were simply fighting for their needs." Interestingly, she did not use the word "rights" but rather "needs." She also took on academics for conducting research studies that did not translate into meaningful change in communities. "While you are conducting studies, you should also try to bring help. The *colonia* residents are tired of being asked questions. They need basic services, such as water. . . . " She added that "*colonia* residents do not appreciate when organizations such as the Border Association for Refugees and Colonia Advocacy (BARCA) try to control us from outside." When one of the academics presented the notion that *colonias* be renamed border housing developments, Socorro quipped that she preferred the term *colonia.*

Like many activists, she tended to help everyone but herself. She seldom made time for herself, sacrificed a lot in order to help others, and met both frustrations and joys in her work. Socorro volunteered at a senior day care center and enjoyed hearing their stories. She tried to get children to visit the seniors as well. The young ones had "an *abuela/o* for the day," and it was a rewarding experience. This program was a source of great pleasure to Socorro.

Cecilia Rodriguez sadly related the beginning of a tragedy that would ultimately end

Socorro's life. Socorro had gone to a conference and returned "in love," which she described as love at first sight. This man was willing to leave everything behind to be with her, a situation that did not set well with her friends who saw this relationship unfold rather too quickly. Some started to see warning signs. When they would pick up Socorro to attend a meeting, her partner would get upset and jealous. Sometimes they invited him to join them at their community meetings but he did not want to go, he just wanted Socorro to stay home with him. The one time he went to a meeting with them, he waited in the car.

In 1996, President Bill Clinton came to El Paso, and Socorro Ramirez was able to get tickets to go see *"el guapo,"* as she put it: the handsome one. She was excited to be able to see the president of the United States. It was a joyous day for her that ended in tragedy, because when she returned home, her angry partner bludgeoned her to death.

At the time of her death, Socorro was forty-six years old. Her obituary listed that she left three sons and one daughter behind. Later it was revealed that her murderer had previously been accused of murdering two other women, including his second wife. His willingness to "leave everything to be with Socorro" was due to the fact that he was escaping arrest for the murder of his second wife. Cecilia was deeply moved by Socorro's death because a couple of weeks before this tragic ending, Socorro told her "Look Ceci, I have been thinking . . . my community now has water, sewer, paved streets, a bridge, a community center. I can die now because everything is in Sparks. . . . " Cecilia said that Socorro was a mentor to her and that she learned the meaning of courage from her. In addition to now having basic services, Sparks Colonia dedicated the community center to her memory.

State Senator Norma Chavez introduced a resolution in the Texas State Legislature that reads:

> 79R10257 KO-D
> By: Chavez H.R. No. 875
> R E S O L U T I O N
>
> WHEREAS, On International Women's Day, which occurred on March 8, 2005, one remarkable woman, Maria del Socorro Ramirez, was on the minds of many Texans whose lives were forever changed by this committed civic leader; and
>
> WHEREAS, International Women's Day is an annual day of tribute to women who have fought and advocated for the elimination of poverty and violence against their gender, and Mrs. Socorro Ramirez was indeed a woman who helped to empower the female residents of Sparks, a colonia located about 15 miles west of El Paso; and
>
> WHEREAS, She was a founding member of the Sparks Housing Development Corporation, a community-based center dedicated to improving the health and well-being of colonia children and families through affordable housing development and social services; also known as the Centro Socorro Ramirez, this nonprofit organization was led by Mrs. Socorro Ramirez as its executive director from 1990 until the time of her death in 1996; and

WHEREAS, A well-known and greatly admired community activist who fought for human rights and social justice, Mrs. Socorro Ramirez devoted her life to improving the living conditions in the colonias and enlightening state and federal agencies on colonia issues; and

WHEREAS, A woman of uncommon integrity, strength, and generosity, Maria del Socorro Ramirez gave unselfishly of her time to others, and her wisdom, warmth, and valued counsel will never be forgotten by those who knew her; her words, Para La Comunidad, or For the Community, have left a lasting impression on all those who continue to strive to make their community a better place; now, therefore, be it

RESOLVED, That the House of Representatives of the 79th Texas Legislature hereby pay tribute to the life of Maria del Socorro Ramirez and join with all those associated with the Sparks Housing Development Corporation in remembering her many accomplishments.

As different as Socorro Ramirez and Mama Dee were, they shared many things in common. Both were recognized posthumously for their achievements and accomplishments. Mama Dee and Socorro both worked with politicians and were able to make meaningful contributions to their communities, Mama Dee by serving on the Texas Tech board, and Socorro by lobbying the county commissioner's court. Socorro and Mama Dee each left something tangible for the community: a *colonia* with infrastructure services; and a beautiful building.

Today several law schools boast that the majority of their student body is comprised of women, however, that was not always the case. Sandra Day O'Connor, an El Pasoan and former Supreme Court justice, lamented that she was not considered for jobs in the legal profession because she was a woman, in spite of the fact that she was one of the top students in her graduating class. Though there is scant research on women pioneers in different fields in El Paso, Liz Rogers, a prominent assistant public defender in Alpine and former El Pasoan, wrote an article for the *El Paso Bar Journal* (October/November 2008) in which she features and highlights several women trailblazers in the legal community here in El Paso.

Ethel Shirley Abbott (née Scarborough) was born in 1887. In 1909 she married W. G. Abbott. Both she and her husband attended Cumberland University in 1917. After they completed their studies, they returned to El Paso, where he became an assistant county attorney, and she worked in private practice. When W. G. Abbott passed away in 1921, she was appointed in his place. It is possible that she was the only woman lawyer west of Dallas, but that is difficult to verify. She was a member of the El Paso Bar Association but was never invited to the association banquet. Her two sons and a grandson have followed in her footsteps to become attorneys.

Elisa Fernandez-Campos attended the University of Chicago Law School in the 1930s. She was the only Mexican and only one of three women in her class. She married Dr. Leopoldo Villareal.

Mary Vance Guinn was married to Judge Ernest Guinn, who also had been a city and county attorney. Mary had six children and stayed home to care for them. She never attended law school but studied law on her own. She was admitted to the State Bar in 1950 and the Federal Bar in 1951, only the second woman to do so. Two of her children and a grandson also pursued a legal career. She died in 1976.

While law schools have become more inclusive, women lawyers still face obstacles and hurdles as they try to make partner in prestigious law firms. Clearly, the pioneers who paved the way have helped to inspire young women to pursue their legal careers, have opened doors and created opportunities for many, and have fought and stood up against discrimination and exclusion. It is interesting to note that several of the pioneers in the legal profession raised children who would later follow in their footsteps. These women have served as role models not just for their children but to many others as well.

Bibliographic Essay

Aguilar, Matthew. "Slain woman was community leader," *El Paso Times,* November 7, 1996, Section B, p. 1.

Basden, Gloria. Personal interview, April 10, 2010, and family files.

Conference proceedings sponsored by the Mexican Center of the Institute of Latin American Studies at The University of Texas at Austin. http://lanic.utexas.edu/project/etext/llilas/cpa/mexcenter/colonias.pdf (accessed September 5, 2010).

Metz, Leon C. "Builder at the Pass," *El Paso Magazine,* July 1987.

Rodriguez, Cecilia. Personal interview, October 23, 2009.

Rogers, Liz. "El Paso Women Lawyers: The Pioneers," *El Paso Bar Journal,* October / November 2008.

Chapter 6

THEY GAVE US THEIR WORDS: EL PASO WOMEN WRITERS

by Lois A. Marchino

Women have always been writers, if they were allowed to learn to read and write. For centuries, however, including throughout the history of El Paso, there has been a gap between educational opportunities for women and those for men, and another gap between publishing opportunities for men and for women. There have also been similar gaps based on ethnic background and culture. These glaring inequities not only affect each individual life, but also affect the way cultures define themselves and perpetuate history and social values. This holds true in all genres of writing.

Literary writing is particularly important, in part because it is often the most read and the most lasting. Literary works—whether poetry, novels, short stories, or drama—provide a way to establish history and to remember history, both of the individual and the cultural. Literature provides aesthetic pleasure and learning, and it affirms the right to voice oneself and influence others. It is a necessity.

Given the obstacles, however, many of El Paso women's stories have become part of oral history and folklore only, never written at all, or never published, or expressed in letters and diaries long ago discarded. It is thus to be celebrated that so many women in El Paso's multicultural history have not only written but have published their works for others, past and present, to read and share. This chapter honors and pays tribute to all women writers in El Paso and the surrounding area by recognizing the lives and writings of some among them.

One of the most remarkable El Paso women writers of the past is Clara Emily Guion Aguirre. She started writing poetry when she was nine and published her last book of poetry in her nineties. In the midst of a full and active life that included six children, she never stopped writing. Her first published book was *The Poplar Tree, Collected Poems 1918-1968,* selections from a half-century of poems she had written. They are essentially love poems, some of romantic love and others of the love of life. They are somehow very comforting. There are sharp poetic images and philosophical musings, often about nature: wind, moon, stars, river, desert, mountains. The poems speak of hard times as well as happy ones, of dreams for the future and an acceptance of the cycle of life leading to death.

Three of the poems in the collection were used as lyrics for music composed by Lew Miller for the High School Choirs of El Paso during the 1950s and '60s, such as this one written in 1954.

To Touch A Star
I reached beyond
To touch a star
And tho it was
Too far, too far,
My feet were lifted
From the dust
And in the cradle
Of my hand
I found a dream
Which I had lost.

Clara Guion Aguirre.
Courtesy of Bernice Mielke.

Clara Guion Aguirre was never without her dreams, particularly those to love and live life fully and to write poetry. Her daughter, Bernice Mielke, describes her as "my best friend" and "a delicate, strong lady, whose thoughts in poetry gave insight to life in the universe. . . . All life had value to this poet."

Hers was a life whose story needs to be recorded. Unique as it was, it also exemplifies the lives of many women of El Paso, both past and present, in her determination, independence, strength in adversity, and dedication to both family and the larger community. Bernice Mielke, a remarkable woman herself, has graciously shared many details and thoughts about this woman and poet who was her mother.

Clara Guion Aguirre was born in Mesilla, New Mexico, but spent most of her life in El Paso. She was the third of four children born to Howard Guion, an artist originally from New York, and Margaret Fountain of Old Mesilla, the daughter of Colonel Albert Jennings Fountain. As an adult, Clara would hold out her small hand and say, "This is how big I was when I was born." The village doctor who delivered her on her aunt's kitchen table put her aside and said, "That thing won't live," and went on his way. To keep the tiny baby alive, her aunt, Theresa, soaked gauze in sugar water and squeezed the sweet liquid into the baby's thirsty lips, wrapped her snugly, and placed her close to the old iron stove to keep her warm. Thus with the care of her aunt and her mother, little Clara thrived and survived her premature birth.

As a child, Clara lived with her parents, two brothers, and a sister on a small farm that never provided much income. The children seldom had enough to eat or new clothes for school. Lunch at school was sometimes only water. Later in life, Clara would frequently say, "What is difficult in life makes us strong."

Clara's parents, hoping for a better life for their daughter, sent her to live with another aunt and an uncle (James Paxton), who was a successful businessman. Although they had money, Clara did not care for the beautiful new room and new dresses. She missed her family. She also rebelled when Aunt Kitty told her that her new name was to be Catherine. "No," she would insist, "I am Clara."

It was this uncle who made her recite poetry and memorize passages from Shakespeare, and whatever his intentions, it altered Clara's life. This was, at the age of nine, her first exposure to poetry, which became her refuge and her delight. When her aunt and uncle were both killed in an automobile accident, Clara returned to her parents. She kept writing, usually by the side of a little hill on the farm, where she could write in solitude.

When Clara was twelve years old, she noticed a boy, then aged fourteen, working in a local drugstore. Later, they would both say that it was love at first sight, and indeed she and Manuel E. Aguirre became high school sweethearts and in 1928, ten years after that memorable first sight, they married and moved to El Paso. Manuel Aguirre had always dreamed of managing his own drugstore, and it was this opportunity that brought them there. He started as a clerk, and then for many years he ran a Warner drugstore, which was situated directly across the street from the main post office on Mills Street. Manuel Aguirre had three more drugstores before he died in 1961, after suffering three heart attacks.

It had been a marriage filled with love. Clara had spent those years raising their six children: Marguerita, Bernice, Gloria, Robert, Jack, and David. She had not worked outside the home since before her marriage. But at her husband's death, she valiantly stepped up to run the downtown stores. What she found was that several of the employees had taken advantage of her husband's illnesses. There was theft throughout the store and in particular the pharmacy department. She fought hard to keep the stores from going bankrupt. She was a good businesswoman and cleaned up the corruption, but it was much too late. She eventually closed the four stores.

Clara then worked for several years as a secretary for her church, St. Joseph's. She was very much respected and liked for her work and her personality. She enjoyed dancing and music. A precocious child, she had studied the piano until her family could no longer pay for lessons, yet playing remained a source of enjoyment for her and those who heard her play. She loved her children and her grandchildren, and they loved her and took care of her in her final months of illness. It was her son David who helped as she put together her second collection of poetry, *Before Winter*, published in 1997, three months before she died, in her nineties.

Many of her family members were at the hospital when she died. Her daughter Bernice says simply, "I held her hand until they took her away." But then Bernice speaks of one of the last poems in her mother's book *Before Winter:*

Pencil and Pad
Bury me
With a pencil
And a pad;
Should I have
The inspiration
In death,
That in life
I never had.

Clara Emily Guion Aguirre clearly seldom lacked inspiration in life, and she was and is an inspiration to others. She would always say that she was never lonely as long as she had pen or pencil and paper so she could write.

One of the most published literary writers of El Paso's past is Estela Portillo Trambley, and it is no coincidence that she wrote during the second half of the twentieth century, when more women's books were being published than in previous eras.

Estela Portillo Trambley's works received several awards during her lifetime, and those works are now recognized internationally. She was a pioneer in Chicano/Chicana literature. The granddaughter of Mexican immigrants, she was born in El Paso and raised in Ciudad Juárez and El Paso. Almost all of her works explore the borderlands she knew well. In numerous stories and plays and one novel, she writes boldly about the need for change and for social justice for all. She knew the limits assigned to women in a male-dominated society, and sometimes, in her work, reacts strongly to those limitations with anger and violence. More often, however, rather than stick to complaints and blame about racial or gender discrimination, Trambley creates portraits of strong women who claimed their own voices, their own lives.

Trambley received her BA in literature at The University of Texas at El Paso in 1956 and her MA in 1978. Her thesis was a 403-page novel, *Women of the Earth,* which she later developed into the novel *Trini,* published in 1986 by Bilingual Press. Her successful writing career helped make it possible for subsequent Mexican American writers to be welcomed by small presses and eventually to attract mainstream publishers as well.

Rain of Scorpions and Other Stories was Trambley's first book, published initially in 1975 by Tonatiuh-Quinto del Sol. This is generally considered to be the first book of fiction by a Chicana writer. Trambley was the first woman to win the Premio Quinto Sol Prize for Literature for her stories. The book was republished in a substantially revised version in 1993 by Bilingual Press. This is a book well worth reading, especially for the title story, a long short story, or novella, "Rain of Scorpions." No specific year is given, but the setting is Smeltertown, the impoverished barrio around the ASARCO smelter smokestack at the western edge of El Paso and immediately across the border from Mexico. The Mexican American workers who have suffered from lead poisoning and other pollution are finally being told to evacuate. One humble worker, Fito, tries to convince the others that they should all move together somewhere else to retain their friendships and community. Another man, Papa At, has had a vision of a green valley somewhere. Three young boys have listened to his stories, and without telling anyone of their plan, they bravely venture off to try to find this ideal space. They think it must be magically hidden in the mountains that enrich the landscape of the El Paso area. The emphasis in this story is not on a woman's quest for her freedom, as is often true in her other stories, but on an even larger goal, peace and freedom for all. The story is also about love, the kind of love Miguel, one of the young boys, realizes at the end: "to feel whole, to be a part of the earth, to believe in mysteries . . . to understand that every breathing being was a miracle, a green valley."

Estela Portillo Trambley.
Achilles Studio, El Paso, Texas.
Courtesy of Bilingual/Belingüe Press, Tempe, Arizona.

In addition to her grace and strength as a storyteller, Trambley was also a largely self-taught playwright. She had performed in many plays, and while teaching drama at El Paso Community College, she created and organized the Chicano Theatre, a group of students who also had a love for the art of drama. As they worked on initial versions of a play, she would then rewrite scenes as needed. In the introduction to *Sor Juana and Other Plays,* she writes that "serious literature is concerned with serious themes that touch human lives," and that it was especially through writing plays that she learned that it is honesty about individual lives that leads to universal themes. She was also one of the founders of Los Pobres, the first Spanish language theater in El Paso. Her 1971 play *The Day of the Swallows* was possibly the first Chicana play to dramatize lesbian issues on the stage. It was controversial, not only for the topic, but because of the violent action of one woman who was afraid of what would happen to her if her sexual orientation was known. But the play was a dramatic and literary success. Trambley followed this with numerous other plays, many of them in her 1983 collection *Sor Juana and Other Plays,* which attracted wide acclaim.

Perhaps it would be more accurate to say the collection of plays, like her stories, attracted wide acclaim in other parts of the country. Although several of her plays were performed in El Paso, even more were performed in other cities around the country. *The Day of the Swallows*, for example, premiered at the Music Hall at the University of California at Los Angeles (UCLA) and then toured California, performed by the Nosotros Theatre Repertoire Company. The distinguished and always credible Betty Ligon, who started work at the *El Paso Herald-Post* in 1970 and was a long-time theatre critic and book reviewer, early recognized the power and importance of Trambley's work. In a phone conversation on May 3, 2010, Ligon reiterated what she had written many years earlier, that Trambley was much better known outside El Paso than in her home city. This often seems to happen to writers. But El Pasoans gradually became more aware of her achievements. Trambley was named Author of the Pass by the *El Paso Herald-Post* in 1990. Trambley's works are now considered Chicana classics, many of them republished, and all available to buy and read. Still, many in El Paso may not know how well regarded her works are—and should be—in the literature of Mexican Americans.

Estela Portillo Trambley was the mother of five children and was also very active professionally in addition to her writing. She taught high school English for many years, served as chair of the English Department at the Technical Institute, and worked as a teacher for the homebound. She hosted an El Paso radio talk show called *Stella Says*, and later hosted *Cumbres*, a Hispanic cultural affairs television program on station KROD. She was resident dramatist at El Paso Community College in 1970. In 1995, she held the Presidential Chair of Creative Writing at the University of California, Davis. She died on December 29, 1998.

Another writer El Paso can be proud of, though many may be surprised to learn of her, is Bernice Love Wiggins. As a young African American who loved poetry, she self-published a collection of her poems called *Tuneful Tales* in 1925, while she was living in El Paso. Dr. Maceo C. Dailey Jr., Director of the African American Studies Program at UTEP, and Ruthe Winegarten, a faculty associate of Women and Gender at UT San Antonio, rediscovered her book and had it republished in 2002.

The introduction for the original publication of *Tuneful Tales* was written by William Coleman, the principal of Douglass School, the El Paso school for African Americans in those days of segregation. This was the school Wiggins attended from first grade through her graduation from high school. Coleman notes that Wiggins was born in Austin, in 1897. Then, orphaned by the death of her mother at age five, she was taken by her aunt to El Paso. With the encouragement of her first grade teacher, Miss Alice Lydia McGowan, to whom Wiggins dedicated her book, she, as Coleman says, "created her own memory verses, the beginning of which she does not remember." Coleman also notes that over the years her poems were published in various newspapers and magazines in El Paso, Chicago, and Houston. He adds that "The poverty, the sufferings, the restricted opportunities of her Race and others lay heavily upon her heart."

In the introduction to the new edition, Maceo Dailey points out that Bernice Wiggins was not only one of the first African American women poets to be published in Texas, but in the United States. He cites her ability to provide perceptive and memorable views of African American life in the Southwest, especially in El Paso. During the first three decades of the twentieth century when Wiggins lived in El Paso, the African American population increased more rapidly than the overall population of the city, and it was a time of progressive talents and development for that community. Dailey agrees with others who have classed Wiggins with the celebrated Paul Laurence Dunbar in sheer talent, in ability to incorporate both standardized English idiom and black dialect in her poetry, and in concern for her people.

Dailey insightfully places Bernice Love Wiggins in conjunction with the Harlem Renaissance and other of her contemporaries, such as Langston Hughes, Countee Cullen, and Zora Neale Hurston. All this she achieved in El Paso, isolated from any large metropolitan African American community or literary influences. Unfortunately, as far as is known, *Tuneful Tales* was her only book. She left El Paso in 1933, headed for California, and no further information about her has been discovered.

Cover of *Tuneful Tales*, Bernice Love Wiggins. *Courtesy of Texas Tech University Press, Lubbock, Texas, and Maceo C. Daily.*

A long-standing organization in El Paso is The El Paso Writers' League, which provides ample proof of the devotion to writing shared by numerous El Pasoans over the years. It was founded in 1935 and is still going strong, with meetings on the second Saturday of each month. Lenore Dils was the initial organizer, bringing together a group of women who led busy lives and only had time to write at night, thus the clever and fitting name of the Night Writers.

Dils had submitted stories to magazines and was getting them published, even paid for some, and she was adamant that if the women supported and encouraged each other they too could have their works in print. As the group grew over the years, men joined as well, and the name was changed to the El Paso Writers' League. The league's record of works written in a wide variety of categories and in publication success was, and is, very lengthy and impressive.

While it is true that a few of the world's acclaimed writers over the centuries have penned away in a lonely garret, or its equivalent, creating a romanticized myth that endures, the fact is that most of the successful writers now, as

Lenore Dils.
El Paso Writer's League, courtesy of Patsy King.

in the past, know other writers, are closely associated with them, and count on them for support and understanding, or at least interest. Lenore Dils knew that; she could not have formed a group if she had not known some writers, and she wanted to know more. It clearly was important for Dils, and for hundreds of later league members over the decades.

Patsy King, the stellar current historian for the El Paso Writers' League, wrote an article for the *El Paso Times* in 2010 about the milestone of the organization reaching seventy-five years of service to writers in the El Paso area, and she has been very generous in sharing her vast knowledge of the league as well as sharing her own works. In 1941, the league published *Sponsor* magazine but had to cut its circulation because of the scarcity of paper in World War II. Under Lenore Dils' leadership, in 1969, some forty-five or so league members created *Southwestern Mosaics,* published in El Paso by Boots and Saddle Press. It is divided into three sections, "Facts," "Poetry," and "Fiction." The "Facts" section is particularly interesting; almost all are essays about the history of El Paso and the borderland. To cite a few examples, Julie Morton, in "The Spirit of Loretto," writes of Loretto Academy, which was built "in the middle of the El Paso desert," and critics said the building was far too big and too far out in the country to attract students. Texas Western (later UTEP) English professor Pearl Olive Ponsford provides a personal and informative essay on her father, Henry Thomas Ponsford, "An Intrepid Pioneer" from Canada who came to El Paso in 1897 because his physician told him that due to his asthma, he would not live through the winter unless he moved to a warm dry climate. He lived forty-five years in El Paso, and his vision as a builder and contractor sweepingly transformed the cityscape. Jessie Peterson writes of Mount Cristo Rey and the inspiration to create the twenty-nine-feet-high statue of Christ the King on the tallest peak of the Sierra Madres overlooking the Rio Grande, El Paso, and Juárez. She follows the progress to its dedication as a shrine in 1940. *Southwestern Mosaics* is a book that should be reprinted, especially since copies are now very scarce.

Lenore Dils' own book, published in 1966, was recently advertised online by a rare book store for $300, for the same reason of scarcity, but Patsy King loaned me her own autographed copy of this as well as her rare copy of the anthology *Southwestern Mosaics.* Dils' book is *Horny Toad Man,* a very odd title which only makes sense when the reader learns it is the story not of one man, but of the men who ran the Horny Toad division of early railroads in the West, most specifically the segment of the Santa Fe Railway from Albuquerque to El Paso, with branch lines to Deming, Silver City, and other towns; for many years there were four regular passenger trains running daily from Albuquerque to El Paso. (It does not explain, however, why the railway had such an odd name.) The author does admit that many of the signs and many of the railroad workers spelled it "Horney," and that she changed it to "Horny" as "a compromise to learned educators." Dils definitely saw the railways bringing civilization to the area, while now most readers would probably not see it that way. Certainly the three civilizations of Native Americans, Hispanics, and Anglos were here before the railroads. She knew a lot about the railroads, since for a time she was the secretary for the superintendent of the Horny Toad division, and her father, John Brown, was an engineer, and her husband, Elmer Dils, a fireman for the same AT&SF Railroad. It was always said about Lenore Dils that, "As long as anyone can remember she was interested in writing."

Another league writer, Dorothy Jenson Neal, also wrote a book about railroads with the delightful title *Cloud-Climbing Railroad,* published in 1966 by Texas Western Press in El Paso. The book is about the building of the railroad to and through Cloudcroft, New Mexico, the highest point on the Southern Pacific railway. A portion of one of the amazing railway bridges in the Cloudcroft area is still there, and no one can look at it without indeed wondering how such a railroad bridge was engineered in the 1890s. The book includes several pictures, some of trains on the S-Bridge, so-called for its S-shaped curves as it winds up part of the mountain, looking more like a rollercoaster than a railroad track. *Cloud-Climbing Railroad* has been described as the definitive history of the railway, the steepest standard gauge railroad in the world. The book sold out almost immediately and was reprinted several times in the late 1960s. It was republished in 1998, again by Texas Western Press, when the Sacramento Mountains Historical Society sponsored a centennial edition of the book, followed by another printing in 2001.

Neal wrote another nonfiction book, *Captive Mountain Waters: A Story of Pipelines and People,* published in 1961. Like Lenore Dils, Dorothy Jenson Neal contributed two essays to *Southwestern Mosaics.* Neal wrote about "Passport Perplexities" on the US/Mexico border (sound familiar today?) and "Mail Order Christmas" (think online holiday shopping today).

One of the more recent participants in the El Paso Writers' League was Lois Elaine Hobart, who lived in El Paso for the last three decades of her life. She published ten books, ranging from children's books to novels, plays, and nonfiction. Hobart was born in Minnesota and spent time in New York City, working for various publications, including *Glamour* and *Esquire* magazines. She married the painter Harold Black, and they lived for twenty-four years in San Miguel de Allende, Mexico, where they established a riding academy. After they divorced, Lois Hobart settled in El Paso.

In a profile of Hobart titled "Diamond in the Rough," Hobart's friend Donna Munch, who met her in the league, describes Hobart as "an individual, multi-dimensional with layers that, when peeled away, revealed a polished gem." Munch writes that although Hobart had little money and lived modestly, she had priceless friends, mostly writers. She never complained about bleak finances or her many trips to Las Cruces, New Mexico, to care for her grown only son, Anthony Black, who had serious health problems. Instead, she concentrated on her writing.

Hobart worked for a few years as an adjunct lecturer in the English department at UTEP, and during this time she was working on her full length play *Dream of Sor Juana,* about the famous seventeenth-century feminist author and nun Sor Juana Inés de la Cruz. Hobart lived to see the play produced in English in Mexico, where the audience called her up to the stage, twice, to take bows. At her death in 2005, the *El Paso Times* headline in the Borderland section was "El Paso Playwright Found Dead at Age 87." In the article, Hobart's writer friend Walker M. Reid notes some of her plays and adds, "Her historical account *Mexican Mural: The Story of Mexico Past and Present* was still being used as a college text a few years ago. She excelled at being the champion of Mexican females." Donna Munch reports that although Hobart was slowing down a bit in her last years, she kept going. An acquaintance spotted Hobart at the Dollar Store on the morning of her death. A volunteer who delivered lunch discovered her in her small backyard, dead from natural causes, with her dear Sheltie dog whimpering nearby. Hobart was apparently gardening, another thing she loved, in addition to her lifelong love of writing.

There are many other notable El Paso women writers of the past as well, such as Mary S. Cunningham, who wrote *The Women's Club of El Paso: Its First Thirty Years.* Anna Hardwick Brand was a novelist who wrote *I Want You for Myself* (1938) and *Thunder Before Seven* (1941), both published by Doubleday, Doran & Co., in New York. In 1950 she participated in the writing of a booklet, *El Paso Centennial Celebration 1850-1950.* Brand lived in El Paso's Lower Valley, which was annexed in the 1950s by the city, and in her history of El Paso for the centennial booklet she includes several pictures of Old Ysleta and the Tigua Indians in that area. Another well-known writer from the Lower Valley was Josefina A. Salas-Porras, one of the first Mexican American women folklorists.

William "Willie" Quinn, one of the always cordial and helpful volunteers in the UTEP Heritage House Commission, who have office space on campus and work to maintain records of the university's past, kindly shared information about writers. One of them was Jeanie MacCallum Frank. Among other works, she wrote her "anonymous" autobiography, *I Can Tell It All Now,* dedicated to the "Old Boys and Girls of Our First Big High School"; it was 118 pages hardbound, printed in the El Paso Schools Print Shop in 1948, with drawings by students at El Paso Technical Institute. She had a very interesting life to write about.

Jeanie MacCallum Frank was born in 1868 in Londonderry, North Ireland, of Scots descent. She was in the second class that admitted women to the University of Glasgow (Scotland) where she completed her MA degree at age eighteen. Upon emigrating from Ireland to the United States with her family in 1886, she taught in a private school for girls in Kansas City. She married Sam Gilbert Frank, a Canadian, and they had two daughters. Her husband died unexpectedly, and suddenly she was widowed at age twenty-eight. They had been living in Chicago, but she returned to Kansas City and taught another five years. A brief marriage to a long-time friend did not last, and she moved to El Paso in 1903, where her brother Malcolm was working with the American Smelting and Refining Co. She was hired as a high school teacher of English, and continued to teach for thirty-seven years.

She was with the El Paso school district February 4, 1903, to May 3, 1940. In her memoir she wrote: "I think I knew, and still know, my subject—English. I had read widely, and I hope, wisely, since I was four years old; I had traveled much and learned much; I have never spoken incorrectly, which is no credit to me, but to my early associations." She knew that languages grow and change, and are always interesting. More, the power to speak and write effectively is essential; command of a language or languages is essential for effective communication.

In 1924, Frank wrote a small paperbound history book that was used in the El Paso school district as supplements for pupils studying Texas history. When that went out of print, she did a second version, *History of the Southwest: An Elementary History of the American Border in Popular Form with Special Attention to the District of El Paso, Texas,* designed for sixth graders. Another version came in 1947: *History of the District of El Paso in Texas and New Mexico: A Reader for Boys and Girls,* published by El Paso Public Schools. She was also a prolific writer and producer of plays and pageants. She wrote newspaper columns on the history of the Southwest and served as historical advisor to the Chamber of Commerce. She also wrote several magazine articles, and in retirement had a radio program, *Frank Speech.* Jeanie MacCallum Frank was inducted posthumously into the El Paso County Historical Society Hall of Honor in 1988.

To mention a few other El Paso writers, Trudy Trafton wrote a column on the Senior's page of the *El Paso Times* for eight years. Mary Ann Herman Bogle, who died in 2009, was a writer for the *Rio Grande Catholic Newspaper,* and among her numerous volunteer activities she taught poetry to children. Kathleen L. Worrell, wife of the first dean of the Texas State School of Mines and Metallurgy (now UTEP) was also a writer. In 1923, Steven and Kathleen Worrell moved to Honolulu, Hawaii, and Kathleen served as president of the Honolulu Branch of the National League of Pen Writers from 1928-1931. She published short stories and poems, including a collection of poetry titled *Hawaiian Moods.*

Susan Magoffin is remembered for the diary she kept as one of earliest women from the East to travel the Santa Fe Trail, arriving in Santa Fe in 1846. She came through El Paso on her way into Mexico. Her husband was the uncle of the pioneer Joseph Magoffin, builder of the Magoffin Home in El Paso in 1875, now a state historic site.

It is clear that a high percentage of the published works of El Paso women writers has been in the areas of nonfiction. In addition to the many nonfiction works published by members of the El Paso Writers' League and others mentioned, another nonfiction writer was Ruby V. Burns, most noted for her major work, a biography of Josephine Clardy Fox, the benefactor for whom the Fox Fine Arts building on the UTEP campus was named in 1978, and whom Ruby

Burns knew personally. The biography, titled *Josephine Clardy Fox: Traveler, Opera-Goer, Collector of Art, Benefactor* was published in 1973 by Texas Western Press. The distinguished El Paso author and scholar Nancy Hamilton has provided some information about Ruby Burns and her career.

Burns's father, H. V. Vermillian, was a Baptist minister, as was her uncle who lived in El Paso. Burns graduated with a degree in English and a certificate in music from Baylor University, to which she left her considerable fortune at her death. In addition, by her bequest, the Ruby V. Burns Endowed Fund for Music at The University of Texas at El Paso was established. She was a newspaperwoman for twenty-four years, retiring as woman's editor of the *El Paso Times* in 1970. She had come to the *Times* as Ruby Stearns in 1948, around the time of a divorce, and she later married Earl S. Burns, who preceded her in death.

Ruby's first years at the *Times* were difficult, as she was the assistant to Mrs. Ollie P. Lansden, who had been the society editor for many years and was then slowly dying of cancer. Ruby had to hold the department together and keep the daily society pages readable while sometimes having to subtly countermand unsuitable orders given by Ollie. After Ollie Lansden's death, Ruby took the helm, writing a daily column. She knew many of the people in El Paso because she attended all of what she considered the important social events. She and her twin sister had been singers as young women, and in her later years Ruby sang in the choir at St. Clement's. (Her sister lived in Fort Worth.) Ruby was always impeccably dressed and liked to wear small hats (unlike Josephine Fox, who had hundreds of very large hats). Those were the days of hats and gloves for parties in their social set.

Ruby Burns.
Courtesy of UTEP Heritage House archives and William Quinn.

Burns's book about Josephine "Josie" Fox was a good "fit" because she knew her well. Josie was a close friend of Ollie Lansden and used to spend a lot of time in the society office at the *Times* visiting with Ollie. Ruby included in the book "warts and all" about her subject, including an episode of the shady art dealer who was suspected of taking Josie Fox for a lot of money, and the time she and Mrs. Kimbrough were rivals in the hospital, each trying to outdo the other with new jewelry, and an episode with a singing waiter —well, it's all in the book.

Josephine Clardy Fox was certainly an excellent subject for a biography, a woman who was very active socially and involved in the arts, including serving on the Advisory Committee of the National Arts Foundation. She made gifts to many local groups and organizations. When she died in 1970, she left her entire estate to UTEP, the largest gift to the institution at that time. Her vast collection of books, many of them collector's items, went to the UTEP library. And yes, her hundreds of picture hats went to the drama department.

Ruby Burns also wrote book reviews and various small pieces for *Password,* the publication of the El Paso County Historical Society. At the time of her death, Burns was working on a biography of Elizabeth Garrett, the daughter of the legendary Lincoln County, New Mexico, Sheriff Pat Garrett, who is most remembered as the man who shot William Bonney, better known as Billy the Kid, in 1881. An excerpt from the biography that Ruby Burns was writing about Elizabeth was published in *Password* vol. 21 no. 2, Summer 1976, titled "Pat Garrett's Daughter and El Paso's Song." Burns writes of her year at the famous Juilliard School in New York in 1924, saying that it was thanks to Elizabeth Garrett that she and her sister were able to be there. She writes: "We lived in the Parnassus Club where Elizabeth also lived, and we had our voice lessons from her there in the practice rooms of the club. We were too poor to study with a teacher like Witherspoon, but we had the benefit of his method in our studies with Miss Garrett. She would go for a lesson with him and upon returning, schedule our lessons while the maestro's teaching was fresh in her mind."

Elizabeth Garrett was the author of the song "O, Fair New Mexico," which became New Mexico's state song. Her controversial father, Pat Garrett, who was himself shot in 1908, lived in El Paso when he was appointed US Customs Collector in El Paso 1901-1905, and Elizabeth wrote the song "El Paso," published by and copyrighted by the Woman's Club of El Paso. Unfortunately, Burns' biography of Elizabeth Garrett was not completed by the time of her death, and the manuscript has never been published. Ruby Burns was listed in *Who's Who of American Women* and in *Foremost Women in Publications* (1970).

The journal *Password* has been a long ongoing publication of the El Paso County Historical Society, and it has been a venue for many published articles and book reviews by El Paso women. Among them is Betty Mary Smith Goetting, who started the El Paso Planned Parenthood Association, was also a leader in the historical society, and wrote many essays for the journal. She was posthumously made a member of the Hall of Honor by the El Paso County Historical Society in 2009. Another was Mary Lil Collingwood, a professor in the English Department at UTEP and head of the composition program there for many years. She served for several years as the editor for *Password* and wrote for it as well.

Certainly the women professors who have taught at UTEP have published abundantly, both in their academic field and in more general areas in addition to their teaching and other contributions to the university. That list would include almost all who have taught there, in virtually every department. To mention just three from the English Department in the latter part of the twentieth century: Roberta Walker, with Dr. Robert Esch, coauthored a textbook that was widely used in freshman English courses at many universities and was republished in a revised edition; Dr. Lurline Coltharp wrote numerous

Sister M. Lilliana Owens, S. L.
Courtesy of Loretto Academy Archives, El Paso, Texas.

books and articles on onomastics, the origin and meanings of names, including *Dual Influences on Chicana Naming Practices* (1981); Dr. Frances Hernandez translated from Spanish to English *The Catalan Chronicle of Francisco De Moncada* (1975) and went on to other articles and books, most notably *The Carvajal Family,* an adaptation of a lengthy book by Alfonso Toro, who gave a historical account of one family's experience in the "New World," particularly concerning, as the subtitle says, "The Jews and the Inquisition in New Spain in the Sixteenth Century."

Certainly many of the nonfiction writers have been interested in history. One who made it a main focus of her life's work was Sister M. Lilliana Owens, S.L., the historian of the Diocese of El Paso. Her written biographies and accounts of phases of the Sisters of Loretto reached well beyond El Paso; she is recognized as an authority on Roman Catholic Church and school history in the West and Southwest and even further geographically, since the Sisters of Loretto started in Kentucky and as members moved west they opened schools and were associated with local churches. Sister Owens seemed to want to cover it all.

Her major biographies are of Father Carlos M. Pinto (1951) and Bishop Anthony Schuler (1953), but she wrote more, including over forty magazine articles. She wrote much for the *Revista Católica,* for decades the only Catholic weekly newspaper in the western hemisphere. The newspaper was published by the Revista Católica Press, founded by the Jesuits in Albuquerque, New Mexico, in 1867, but it operated in El Paso from 1918 until 1958. Sister Owens served as its associate editor for several years. One of the books she published with that press was *Jesuit Beginnings in New Mexico 1867-1882.*

Sister Owens had a PhD from St. Louis University. She lived to be over 100. She also wrote comic strips about historical and religious stories. Her booklet *Loretto, the Monument of Nerinckx,* was done in comic format, what would now be called a graphic novel, telling of the work done by Sisters of Loretto in different parts of the world. Forty thousand copies of this booklet went out to various places in Europe, the Orient, and the United States.

It is fitting to end this chapter on women writers of the past in the El Paso area with another accomplished poet. Like Clara Guion Aguirre, Renee Jeannette Berta insisted on the value of poetry and was involved in writing throughout her life. Renee Berta was born in 1951 in Pueblo, Colorado, the daughter of Evelyn Le Fevre Berta

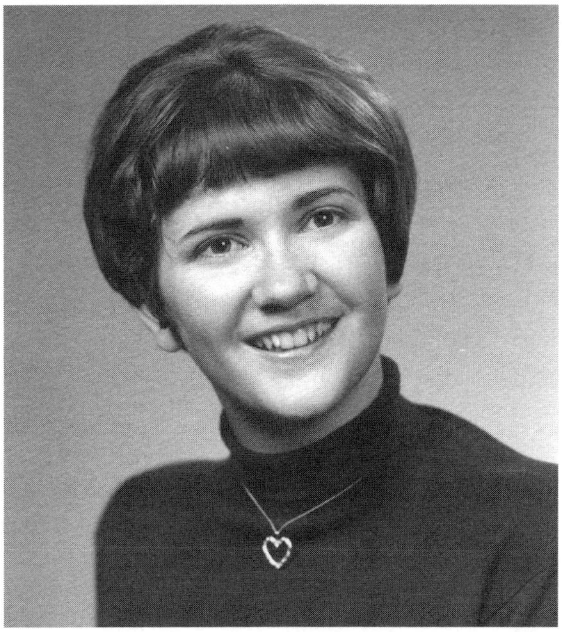

Renee Berta.
Courtesy of Andrea and Evelyn Berta.

and Alexander Berta. In 1970 the family moved to El Paso. Renee had already started college in Colorado at that time but transferred to The University of Texas at El Paso, where she received both her undergraduate and graduate degrees in English. Her thesis for the master's degree was *Sunflowers at Midnight,* a collection of original poems. Several of these poems were subsequently published in various journals, including *The MacGuffin* and *The Centennial Review.*

By the time she had completed her thesis, Renee Berta was already struggling with rheumatoid arthritis. She suffered from this severe illness for over forty years, increasingly forced to deal with major physical limitations. Yet as she fought against this disabling disease, she remained always a cheerful and loving woman, a pleasure to be around. She was determined to have a job where she could help others. She was a writer, and she wanted to help others develop their writing skills. She was instrumental in making the UTEP Writing Center a high caliber service to students, and she served as the writing coordinator for many years before retiring because of health issues.

When Renee Berta died on August 30, 2009, Judith Fourzan-Rice, a friend and UTEP colleague, wrote an e-mail giving the sad information, commending Renee's important work, and ending by saying, "She was a sparkle of intellect, humor, grace, and goodwill."

Renee Berta also contributed much to the El Paso community. Her sister Andrea, who works at UTEP, and her mother, Evelyn Berta, shared information about Renee, including the fact that when Renee was undergoing occupational therapy at Providence Hospital, she felt sorry for the other patients she saw there and volunteered to help. She also created and edited a newsletter for current and past patients. In another significant volunteer project, she worked with Amnesty International and was for a time president of the local chapter. She wrote hundreds of letters to help the organization in freeing political prisoners throughout the world. Her career and her volunteer work were outstanding.

Through all this, Renee was at heart a poet. Renee Berta dramatically represents the determination, dedication, and achievement despite adversity that characterizes not only the writers included here, but others. Writers provide inspiration to us all.

What we have are the written words of women who came before us. Current writer Janice Woods Windle, long the head of the El Paso Community Foundation, a force behind the reopening of the Plaza Theater, and a justly well-known author, sets her novels, such as *True Women,* in the past. Windle perhaps says it best in the title of one of the papers she presented at a local conference: "Every Woman has a Story." Whether women's stories are fiction, autobiography, poetry, or nonfiction, and whatever the subject, in those stories we have a record of their thoughts and knowledge for us to read.

Bibliographic Essay

Information about major works by writers included in this chapter is given in the text in most cases. One item that needs some additional information is Susan Magoffin's diary. It was edited by Stella M. Drumm Magoffin and published in hardcover in 1926 with the title *Down the Santa Fe Trail and into Mexico: The Diary of Susan Shelby Magoffin 1846-1847.* It is also worth noting that Susan Magoffin's diary was unknown for many years until it was found in her descendant's attic in 1926 and then published, a reminder that there may be written treasures yet to be passed on.

Much of the information in this chapter about the writers themselves was provided by persons who knew the writer under discussion or who are especially knowledgeable about El Paso history. The most prominent of these contributors, often contacted repeatedly, are, in alphabetical order: Andrea and Evelyn Berta, Nancy Hamilton, Patsy King, Betty Ligon, Bernice Mielke, Donna Munch, and William "Bill" Quinn, whose covolunteers at the UTEP Heritage House were also eager to assist. Claudia Rivers is always a valued resource, as is her team at the Special Collections section of the UTEP library. Those at Texas Western Press shared their information. Other resources include *Password,* the journal of the local historical society and Borderlands, the historical research work by El Paso Community College students under the expert direction of English professor Ruth Vise. Many thanks to these and all who helped with this topic.

Chapter 7

MAKING THE DESERT BLOOM: EDUCATION IN EL PASO

by Deane Mansfield-Kelley

EL PASO IS A CITY built around mountains and surrounded by desert. Any person seeing a thunderstorm sweep across that desert knows that only water can make that parched land bloom. After the rain, flowers of every type appear, displaying vibrant hues and bringing beauty to our part of the Southwest. Thus the desert, with its variety of blossoming plants of varied colors, becomes a symbol for El Paso, a multicultural city that blooms for a variety of reasons. One of those reasons is a long history of valuable women educators who have brought knowledge to El Paso students thirsty for learning.

Although El Paso is blessed with a large diversity of cultures, the two dominant ones are Hispanic and Anglo. From a small village on the Texas/Mexico border to the thriving metropolis that it is today, El Paso has seen itself as a bilingual community. To live with both languages adds richness to life; to educate effectively with a dual language situation is an educational challenge that requires not only dedication but innovation as well. From early El Paso educational history to the present, there have been women of brilliance and determination who have met this challenge.

The group of women with the longest continual educational history in El Paso are the Sisters of Loretto. According to *The History of Loretto Academy,* they were founded in Kentucky in 1812 and became the first fully American Catholic religious order. All other orders of the time had originated in Europe. The Sisters of Loretto rapidly attracted new members, and their work grew throughout the Southeast and Midwest. Their main focus was on education and the building of schools in the communities that they served.

Finally in 1852, the Sisters of Loretto were asked to come to Santa Fe by John Baptist Lamy, then bishop of that region. The story of Bishop Lamy's journey to Santa Fe and his life there was presented in Willa Cather's famous novel, *Death Comes for the Archbishop,* in which the sisters are mentioned. In June of 1852, six sisters began their trek to the Southwest, traveling on a steamboat from Independence, Missouri. While on board, cholera swept through the boat, killing Mother Mitilda, the superior of the group, and leaving another sister very ill with the disease. It took her three years to finally reach Santa Fe. The other four sisters and Bishop Lamy, who made the journey with them, traveled for four months in covered wagons to reach the small town, at one time accompanied by three hundred Indians.

Once in Santa Fe, Mother Magdalen Hayden became the first superior of Santa Fe and led the order from 1852 to1881. One of her first priorities was for all the sisters to learn Spanish, as most of their students did not speak English. Mother Magdalen and the other sisters also translated the traditional Catholic prayers and the rulebook of the order into Spanish. Mother Magdalen pushed hard to expand the educational outreach of the sisters by establishing schools and supplying teachers in Taos, Denver, Albuquerque, Las Vegas, Bernalillo, Socorro, and finally in San Elizario, just outside of current El Paso. The teaching sisters learned to live in adobe buildings with dirt floors and stretched muslin for windowpanes.

The school at San Elizario was named St. Joseph's Academy, founded in 1879. It was staffed by one sister from Santa Fe and four others from Las Cruces. In *Light in Yucca Land, 1852-1952,* written by Sister Richard Marie Barbour, she quotes Sister Mary Bernard on her arrival at St. Joseph's:

> We were met [at Franklin, now El Paso] by two Sisters in a canvassed-top spring wagon. The driver looked like he had never known soap, water or comb. Finally we reached San Elzeario [Elizario] after dark the same evening. When daylight dawned upon us, really my impressions were not very encouraging, as it seemed we had reached God's forsaken part of the world. Some of the rooms had mud floors and were . . . swept with a bunch of broom straws tied together . . . the church had no pews, a mud floor, the highways were full of ruts and holes . . . Our boarding and day school began to increase, so I found myself very busy trying to teach music and classes. We were only five Sisters. We had twenty-five boarders which required a great deal of extra work.

Sister Magdalen Dietz, another teacher at the school, made it clear in her comments that the main priority of the sisters was to educate the young women of the area:

> There was a public school there but nearly all the girls came to us. We did not teach boys. We took boarders from the country round and some from across the border. Sister Sylvia Roy and Sister M. Bernard Doyle taught the high school studies during the later '80s and music between times, and about 1890 graduating honors were conferred on Mary Garcia, a handsome intelligent Mexican girl who afterward married a Mexican lawyer, O. A. Larrazola, who served as Governor of New Mexico.

Although St. Joseph's in San Elizario was certainly a success, the decision was made by the motherhouse and mother general, Sister da Frosa, to move the school to El Paso in 1892. They felt that the educators could reach more students in the growing town. The move was a surprise to the sisters, and they were asked to move to El Paso only one week before school was supposed to start. In the historical book *Loretto in El Paso,* Sister Bernard Doyle speaks of the hurried move to El Paso:

> On Friday afternoon, about three o'clock, we received a telegram to pack everything as we were to take the school to El Paso. Sister Petra and I tramped the rough and rutty roads of San Elizario trying to secure teams to haul the furniture. We succeeded in procuring five. Sister and I stayed up all night and packed everything we could. By five-thirty the next morning the five wagons loaded with parlor furniture, two pianos, mattresses and other furnishings were on their way to El Paso.

The sisters not only moved belongings, faculty, current students, and welcomed new students, but school began exactly as scheduled at the new St. Joseph's. Soon the sisters were asked to staff four more schools in El Paso: St. Mary's, St. Ignatius, Guardian Angel, and St. Patrick's. Very soon St. Joseph's had increased to the point that it was obvious a new teaching facility was desperately needed.

Into this situation came Mother Praxedes Carty, a true legend and one of the great Loretto leaders. According to the Catholic Diocese of El Paso's Historical Archives, Susan Carty was born at Bawnbay, County Cavan, Ireland, March 4, 1854. She emigrated with her family to America at the age of ten. Joining the Sisters of Loretto at age twenty, Sister Mary Praxedes was ordered to serve in Santa Fe, and took her final vows before the revered Bishop Lamy.

Almost everyone who writes about Mother Praxedes calls her a "human dynamo." She was petite in stature, but powerful in personality and purpose. Unfamiliar with Spanish when she reached Santa Fe, she learned the new language from her students while she was teaching them English, stressing the importance of both languages. When she was transferred to Bernalillo in 1878 to rebuild and supervise the school, Sister Praxedes found her true calling, as a builder of schools. She was later to create educational facilities all across the Midwest and Southwest.

In 1880, Sister Praxedes was sent to head the school in Las Cruces and stayed there until 1893 as Mother Superior. She was in close touch with the El Paso sisters, and very supportive of the move of St. Joseph's from San Elizario to El Paso. El Paso, the rapidly growing city near Las Cruces, was a place dear to her.

Then in 1896, Mother Praxedes became the head of the Order of the Sisters of Loretto. For twenty-five years she traveled across the United States as superior general, checking on the Loretto convents and schools. She greatly strengthened the funding of the order, and even made two trips to Rome to assure approval of the constitution of the Sisters of Loretto. Completing her term of office as superior general in 1922, Mother Praxedes Carty returned "home." She was made Mother Superior of the El Paso sisters, and put in charge of building the new Loretto Academy. In control of the entire building project, she chose the site, land composed of twenty-nine lots on Trowbridge where the academy still stands.

Mother Praxedes helped design the three main buildings: the convent, the school and the chapel; she constantly raised funds for the completion of the school. In a symbolic gesture, she insisted that the architect completely change the direction of the buildings, making them face Mexico, welcoming its women with open arms. There are many generations of women from Mexico who can fondly remember their years at Loretto Academy, thanks to Mother Praxedes.

Loretto Academy, one of El Paso's finest private academic institutions, opened in September 1923, although building was far from complete. It took fourteen years to finally complete all three main units, with Mother Praxedes somehow managing to obtain the financing. In failing health, she managed to direct the building project from her bed until her death in 1933. The students chose to name the student newspaper *The Prax* in her honor. Still today, every student at Loretto Academy knows her story and how much of their education they owe to her.

The present Loretto Academy has expanded its facilities, has beautiful and spacious grounds, and students who absorb knowledge like water in the desert. It now has coeducational classes through fifth grade, with girls-only education from sixth to twelfth grades. The new 2010 Loretto Academy informational packet describes it as " a community of Faith, Justice and Respect." Statistics reveal that 100 percent of the 2010 graduates applied for college; 100 percent of those applicants were accepted in at least one college or university. This was the plan of one strong, determined woman. Now the Sisters of Loretto and other teachers at the academy have made it happen. This is their contribution to making the desert bloom.

Mother Praxedes.
Courtesy of Loretto Academy Archives.

As the Sisters of Loretto were continuing to increase their opportunities to give students an excellent private education, public educational facilities were streaming into El Paso. According to the history found in *The Woman's Club of El Paso: Its First Thirty Years,* the first public high school in the city was established in 1885-1886, with Miss Emma Seabough as principal. Kate Moore, a graduate of El Paso High School, began teaching music in the schools in 1890, the first time music instruction took place in public schools in Texas. In 1892 the first free public kindergarten in Texas was opened in El Paso, taught by Lucretia Hoard Jones with assistant teachers Belle Blacker and Findley Borem.

The early 1900s brought to El Paso one of its most important and influential woman educators in the person of Maud Isaacks. According to *The Handbook of Texas,* Isaacks was born near Austin in the mid-1880s and moved to El Paso to teach in 1916. A middle school teacher from 1916 to 1921, she became a much-loved high school English teacher from 1927 until 1954 at El Paso High School. She served as chair of that English Department for fourteen years, helping shape the early English curriculum for the school. Having a reputation as a gifted educator, Isaacks also served as a member of the State Textbook Committee, influencing education statewide.

In 1954, when her father retired from the Texas House of Representatives due to illness, Maud Isaacks ran for and won a special election to the house to take her father's place. She was one of only five women in the House of Representatives. She left the El Paso school system in 1955 to serve in the legislature. She was then elected to five more consecutive terms, finally retiring in 1966 at age eighty. When she retired, she was the only woman in the Fifty-ninth Legislature.

Although Isaacks left the role of teacher in 1955, she did not lose her interest in education. In fact it became her focus in her legislative career; her special concern was the improvement of Texas public schools. She advocated for higher salaries for teachers, examined school administration policies and procedures, and pushed to raise academic standards in Texas public schools and colleges. In 1961, Isaacks was selected as a member for the Special Interim Committee on Education, which combined with the Texas Legislative Council to study teacher certification. Although no longer in the classroom, she affected what was taught in the classrooms all over Texas.

Her reputation as a hard-working and dedicated legislator who constantly kept in touch with her El Paso constituents is reflected in her letters found in the *Maud Isaacks Papers 1953-1966* in the Special Collections at The University of Texas at El Paso library. On March 14, 1963, Maud Isaacks wrote to Dr. Wade Hartrick, a professor at Texas Western College, about her work on a bill "providing political freedom for college teachers." She is optimistic about the bill, but apologizes for not writing sooner. She has had eye surgery and writes, "I am trying to keep up with a little correspondence from my hospital room." She further mentions that the doctor will allow her to meet with the education committee for only one hour on the next Tuesday. Her determination to get back to work as soon as possible is evident.

Other letters in the *Maud Isaacks Papers* clearly show her support of Texas teachers. In a letter to Janie Alexander on March 9, 1965, she explains why the teachers' requests for pay raises do not appeal to the legislators because of the hostility created by the Texas State Teachers Association. She advises the classroom teachers to separate themselves from the school administrators in their actions. However, she definitely states "if the revenue is raised and appropriated, I shall vote for a teacher salary increase." Her decision is that pay raises should be based on merit, the belief that "a teacher who has made a career of her work, deserves more than a beginner or a less experienced teacher." Whether in Austin or El Paso, Maud Isaacks had an important effect on the educational process in Texas.

It is no wonder that she was selected for *Who's Who of American Women (1966-1967)*.

A few years before Maud Isaacks came to El Paso to teach, another wide stream of education came to the city. Senate Bill 183, signed by Governor O. B. Colquitt, established the Texas State School of Mines and Metallurgy on April 16, 1913. It opened in September of 1914 with an all male enrollment of twenty-seven students. Women students entered the college in 1916. According to *Diamond Days: An Oral History of The University of Texas at El Paso*, the School of Mines was first located in the old El Paso Military Institute near Fort Bliss. In October 1916, a fire destroyed the Main Building, one of several factors that caused the campus to be relocated, along with increased enrollment and the demand for increased military due to the Mexican Revolution and World War I. With $100,000 from the state legislature and money from El Paso civic leaders, a new site was purchased for the school on the west side of the Franklin Mountains near downtown and the American Smelting and Refining Company. The new campus began with the construction of four buildings, all of which are still in use at the current university.

The most influential person in the choice of architecture for the new campus was Kathleen L. Worrell, wife of Dean Stephen H. Worrell, the head administrator of the college. In April 1914, *National Geographic* magazine published an article entitled "Castles in the Air," about the Kingdom of Bhutan. Having read the article, Kathleen Worrell noticed the similarity of the Bhutanese landscape to that of the new college site. The article pictured buildings with high sloping walls, red brick friezes, colored tile mandalas, and deep inset windows, suitable for the rugged terrain of Bhutan, and for the Southwestern desert. A most persuasive woman, Mrs. Worrell convinced the college officials to use this style architecture for the four new buildings. To this day all buildings on this campus adhere to the Bhutanese design. The distinctive architecture makes the current University of Texas at El Paso one of the most attractive and unique campuses in The University of Texas system. The credit for this belongs to Kathleen Worrell, who left her mark on the university as well as El Paso.

By 1921, the college was renamed the Texas College of Mines and Metallurgy with its emphasis still on the training of mining engineers. In 1927, the school merged with the El Paso Junior College, and new groups of students arrived on campus. A strong rivalry developed between the "Engineers," the students majoring in mining and engineering, and the "Academs," students majoring in arts and education. Before too long the number of academs passed the number of engineers.

The Texas College of Mines and Metallurgy acquired a number of outstanding women on its faculty. One of the foremost was Dr. Gladys Gregory, political science professor from 1928 to 1962. She received her BS from Southwestern University, and her MA and PhD from The University of Texas. Acknowledged as an excellent teacher and scholar, she was the first woman on the faculty to achieve the rank of full professor.

During her teaching career the Texas legislature mandated several courses that all students at the university were required to take. One of the mandatory courses was Dr. Gregory's govern-

Gladys Gregory, 1930. *Courtesy of the archives of The University of Texas at El Paso Library.*

ment course, so for many years she taught every student on campus. Clearly involved in many campus activities, she was also the faculty sponsor for Zeta Tau Alpha, one of the major sororities that then had a lodge on campus. This association with the sorority resulted in the Dr. Gladys Gregory/ZETA Endowed Scholarship Fund currently available at The University of Texas at El Paso.

There is no question of the importance of her scholarly work. Her book entitled *The Chamizal Settlement: A View From El Paso* provided a background on the long dispute over a strip of land along the Rio Grande between El Paso and Juárez. Her assessment of the situation and her proposals for a settlement were so astute that her entire work was reprinted in the *Congressional Record.* She is credited with being an important influence in settling the disagreement between Mexico and the United States. Dr. Gladys Gregory's knowledge of government not only benefited her students and her university, but also her state and country.

Another noted faculty member of the Texas College of Mines was Vera Wise. She was born July 26, 1892, in Iola, Kansas. Her early years were spent in southeastern Kansas and then in the Pacific Northwest. Wise received her BA from Willamette University in Salem, Oregon, in 1920. She was accepted to study at the Chicago Academy of Fine Arts and there specialized in watercolor in 1924 and 1925.

Vera Wise then studied landscape art with regionalist painter Thomas Hart Benton in 1931, and later in 1938-1939 at the Kansas City Art Institute. Benton clearly had a large impact on her choice of subject matter for her paintings. Vera Wise chose to be a regionalist painter herself, but her region was the desert Southwest, especially around El Paso. She captured the bright colors, the arid mountains, the golden adobe houses, and unique landscape in her watercolors. She was a well-known and respected artist, prominent in the El Paso art scene. Today her work is still collected in excellent watercolors of Southwestern landscapes.

Vera Wise joined the faculty of the Texas College of Mines in 1939. She remained a major figure in the Art Department until she retired in 1962. As an educator she was noted for her careful attention to her students' work and her constant encouragement to her students to explore and expand the art world. She also had a reputation for teaching her classes impeccably dressed, shattering the frumpy, paint-splattered artist image of the time period.

Like Gladys Gregory, Vera Wise was active in campus activities, serving as faculty sponsor for the Chi Omega sorority. She was also among the first women to become full professors. Wise was the first woman academic department chair of the college, serving as the chair of the Art Department for most of her academic career. Renowned as an excellent educator and artist, Vera Wise made the desert bloom academically in her classroom and artistically in her watercolors.

Another important woman professor who taught in the college when it was both Texas College of Mines and Texas Western College was Myrtle E. Ball, who taught speech and drama. An interview with Myrtle Ball, recorded for The University of Texas at El Paso's Institute of Oral History, reveals some interesting aspects on early teaching at the college. For example, all college professors were expected to teach four courses one semester and five the next. A number of the professors gained experience in the public schools for a year or two, and then went on to teach at the college. There were very few buildings on campus, and so some classes were taught on the steps of the buildings to provide more room. But regardless of the difficulties, the desire for an education seemed to prevail. Ball said, "But I can truly say that I don't believe that ever, I had ever known as fine students and the quality of students as I had in those years. They worked their fool heads off and I worked my hair grey."

Myrtle Ball, 1930.
Courtesy of the archives of The University of Texas at El Paso Library.

Myrtle Ball recalled that her drama students had to practice their plays in the classrooms because the college didn't have a theater. They performed the plays in the Scottish Rite Temple, but they had to pay to rent that location. When they presented *Our Town*, Ball said, "We had nothing apportioned for us or any of the arts, really. And *Our Town*, I guess we had just one rehearsal and we couldn't afford it, and it was a rather memorable thing."

Although she didn't have proper funding or her own theater, Myrtle Ball was an unforgettable teacher of acting. When she took her students to a competition, they were prepared to win. She tells of the state-wide competition in one-act plays that was held in Lubbock, Texas. Before the contest, she had contacted a man at Paramount Studios in Hollywood, and told him that she had a girl named Donavie who would be good movie material. He and three other studio men arrived. Because Donavie was poor, "as we all were," Ball said, they had to borrow a white dress for the girl to do a brief acting test.

Then Ball related, "And Twentieth Century was there and Paramount and she got two offers of screen tests and she went to Paramount and that was our night." Her acting company also won Best Actor, Best Actress (Donavie), and Best One-Act Play. They had beaten their arch-rival, The University of Texas. When they stopped to eat on the way home, Ball recalled, ". . . all at once we looked at Donavie and I says, 'What's the matter with you, Donavie, you're all breaking out?' She had the measles."

Myrtle Ball was in charge of drama and speech at the college for many years, and was a nationally and internationally known theater figure. For her many contributions to the university, she was named professor emeritus when she was ninety.

Another renowned woman faculty member, Dr. Lurline Coltharp, came to the College of Mines at age fifteen as a student and later returned to become one of the outstanding professors in the Languages and Linguistics Department of Texas Western College. In her interview for UTEP's Institute of Oral History, Dr. Coltharp reminisced about her early days as a student, "The gathering place was the bookstore. You went inside Old Main and the first room to the right was the bookstore and we had a lot of fun going in there. There were not only books, but you could buy Cokes and you could stand around and visit with the boys." She also commented, "We always had to wear old shoes on campus because every place you went there were rocks." Later noted for her sense of style and elegance in the classroom, she returned to a Texas Western College that excelled in many areas of academics, and had certainly paved its streets.

Dr. Coltharp made it clear that when she entered the College of Mines she intended to be an engineer. Her father was an engineer, and she wanted to follow in his footsteps, but she did not count on the prejudice against women in engineering at the time. She relates the story of the male calculus teacher who told her, "I don't care if every paper you turn in to me in calculus is 100 percent, I'll still give you an 'F' and I will fail you in calculus so that you can never be an engineer." He was the only teacher of calculus at the college at the time. She changed her major to history, and then added education as a second major.

Her extracurricular activities certainly reflected the life on campus at the time. She joined a sorority, was the only woman on the rifle team, and was elected one of the school beauties. She also participated in the founding of the Golddiggers, the girls' cheerleading and marching squad. The name, she admitted, was tongue-in-cheek, because "we were the kind of girls that had been brought up, when a boy took us on a date and we stopped at a drive-in for a drink and he said, 'What will you have?' we'd say, 'I'll take a small Coke, please,' because we weren't going to spend more than five cents of the boy's money. Money was too scarce a commodity then, so we thought the name 'Golddiggers' was

Lurline Coltharp, 1965.
Courtesy of the archives of The University of Texas at El Paso Library.

funny." Dr. Coltharp then left the College of Mines to pursue her education at The University of Texas, the school she laughingly referred to as "the wicked university."

She returned to Texas Western College with her doctorate, and rose to prominence in the Department of Languages and Linguistics. She is still regarded worldwide as one of the important scholarly figures in onomastics, a branch of lexicology devoted to the study of the origin, form, meaning, and use of names. Her presence brightened and enlightened the lives of her students and made them think and bloom on this desert campus.

In 1966, the college was renamed, again. The Texas Board of Regents, unifying the educational institutions in The University of Texas System, changed Texas Western College to The University of Texas at El Paso. In 2010, UTEP now has over 21,000 students and sixteen PhD programs, with more in the making. There are many excellent women now teaching at this university in various fields. We remember the women in education, past and present, who continue to inspire us. In early El Paso, the Sisters of Loretto had a saying, "*Esperamos que florezca el desierto en este mundo nuevo.*" [We hope that the desert will bloom in this new world.] Every day the women educators in El Paso are striving to make that happen.

Bibliographic Essay

Information for the first section of the chapter was found in the library and archives of the Loretto Academy of El Paso, Texas. The staff at the academy was most gracious about supplying a number of photographs also, some of which appear in this book. I owe them many thanks for their help and support in this project. Works that were particularly helpful were *The History of Loretto Academy, Light in Yucca Land, 1852-1952,* and *Loretto in El Paso.* The Catholic Diocese of El Paso's Historical Archives were likewise rich in information that helped create a clearer picture of the Sisters of Loretto.

Public education in El Paso and the history of The University of Texas at El Paso's outstanding women professors was supplied through such sources as *The Woman's Club of El Paso: Its First Thirty Years,* the Maud Isaacks Papers in the Special Collections at The University of Texas at El Paso, *Diamond Days: An Oral History of the University of Texas at El Paso,* and interviews done with prominent UTEP women professors found at the university's Institute of Oral History. Other comments about the professors come from personal knowledge. There was so much that was of historical interest that it was difficult to do justice to it all. I also owe much gratitude to Bobbi Gonzales, my research assistant on this project. All the women discussed illustrate why education in El Paso is thriving in the twenty-first century.

Chapter 8

WITHOUT COOKING, THERE IS NO COMMUNITY: WOMEN FEEDING EL PASO

by Meredith E. Abarca

"Cooking for me is a blessing . . . the opposite of work."

Aída Gabilondo,
El Paso native and author of
Mexican Family Cooking (Fawcett, 1986)

POET PAT MORA, a native El Pasoan, once said that we "need to get recipes while we can, [to] absorb *el pasado,* the past, nourishment and delight for the body and soul." Recipes are sources of nourishment and delight, for they go beyond offering instructions and directions to prepare a dish. Recipes convey *historias,* the Spanish word for both stories and histories. Such *historias* address issues of social, geographical, and economic changes affecting families, cultures, and communities. Stories embedded within food narratives add to our knowledge about women's lives. Their strength, generosity, hospitality, and creativity are expressed in the acts of preparing and serving meals and in the management of their kitchens. When consuming such meals, not only is basic hunger satisfied, but we also are nourished and delighted by the *historias* enmeshed in the recipes of women who build a life for themselves in the desert of El Paso by feeding its multicultural and multiethnic inhabitants.

To speak about the kitchen, the heart of food preparation and provision, is to recognize a talent often gone unnoticed; yet the skill of cooking holds multiple layers of *historias.* Cooking is the human activity *par excellence;* it is the act that transforms a product from nature into something profoundly different. Women have been the forerunners of such transformations; with their culinary abilities, they have cooked and seasoned the histories of families, of social classes, of entire communities. This has been the case from medieval times, as Cristina Mazzoni illustrates in *The Women in God's Kitchen,* to more recent times as Aurora Levins

Morales declares in the opening lines of *Remedios: Stories of Earth and Iron from the History of Puertorriqueñas* that Puerto Rico is a women's country for neither town nor fortress could have been built without women's "cooking." With their food, they literally and symbolically nourished a multitude. A book honoring social and cultural contributions made by women to a particular area acknowledges the humbling, but essential, act of building a community by feeding its people.

Within the United States, the ultimate harvest ritual that brings families to the table to share a meal is Thanksgiving. There are debates as to when the first recorded act of Thanksgiving took place in the Americas. Some historical and folkloric sources date and place the "myth" of the first recorded Thanksgiving on April 30, 1598, in the region now known as El Paso del Norte. While this celebration is connected to the expedition of explorer Juan de Oñate, a historical figure who can provoke strong controversy among residents of the area, the native Manso people made contributions to that dinner as well. References to this meal often mention that the feast included fish, crane, duck, and geese. However, the Mansos were both an agricultural and hunter-gatherer society. As many of the Native peoples throughout most of the Rio Grande and Southwest area did, they structured their community through a gender division of labor where men hunted and women gathered. Some scholars have argued that this division "did not necessarily mean that the men's task was thought to be more important. Indeed, . . . the actual weight of food collected by the women was probably greater than that killed by men." The cultivated staples, a task undertaken by women, included corn, squash, beans, as well as other plants and seeds such as *quelites*, amaranth, and of course, cacti. Surely these vegetables, cultivated and harvested by women, were also part of such first Thanksgiving feast. Women's contributions to a meal had a spiritual component, since agriculture was seen as a holy occupation. *Maíz* (corn) in particular was held in high regard as the sustainer of human life, and corn is also integral in many indigenous myths of creation.

If Europeans marked the diet of the region with their contribution of livestock, a few centuries later with the arrival of the railroad to El Paso, a wave of seafood—especially oysters—entered into the diet of El Pasoans. These could be enjoyed at the Grand Central Hotel, "The only First-Class House in the City," as well as at the El Paso Coffee and Oyster House. In 1882, the *Herald* had an ad for the "El Paso Coffee and Oyster House," which indicated that a customer could enjoy fresh oysters, spring chicken, and good coffee for lunch. The railroad had other implications for the diet of El Pasoans as new fresh products were more easily brought into the area. For example, Mrs. T. F. Early, who in 1883 managed, first with her husband then by herself, the Nevada House, which later became El Paso House, served home-like meals all week long that included "meats of all kinds, ham, and eggs, fresh vegetales [*sic*], and all the market affords." In 1883, the *El Paso Times* recognized El Paso House for always offering the "best of coffee, hot pancakes, and gems in the morning."

Historically, food preparation has been a task under the care of women's hands, even when a restaurant is owned and managed by a man. This has been the case at L & J Cafe: The Old Place by the Graveyard, located at 3622 E. Missouri Avenue. This restaurant has been serving meals since 1927, and since its opening day has

L & J Cafe: eighty years of history. *Courtesy of Leo Duran.*

remained a family owned business, originally known as Tony's Place. Antonio O. Flores opened it just before the Great Depression in what was then the outskirts of town. Nowadays, L & J Cafe sits literally in the center of the city. Tony's Place, the story goes, was famous for two things: "bootlegging" activities and Juanita G. Flores' (Antonio's wife) cooking. The cavalry stationed at Fort Bliss were the regular consumers of Juanita's homemade cooking and homemade brewing. When Tony's Place officially opened after Prohibition in 1934, the brewing activities were kept quiet. In 1968, Antonio and Juanita's daughter, Lilia F. Duran and her husband, John G. Duran, took over the restaurant and renamed it L & J Cafe, with the L standing for Lilia and the J for John. After John Duran's passing in 1987, the third generation of family members (Leo Duran and his wife Frances) have the responsibility of managing what is known in El Paso as one of its legendary eating spots. Just as Juanita was integral to the success of Tony's Place, so was Lilia, who offered her support and assistance to her son Leo and his wife Frances, up until her own passing in March 1999.

The pillars sustaining Tony's Place and later L & J Cafe's success for more then eighty-four years, according to Leo Duran, are the women integral to the business: his family members Margarita (great-grandmother), Juanita (grandmother), Lilia (mother), Frances (wife), and hired cook Paula Rocha, who worked at L & J Cafe for almost forty years. During an interview for the *El Paso Times* in 2005, Frances mentioned that Paula had been with them for more than thirty-seven years, and that she was "more than a cook; she [was] also a consultant on everything" they did. Juanita Flores and Paula Rocha's spirit continues to mark their presences through the recipes they developed, which are still served today. With the use of simple ingredients and her unique *sazón,* or culinary touch, Paula created the spicy red salsa served today with chips at L & J Cafe. The popularity of this salsa has been such that in 2005, Frances and Leo Duran began working on marketing a jar label to sell in grocery stores throughout the city so people could enjoy L & J salsa in their own homes. Lilia's spirit has also not left the restaurant's kitchen. In 2005, the Durans invited a psychic, Grace Neauhaus, to visit the establishment to confirm the legendary stories that L & J Cafe is haunted. While walking through the kitchen, Neauhaus said, "I'm sensing a woman, a large woman, and she loved to dance—I mean she really enjoyed it. I feel she died of some kind of heart trouble." Leo Duran affirmed that such a woman was his mother, Lilia.

While Paula Rocha did not leave her image captured in a photograph, as she did not like having her picture taken, her memory lives on in what Leo Duran describes as the making of a true cook. A true cook teaches values and practices that build a character of integrity, confidence, and respect of self and others. The basics of a true cook consist of cleanliness, efficiency, and passion—three elements that Leo Duran remembers affectionately and respectfully about Paula and her cooking. Regardless of how many dishes Paula prepared each day—even in her advanced age as she worked at L & J Cafe for almost forty years—her kitchen was always clean and in order. In the process of cooking, she would not waste anything; when using a green onion, the white head would add flavor to grilled meats, while the green stems would add nutrition to a vegetable, chicken, or beef stew. When she chopped celery, Leo remembers how she cut the tail end of it, washed it, and threw it in the soup, saying this added more healthy substance to the soup. By observing Paula's cooking, Leo learned to demystify the notion that Mexican food is not healthy. "She had her way of cooking her meats [and] her sauces," says Leo, that he "never realized were actually a healthy way of cooking." When comparing how food was cooked in his home versus how Paula cooked in the restaurant, Leo states, "I was more used to *el estilo casero.* We used more lard, and grease, and shortening at home than here [at the restaurant]. So I was really overwhelmed when I saw Paula's cooking. So I would ask her, 'is this something new, did you change the recipes?' And she would say, '*No, mijo. Así se han hecho estas recetas desde que me enseñaron a mi.*' My major surprise was the very minimal use of oils and shortening for *guisados.*" Paula's healthy cooking practices have earned L & J Cafe recognition as a spot for eating healthy Mexican cuisine by *Saveur,* a food magazine.

When I asked Leo Duran if he could describe Paula Rocha with one phrase, this task became quite difficult. In his effort, with a bit of a broken voice, he said, "Paula was a woman of strength, a woman of passion. She was a beautiful woman who loved her work; loved her kitchen; loved her life. Loved her family." For Leo, Paula's passing singled out the end of what he feels was a generation of people—in specific cooks—who worked knowing that their jobs had a purpose. According to Leo, Paula was an "inspiration and a tribute to women in the kitchen." Her presence in L & J Cafe's kitchen was not simply to do a job, but it carried with it a sense of self-fulfillment that comes from knowing that one's job contributes to the well being of others—a knowledge that brings with it pride in one's occupation. Her sense of pride went beyond her culinary talents and extended to the management of her kitchen, for she mostly cooked by herself until advanced age prevented her from doing all the physically demanding aspects of cooking in a restaurant's kitchen.

Paula Rocha's pride about her culinary talents remains in what Leo Duran identifies as L & J Cafe's five signature dishes: green chile enchiladas with chicken, *chile con queso,* steak tacos, *caldo de res,* and the combination plate. The connection between the preparation process of these dishes and Paula's culinary seasoning is that she was a cook from the old school, and cooking practices at L & J Cafe remain from the old school. Paula's "very, very private" nature found an expression in the many dishes she prepared with much passion. Paula Rocha was in Leo's opinion, "a legend in her own time."

If from Paula Rocha, Leo Duran (and by extension the rest of us) learned that the value of integrity, confidence, and respect of self and others derive from a job done with passion, from his own mother, Lilia Duran, Leo gained a work ethic that comes from struggling to build and maintain a business. He remembers how his mother struggled to "build a business during a time, back in '76, when we had our first Arab oil embargo and the United States felt the effects. Business started tapering off—not just here [in El Paso] but everywhere. I could see my mother struggling in the kitchen. [I could hear] the sounds of sweat and tears." For Leo these are powerful memories of his mother in the kitchen because as he says, these memories "instill in [him the] principles of determination, hard work, [and] perseverance."

The fact that Tony's Place/L & J Cafe has been in operation since 1927, under the ownership and management of one family, is a testament of lessons well learned. From the days of the cavalry, when customers came on horses, to modern days of SUV-driving customers, L & J Cafe has delighted the palate of multitudes with the recipes of the women who have been the pillars of this legendary food establishment. Leo Duran hopes to see L & J Cafe celebrate its 100 years of service while remaining a family business. If once Leo tried to encourage his own mother to sell the business, now he knows why she couldn't let it go: "There is something here that has sustained and continues to sustain three generations in business." The root of such sustainability comes from the principle of reciprocity integral to the act of giving and sharing food that Leo Duran fully captures when he says, "I feel we are contributing to the community."

El Paso's population in 1949, according to the US census, was 115,000 and by 1960 it increased to 276,687. During this time, more than 162,000 people enjoyed tea luncheons, dinner parties, wedding receptions, fundraising events, and other cultural and social engagments at El Paso's El Patio Verde, owned and managed by Grady (Geneva) M. Causey. A testament of her success was that after only three years in business, she had to relocate her site of operation. El Patio Verde enjoyed two different locations, the first was the Causey's private residence located at 1009 Park Road in Kern Place, the second at 1406 Montana Street.

Grady (Geneva) M. Causey, native of Mayfield, Kentucky, and graduate of Western Kentucky State University, moved to El Paso with her husband and their daughter in 1932. Upon arriving in El Paso, the Causeys became members of a number of organizations that later provided key networks for the success El Patio Verde enjoyed for eleven years. The Causeys became active members of St. Clement's Episcopal Church, the Planned Parenthood Association, El Paso Medical Society and its Auxiliary, the Parent-Teacher Association, and El Paso Chamber of Commerce. Geneva also served on the board of directors of the Woman's Department of El Paso Chamber of Commerce; furthermore, several times she served as the chairperson for the St. Clement's annual Harvest Festival, and she founded the Alma Rodge Sewing Guild.

The art of hosting came naturally to the Causeys, who often held gatherings in their spacious Kern Place home with its 20' x 36' living room, spacious dining room, and enclosed patio. The transition from private entertaining to public hosting was precipitated by Dr. Causey's death in 1948. Faced with the responsibility of supporting her family financially and the desire to "change as little as possible her life and those of her children," she decided to introduce a new business to El Paso. "It occurred to me," she said, "that I might open my home to the public and charge people to entertain or be entertained there. . . . Nothing similar was operating in El Paso and there appeared to be a need for such accommodations." Geneva Causey's Southern values of propriety and hospitality proved key ingredients to her business venture.

In addition, with the opening of El Patio Verde in a private residence, Geneva Causey joined a growing number of women who entered the hospitality industry and infused it with a home-like coziness. This new ambience, Nieves Pascual Soler says, altered the "male-dominated sphere of food production and consumption" by "introducing a middle-class dining-room culture into a market place previously bifurcated into high-class eating places." At this time, the high-class public spaces for social gathering in El Paso were hotel dining rooms, reception halls, and the members-only country club. El Patio Verde provided a setting for personal entertainment with a home-like ambience and privacy.

A personal touch also sealed the first "announcement," not advertisement, made to communicate the new services provided in El Patio Verde. Geneva Causey ordered 200 announcement cards and personally mailed them to her network of acquaintances. The announcement included the following information: "El Patio Verde, 1009 Park Road; Party Service: Coffees, Luncheons, Teas, Dinners, and Wedding Receptions. By Reservation Only; Wednesdays open for Luncheons and Bridge. Geneva M. Causey. Telephone 3-0923." As the business increased, in order to offer this home-like public setting to more people, Geneva Causey didn't book private gatherings on Friday afternoons—as El Patio Verde was open to the general public. Besides the personal touches, another factor that greatly contributed to her accomplishment was the significant attention El Patio Verde events received from the society pages of the *El Paso Times*. Finally, of course, at the root of the eleven years of success were Geneva Causey's gracious style, Southern hospitality, and most of all, her skills as a superb cook.

Mrs. Geneva Causey in 1949 when El Patio Verde opened. *Courtesy of* The Receiving Line was 11 Years Long: Reminiscences and Recipes from Geneva Causey's El Patio Verde in El Paso 1949-1960.

Her menus, known for their creative innovations, clearly reflected the different regional foods that have become native to El Paso. As a Southern transplant to the Southwest, she combined spoon bread with chile and chicken to create what become known as one of her specialties: chicken fiesta. She always cooked with the finest ingredients: never margarine, always butter; heavy creams; choice meats; and rich sauces. Items on the menus, which Geneva Causey took care not to duplicate, included: tamales, ham, curry sauce, cold vegetables, chicken wiggle, spiced peaches, buttered asparagus, pumpkin tarts, beef and cheese balls, barbecued meatballs, shrimp Creole, vinaigrette strawberry salad, and

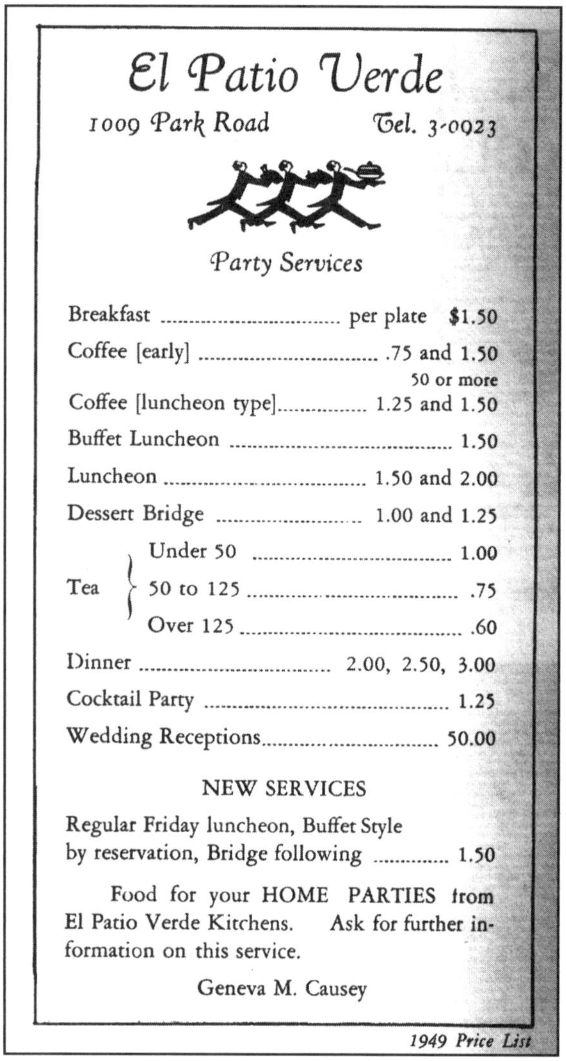

El Patio Verde

1009 Park Road Tel. 3-0923

Party Services

Breakfast ... per plate	$1.50
Coffee [early] ...	.75 and 1.50
	50 or more
Coffee [luncheon type] ...	1.25 and 1.50
Buffet Luncheon ...	1.50
Luncheon ...	1.50 and 2.00
Dessert Bridge ...	1.00 and 1.25
Tea — Under 50 ...	1.00
Tea — 50 to 125 ...	.75
Tea — Over 125 ...	.60
Dinner ...	2.00, 2.50, 3.00
Cocktail Party ...	1.25
Wedding Receptions ...	50.00

NEW SERVICES

Regular Friday luncheon, Buffet Style by reservation, Bridge following ... 1.50

Food for your HOME PARTIES from El Patio Verde Kitchens. Ask for further information on this service.

Geneva M. Causey

1949 Price List

Left: El Patio Verde list of prices in 1949.
Above: Geneva Causey: Always a hostess.
Courtesy of The Receiving Line was 11 Years Long: Reminiscences and Recipes from Geneva Causey's El Patio Verde in El Paso 1949-1960.

key lime pie, just to mention a few. What makes this selection of dishes remarkable is the variety of ethnic culinary traditions they represent.

Geneva Causey's records of events and menus left in the annual planners are chronicles of El Paso's history. They reflect economic changes, social networks, distinguished visitors as well as new transplants to the city; these events are intertwined with private family affairs. During the first years of business, Geneva Causey recorded prices of food, lists of guests, menus, recipes, and the origin and history of food, as well as her family doctor appointments, family invitations to social gatherings, and a diary of inspiring thoughts. As her confidence increased as a professional hostess, however, the information in the notebooks decreased. When Geneva Causey closed El Patio Verde in 1960, for a few years in California, Arizona, New Mexico, and Hawaii, she continued to be a gracious hostess at university fraternity houses. If a society newspaper today reported the era and the ambience of El Patio Verde, the description might read something like this: "Gorgeous weather, spacious entertaining rooms, and delightful refreshments contributed to one of the century's most successful entertainments when El Paso played hostess to more then a quarter of a million old and new friends. Calling hours were from the late forties to the sixties, and the receiving line was eleven years long!"

Born on May 8, 1933, in Pozzuoli, Italy (near Naples), Maria Vincenza Rosaria DiBonito was a "trailblazer" who surpassed gender and socio-economic limitations of her time to become an educator of generosity, hospitality, and cosmopolitan palates. For thirty-two years, she was the backbone of Ardovino's Italian Gourmet Shop on Cincinnati Avenue. Shortly after her marriage to Joseph Ardovino in 1962, Maria DiBonito Ardovino became "integral to the [restaurant] business" her husband had just opened a year earlier in 1961. She infused the shop with her spirit until the Ardovinos retired and sold the business in 1993. Her presence was such that people would eat at Ardovino's because of her. As her daughter, Marina Ardovino, says, "my mom would be part of people's families. You would go to Ardovino's, and she would invite you to her table." On these occasions, she delighted people with her great storytelling abilities. Maria DiBonito Ardovino fed generations of kids, who now, as adults, think of growing up eating at Ardovino's—just like we all think about eating our own mother's food. Her appreciation for food, hospitality, and generosity were perhaps born out of her own tenacity and determination to make the best of life, especially when life offered so little.

Maria DiBonito grew up in the small town near Naples, Italy, during World War II. Her father, Luigi Amadeo, was a farmer and her mother, Rafaella Pilato, was a nurse. Her father passed away when she was only six years old, leaving Rafaella with the responsibility of supporting all of their children on her own. The circumstances were such that as the oldest child Maria ended up living in a convent. The difficulties caused by the war, geography, and economic limitations led to a challenging childhood. Growing up eating "crusted bread" and often feeling hungry, gave Maria her life-long interest in food and, more importantly, in feeding others.

Living in the convent left Maria experiencing literal hunger, but it also provided the opportunity to eventually cross the Atlantic and settle in the blissful desert of El Paso. The story surrounding her long journey to El Paso goes something like this. According to the accounts Maria shared with her own daughter, Marina, about her youth: a princess, who had nine children, came to the convent and asked if someone could accompany her to the park, and Maria volunteered saying she had permission to leave the convent. During these outings, she played with other kids who happened to be the children of a British colonel stationed in Naples. Since Maria did not actually have permission to leave the convent premises, once the nuns found out what she had done, they expelled her. But this was a fortuitous event. The British colonel and his wife, the Bradleys, were in need of a nanny and offered her the job. When he had to report back to England, they asked her if she would like to go with them and continue with her new post as a nanny. She accepted. As fate would have it, after a few years the colonel was deployed again, this time to Fort Bliss. While Maria without hesitation embraced such an opportunity to relocate temporarily to the United States, her mother Rafaella did not. In order to achieve such a goal, Maria knew to hide her passport from her mother

Top: Maria and Joseph's engagement, 1962. *Courtesy of Marina and Joseph Ardovino (family photos).*
Left: Maria, Joseph, and Colonel Bradley at the shop, 1964. *Courtesy of Marina and Joseph Ardovino (family photos).*

by keeping it under her pillow. She left Europe and traveled to El Paso. Shortly after her arrival, she met Joseph Ardovino. Eventually they got married, making her stay in El Paso a permanent one, and she became the backbone of Ardovino's Italian Gourmet Shop. She gave her entire life to it.

It is impossible not to give yourself in the process of providing food for others—even when this happens in the professional public kitchen. But beyond reading this act as one more example of a woman selflessly giving herself to the service of others, we have to remember the social and cultural power involved in the very act of providing food. In the case of Maria DiBonito Ardovino, preparing and sharing food provided a channel for her creativity, a space to build community, and the opportunity to develop cosmopolitan cultural palates—while also delighting many with her storytelling ability.

While anyone can follow a recipe and hope to create a good meal, not everyone can do what Maria DiBonito Ardovino could—create art guided by her senses. Marina, Maria's daughter, describes her mother's cooking in this manner:

> What was really amazing to me about my mom was something that I think very few people have the ability to do. If we had leftovers in the kitchen—this and that—she could whip [them] up, throw [them] together and make a new delicious dish. She would combine all these weird, different things and come up with something fabulous. That's an art. She was a natural.

Maria's culinary art was not based on reconfigurations of family recipes—as she never cooked with her own mother—but on an acute awareness of traditional regional cooking from Naples.

Her artistic ability to just create dishes using the knowledge of her hometown culinary style filtered into the restaurant despite, or perhaps because of, the simplicity of the menu: pizzas, sandwiches, salads, a few pastas, and minestrone soup.

Some of the influences of traditional Neapolitan cooking included a few fundamentals for Maria's approach to food: cook everything from scratch; use quality, fresh ingredients; keep it simple. To end with a final recipe following these guidelines was for her a process of trial and error until the perfect combination came along. In this manner, Ardovino's Italian Gourmet Shop provided "consistently great food for thirty-two years." Furthermore, through the re-creation of Neapolitan recipes, an international palate was added to the unique regional cuisine of El Paso. By the very process of following traditional Neapolitan cooking guidelines, Maria DiBonito Ardovino helped many local residents develop an international community with a shared palate. Food makes such community possible. In the act of feeding people and sharing meals, food is transformed from the most basic individual and biological necessities into a medium for social relationships, which ultimately brings about community.

For a restaurant to stay in business for so many years, it needs consistent and loyal customers—something else that Maria DiBonito Ardovino created. In the early days, the customers that kept the business alive were "wealthy Mexicans from Ciudad Juárez," already familiar with some of the items sold at Ardovino's. In order to attract more El Pasoans,

Top left: Maria Ardovino in front of the shop, 1964.
Bottom left: Maria and Joseph in front of the shop, 1965.
Above: Maria's home dining table, 2002.
Courtesy of Marina and Joseph Ardovino (family photos).

the process of educating palates took place by introducing people to imported specialty items such as olives, capers, anchovies, hearts of palm, and frog legs. To share her traditional Neapolitan flavors with a community beyond the one created within the restaurant, Maria engaged in structures of taste. By creating baskets with pastas, sauces, cheese, crackers, olives, wine, etc., that people bought and took home, Maria helped structure the taste in the preparation of a particular Italian meal. At times she also prepared a set menu from her native land for customers who requested catering services. The process of structuring taste emphasizes collective and communal values of a given experience, and it is in this process where communities of similar palates are born.

What brought together such communities of different cultures were Maria's generosity, hospitality, and talent as a cook. At Ardovino's, it was not uncommon for customers to have a meal without paying. The system of keeping a tab was a common practice; sending kids home with a treat of an imported chocolate or candy was also not unusual; and enchanting everyone with her stories was a frequent occurrence. Welcoming people to the restaurant as she would at her home was the trademark of Maria's hospitality.

Every cook has at least one, if not more, signature dish(es). When I asked Marina, Maria's daughter, what she would consider to be her mother's signature dish, without hesitation she said, "definitely her meatballs." Maria's meatballs, says Marina, "were the best on the face of the earth." They were made with traditional and basic ingredients: golden raisins, pine nuts, ground beef, ground pork, and Parmesan. The combination of ingredients, the quantities, and the timing for the right degree of frying holds the secret of such perfection. This perfection lives in the sensory memory of those who were fortunate enough to be invited for dinner at Maria's home, for it was cooking at home when she would go to town with her culinary creativity.

While the meatballs might have been something she prepared mainly for her family, personal friends, and neighbors, some of her other distinctive recipes are still prepared and served at Ardovino's Desert Crossing in New Mexico. Maria and Joseph Ardovino's two children Marina and Robert own and run this restaurant, which was once owned by their paternal granduncle, Frank Ardovino. At Ardovino's Desert Crossing, Maria's children share their mother's spirit with their customers via certain items in the menu, such as Mamma Ardovino's spinach lasagna. When the Ardovino siblings opened Desert Crossing, Marina would tell her mother, "Ah, Mama, I wish you were twenty years younger. We [would] go to the moon having you as our chef." Maria Vincenza Rosaria DiBonito Ardovino's spirit of generosity, creativity, and hospitality remains present at Desert Crossing, as these are the same qualities exhibited by its owners. A community continues to be built as we savor the culinary creations of a woman who dedicated thirty-two years of her life to feeding El Pasoans.

"Ever since I can remember," says David Jurado, "[my mother] was always cooking." His mother, Estela Borrego Jurado, was a renowned chef in El Paso in her day. Her reputation as a cook began in the 1950s through a catering service she ran out of her home in Sunset Heights—a neighborhood in El Paso from where Ciudad Juárez, Chihuahua, is clearly visible. Her inclination for cooking predates this catering service, as she took cooking classes in Ciudad Juárez and

Estela Jurado, ca. 1940s.
Courtesy of Henry Jurado (family photos).

joined a group of friends who rotated meeting in their respective houses to prepare different dishes. In her initial years of catering, neighbors and acquaintances were among her earlier customers. She catered for a range of personal and social events with a variety of traditional Mexican meals such as *cochinita pibil* (roasted suckling pig) and chicken *mole*. Among her many clients, the Schwartz family, one of the oldest Jewish families in El Paso who owned the Popular Dry Goods Company, often requested her catering services.

As her success as a caterer increased, so did the necessity for a bigger cooking facility. With the eventual 1972 opening of Casa Jurado at 226 Cincinnati Avenue, a partnership venture with her oldest son Henry, Estela Borrego Jurado met such a need plus more. The initial success of the restaurant, which remained in the family until 2004, was a fortuitous coincidence because most of her catering customers lived in the Kern Place area, where the restaurant was located. One such loyal customer, who remembers Estela as pleasant, compassionate, and down-to-earth, made Casa Jurado a regular dining experience. With Estela's exceptional cooking and Henry's innovative hosting/managing abilities, they complemented each other as business partners and successfully sustained Casa Jurado for thirty-two years.

Born in Ciudad Juárez, Chihuahua, Estela grew up cooking next to her own mother, Antonia Borrego. David recalls weekend family gatherings at his grandmother Antonia's house where "she had a big kitchen with a big table for all [the] aunts and uncles to get together." Cooking and eating at Antonia's were events for *convivencia,* the act of creating unity, with family members but also with nature. David remembers the preparation of different foods, many of which included harvesting vegetables and fruits. Corn was planted, harvested, and then cooked over an

Estela and her sons, Henry and Louie. August 13, 1944.
Courtesy of Henry Jurado (family photos).

open fire, an activity in which the grandchildren took part. The Borrego's agricultural venture also delighted the palates of wine lovers, particularly those who consumed wines made by James and Susan Magoffin, as they often bought grapes from the Borregos. Estela's children also learned to make cheese from scratch, such as *jocoque* and *asadero,* by first milking the cows. The Borrego's household offered Estela's children an upbringing infused with the wonders of growing, preparing, and serving food. Testimony of this culinary embrace is the fact that two of Estela's four sons, David and Henry, became restaurateurs.

Estela Jurado's culinary talents found their strongest expression in her desire to build community by feeding others. Instrumental to her endeavors into the commercial kitchen were the numerous elaborate meals she helped produce as acts of charity. For years, she helped various organizations, mainly through Sacred Heart Church, both in Ciudad Juárez and El Paso. In Ciudad Juárez, she cooked and delivered food to an organization that looked after elderly people. For the church, she often helped raise funds for different events, benefits, and even a church expansion by cooking and selling food and then donating the profits to the church. David Jurado remembers his mother as a woman who "helped people in need who passed through El Paso." Her desire to feed others, a desire vested with the principle of generosity extended from charity work, to catering, to Master Chef at Casa Jurado.

The food magazine *Saveur* labeled the food served at Casa Jurado not as Tex-Mex but as border food. Tex-Mex means "oversized combo platters blanketed with melted orange cheese, or crisp-fried tacos filled with greasy ground beef." Border food, on the other hand, "is marinated cactus salad wrapped in a just-made tortilla, or enchiladas, stacked instead of rolled, and smothered in delicate red chile sauce. . . . It is plain cooking, served up unadorned, with a distinct regional character—pure, complex, and unambiguous." The idea of complexity as a category defining border food seems rather appropriate for the style of cooking at Casa Jurado that Estela Borrego Jurado and her children learned in the years of cooking next to Antonia Borrego. The meals Antonia Borrego prepared were elaborate and reflected not only her culinary ability, but also the historical and geographical trajectories that some recipes have traveled. These processes ground people to a place by giving them a sense of familial and cultural history that goes beyond the region of their birthplace.

For example, while visiting his grandmother David fondly remembers learning to make *jocoque,* a cheese that we can safely assume his mother also made. While recipes and cooking processes always have distinct regional components to them, people throughout Mexico make (or at least eat) *jocoque,* a cheese that has the consistency and distinctive taste of sour cream or dense yogurt. Because culinary border zones are spaces where different cultural practices come together to create something uniquely new, the most visible border that *jocoque* implies is a trans-Atlantic one. According to ethno-botanist Gary Paul Nabhan, the original creators of this yogurt/cheese-making process are Arabs who introduced it to Europe and later the Americas. Nabhan states that 1492, besides marking the so-called "discovery" of America, also indicates:

> . . . the year that tens of thousands of Jews and Moslems were forced by the Spanish Inquisition to convert to Catholicism or to leave the Iberian Peninsula or die. . . .

> Although many Sephardic Jews and Moorish Moslems fled to Morocco and other countries of the Maghreb, others sought refuge in the Americas. . . . In the first wave of immigration from Iberia to Mexico, roughly one-third of all immigrants were originally from Andalusia, where Moslems and Jews had formally lived in the greatest numbers.

These immigrants influenced the culture and cuisines of Mexico and the US Southwest, argues Nabhan. The word *jocoque* comes from the Nahuatl *xoco,* which means sour, dating this process to the arrival of people from the Old World into the New World. When the Aztecs tasted the sour, dense, cheese-like substance for the first time, they named this dish (and its culinary technique) using their own language. The etymology of *jocoque* marks a culinary practice that bridges food, knowledge and people.

Cochinita pibil is another dish in which regional borders are bridged. *Cochinita pibil* (roasted suckling pig) is a traditional Yucatecan dish marinated in strong acidic citrus juice and colored with *annatto* seeds, which are used to make *achiote* paste. Preparing this dish in El Paso gives multiple meanings to the very concept of border food. Speaking within the context of Mexican culinary history, this dish provides a culinary oasis in the desert as it originates from the peninsula of Yucatán, Mexico. How did Northern Mexicans from Chihuahua, as were Antonia and Estela, learn to make Yucatecan food? While the easy answer could be cookbooks, David Jurado provides a different answer, which adds to the very notion of *convivencia,* creating unity and community by sharing knowledge and food with others. While not directly speaking of *cochinita pibil,* David recalls a "couple who were tenants of [his] grandparents, [who] were from Yucatán. When it was time to make tamales, they would say, 'No, this is how we make them, with banana leaves.' Tamales Yucatecos." Since Ciudad Juárez has a large community of Yucatecos, and it was not uncommon for Estela Jurado to further develop her culinary abilities "by meeting acquaintances who were interested in food." A high probability exists that the recipe for *cochinita pibil* was learned from Yucatecos.

For Estela Jurado, the cultural borders that came together with the making of *cochinita pibil* were tradition and modernity. The very word *pibil* comes from a Mayan word that means "buried." The traditional cooking of this dish requires it to be buried in a pit. As the Borrego and Jurado family gathered in Antonia's house to cook, Estela's brother would prepare the "pit with bricks and rocks and light the fire . . . buried the meat and cooked it overnight." This was done not just for *cochinita pibil,* but also for *barbacoa de olla.* However, *cochinita pibil* was often buried in the modern pit of Estela's gas oven.

One more aspect by which Estela Jurado connected tradition and modernity to the practices of continuity was manifested in the ritual of remembering, as David says, "*la manzana!*" Estela would set her pork dish in a large platter and would always decorate it with a large apple. Numerous recipes exist that call for the use of apples when roasting pork. The root of this correlation comes from the time when cooking was governed by the seasons. Before the advancements of modern mass production, pigs were only slaughtered in autumn after growing and fattening them up in the spring and summer. Due to this seasonal eating of pork, apples were added to the preparation as they too were harvested in late summer and early autumn. Nowadays, we can eat pork and apples all year round, and the combination of pork and apples remains a staple in contemporary recipes.

Estela Borrego Jurado dazzled many of her customers' palates with dishes she learned from her mother, from cooking classes, from other people, but most of all with dishes she perfected with the touch of a naturally gifted culinary artist. Like all great cooks, the development of her distinctive recipes was mainly a result of "just trial and error." She perfected the *masa* for tamales by making it "not too heavy." What she added or took away to achieve its lightness remains a shared secret of cooks at Casa Jurado. Casa Jurado was known for Estela's *mole, salpicón*, and red and green chile sauces. She made *mole,* the thick brown chocolate-chile sauce, in a way that not many people do nowadays, especially in the context of a restaurant's kitchen. Estela's *mole* was made from scratch. The preparation often began with a trip to El Mercado in Ciudad Juárez where she would go with her son Henry. There she would buy large bags filled with five different types of chiles, almonds, chocolate, garlic, and all the other ingredients she needed for her *mole.* Estela Jurado's dedication in making this laborious dish, highly sought by her loyal costumers, was commemorated by her son Henry when he presented her with a plaque acknowledging her as a source of inspiration. The plaque was mounted on the center of the large skillet she used for making *mole* in Casa Jurado, dating back to 1972.

Henry and his wife, Luz, continued operating the restaurant after Estela Jurado passed away in 1981. In 2004, Henry sold the business, but his mother's legacy continues. We can visit David Jurado's second Casa Jurado, located at 4772 Doniphan, and enjoy some of Estela's recipes prepared by cooks she trained in the kitchen of the original Casa Jurado, who now work for David. In their *sazón,* Estela Jurado's culinary talent lives on.

A significant aspect of El Paso's history has been (and continues to be) seasoned with women's culinary flair. It is the history of Native Americans, of colonial times, of slavery, of immigrants, and part of their stories are embedded within the culinary practices of women who have cooked for El Pasoans throughout the years. In addition, the personal *historias* of the four women mentioned here, Paula Rocha, Geneva Causey, Maria Ardovino, and Estela Jurado, are a testimony to a generation of women who belonged to a period when "pride still mattered." They knew something we forget today about the value of food work: gathering, preparing, sharing, and serving food. They knew that it takes food work, as Janet Flammang says, "to make a community, craft a civilization, and impart wisdom from one generation to another." To honor the generosity of spirit of this generation of women as well as the social and cultural values of their labor, we must make their lives visible, their work rewarded, and their teaching universal.

Bibliographic Essay

The sources for "Without Cooking, There Is No Community," come mainly from personal interviews with either family members and/or owners of restaurants. The three central interviews were the following: For L & J Cafe, Leo Duran, third-generation owner and manager along with his wife, provided all the information on Paula Rocha; Maria Vincenza Rosaria DiBonito Ardovino's daughter, Marina Ardovino, shared memories of her mother and her life as the backbone of Ardovino's Italian Gourmet Shop; David and Henry Jurado, as well as Henry's wife, Luz, reminisced about Estela Borrego Jurado's powerful connection with food. Information about Casa Jurado also came from two articles that appeared in *Saveur:* Peggy Knikerbocker's "Border Food," and Beth Kracklauer's "El Paso" (www.savuer.com). For Geneva Causey and her business, El Patio Verde, I gathered all the information including pictures from Mary Margaret Davis' book, *The Receiving Line was 11 Years Long: Reminiscences and Recipes from Geneva Causey's El Patio Verde in El Paso 1949-1960.* Guynes Printing Company published this book in 1975.

The other central sources for this article come from books and articles addressing key issues about the social value found in women's culinary talent. These books also provide excellent material on the powerful influence women have had in the preparation, consumption, and distribution of food. These included Janet Flammang's *The Taste for Civilization: Food, Politics, and Civil Society* (University of Illinois Press, 2009); Donald J. Hughes' *American Indian Ecology* (Texas Western Press, 1983); Pat Mora's "Layers of Pleasure: Capirotada" comes from Arlene Voski Avakian's collection, *Through the Kitchen Window: Women Exploring the Intimate Meanings of Food and Cooking,* (Beacon Press, 1997). Four other sources providing general information about food were: Cristina Mazzoni's *The Women in God's Kitchen: Cooking, Eating, and Spiritual Writing* (Continuum, 2007); Aurora Levins Morales' *Remedios: Stories of Earth and Iron from the History of Puertorriqueñas* (South End Press, 2001); Nieves Pascual Soler's *A Critical Study of Female Culinary Detective Stories: Murder by Cookbook* (The Edwin Mellen Press, 2009); and Gary Paul Nabhan's *Arab/ American: Landscape, Culture, and Cuisine in Two Great Deserts* (University of Arizona Press, 2008).

Chapter 9

LAS COMADRES: THE ORAL HISTORIANS

by Marcia Hatfield Daudistel and Susan Goodman Novick

WHENEVER WOMEN would gather in the parlors or kitchens of their homes, stories were told of their families and the intricate connections between them through marriage, birth, and death. We can all remember when our aunts, grandmothers, mothers, and their friends would gather and tell the stories of their own families. Most of us remember hearing these stories by listening at doors as children and when we were older finally being allowed into those kitchens and parlors while the women talked. This is what formed our own early oral histories about our families and the families of our friends, not a formal genealogy. Through these stories we found our identities as family members and as part of our communities.

Because of these informal narratives heard by granddaughters, daughters, and nieces, we are connected with the women who came before us—relatives, lifelong friends, and other women who established homes and families in our fledgling hometowns. *Las Comadres,* an informal organization of the female descendants of El Paso's pioneers, continues the tradition of sharing these narratives and friendships with succeeding generations as well as their admiration for the place in which they live—El Paso.

The beginning of *Las Comadres* is also the story of a border city. Over 11,000 people lived in El Paso in 1895, a city whose population had soared from 736 inhabitants in 1880 as a result of the arrival of the Southern Pacific, Texas & Pacific, and the Atcheson, Topeka, & Santa Fe railroads in 1881. By opening up the area to markets near and far, the railroads dramatically changed El Paso and the opportunities it provided to newcomers. People came from all directions to settle in a place that promoted business opportunities and a healthy climate year round. The railroads also brought touring companies that performed in the many theatres and opera houses, increasing the town's cultural development. A sense of community was established with the founding of schools, libraries, and churches.

In what was called "The Gay Nineties," a group of young women, daughters of pioneer families who came to El Paso in the 1880s, attended the Central School at the corner of Myrtle and Campbell Streets. A few members of their group attended boarding schools in other cities. It was in their neighborhoods near what is now downtown El Paso—on San Antonio Street, Magoffin Avenue, and Olive Street, as well as on Mesa Street—that they would forge friendships that would continue for many years.

These friendships lasted as the young women married, had children, and participated in El Paso's social and charitable activities. They realized that, in spite of their cultural and civic activities, which were very much a part of the life of the women of the early families in El Paso, they were not in frequent contact. They wanted to strengthen and maintain their girlhood friendships in a strictly social atmosphere. In 1931, they founded an organization that, eighty years later, is still going strong. They called it "*Las Comadres.*" The Spanish word *comadre* can mean "godmother, neighbor," and is used now to mean a close female friend.

Throughout the years, there have been several attempts to write down an exact account of the beginnings of this organization. Considered the moving spirit of the group, Mildred Tilton Oliver related the reasons behind the organization of *Las Comadres* to her friend, Lula Hasam McAfee in the 1930s:

> I met Lena Falvey Lynch on the street. We were so glad to see one another. She said she'd just been talking with Anna Shelton Kemp who remarked that it was too bad we old girls could not see more of each other. I said I'd consult with Ora David, Anne White, and you and work out some plan. You all thought it was a good idea. We were not to form a club, or burden people with entertaining—no dues.
>
> I then called a group to make plans. Everyone liked the idea. Maude Crouse who lived at Arizona and Mesa asked us to meet at her home as her husband and mother were invalids and she could not leave home very well. We met and decided on a monthly luncheon at a hotel or café either in El Paso or Juárez.

Although some of the original fifteen members of *Las Comadres* were from privileged families, most had attended the same public schools and grown up within a few blocks of one another. The early records of *Las Comadres* document these friendships made through the years. Included in the records is a scrapbook with photographs of two of the original members in their youth before *Las Comadres* was organized. Their stories present a perspective on El Paso and the opportunities it provided to its newcomers in the late nineteenth century.

The life of Josephine Clardy Fox was not typical for a woman of her time. The daughter of Missouri natives Zeno Clardy and Allie Davis, Josephine was born in 1881 and brought to El Paso the following year when her father, a former prosecuting attorney in St. Francois County, Missouri, was drawn to El Paso and its reputation as a boomtown with the arrival of the railroad. Zeno was a very successful attorney in El Paso and acquired many valuable properties in lieu of fees. Josephine attended the Academy of the Immaculate Conception, and then entered public schools until the end of the eighth grade. She grew up with the women who would form *Las Comadres,* but was one of the few who were sent to a finishing school, Hosmer Hall in St. Louis.

At Hosmer Hall, Josephine began her life-

Left: Josephine Clardy in Shakespearean costume at Hosmer Hall, age eighteen, 1900.
Courtesy of Texas Western Press.
Above: Josephine Clardy Fox, 1915.
Courtesy of Texas Western Press.

long interest in theatre and music. Although she did not continue as a performer, she became a patroness and benefactor of theatre and music in El Paso. When she was twenty, her father died suddenly of a heart attack at the age of forty-five in El Paso.

Josephine's mother decided not to keep her grief-stricken daughter at home while they learned to cope with Zeno's death, but sent her to friends in Berkeley, California, to study music. Allie Clardy had been told from various music teachers that Josephine's contralto voice was worth cultivating, along with her other musical talents. Josephine looked forward to her time in a sophisticated city, much as she had enjoyed her time at school in St. Louis. San Francisco, with its operas and plays, was a vivid contrast to her hometown; the El Paso that Josephine left behind was essentially a frontier village without sidewalks or paved streets. She stayed with family friends and soon after her arrival was enrolled in a fine music school in Berkeley.

In Josephine's absence, Allie had to learn how to manage her husband's business affairs, including the management of his vast property holdings. During the next few months, Josephine did not come home to El Paso, but remained in Berkeley. She did not lack for suitors among the dashing young army officers that came to call, but in May she returned to El Paso because her mother was ill and lonely. Josephine, then twenty-one, divided her time between New York City and El Paso. She pursued her voice and piano lessons in New York and returned every year to enjoy the opera, theatre, fine restaurants, and luxurious hotels. It was in New York that Josephine met Charles McGhee, a widower and a member of the New York Cotton Exchange. A cultured and educated man, he fell in love with Josephine, and it appeared that she consented to become engaged to McGhee. He was plagued with health and financial problems. Early in their relationship, Josephine suffered an eye injury that affected her sight.

However, by 1907, the relationship between Clardy and McGhee was suffering because of the attraction Josephine felt for a man she had met four years earlier in El Paso. Eugene Fox was persistent in his courtship, and Josephine eventually married him, but not until she spent a year in Europe with her mother beginning in June of 1908.

Eugene surprised them by accompanying them for part of their journey. The trio traveled much of the year to London, Florence, Venice, Vienna, and Berlin before spending the winter in Paris. Eugene left to return home before Josephine and her mother went to Paris. Allie and Josephine also consulted medical experts about Josephine's eye injury, but nothing could be done to improve her sight. Josephine claimed that one European specialist made the condition worse by using the wrong poultices on her eye.

In her travels, Josephine had a papal audience and was presented at the Court of St. James. She kept the gloves and fan from that event in a box that was displayed to her friends. In the summer of 1909, Josephine and Allie booked passage for New York and asked Eugene Fox to meet them there. Allie settled Josephine into the Waldorf-Astoria Hotel while she hurried home to El Paso, as several of her commercial properties had burned in downtown El Paso.

Josephine Clardy Fox and her mother, 1912.
Courtesy of Texas Western Press.

Eugene Fox came to El Paso in 1904, and the friends he made in his new city were some of the most successful and influential business leaders. Eugene worked for the El Paso & Southwestern Railroad (EP&SW) as a freight and travel agent and, although not as wealthy as his new friends, he became a very popular member of The Social

Club. Fox was a tall and handsome man with a pleasant personality. When he met Josephine Clardy, a beautiful and cultured young woman, he immediately fell in love. As the bachelors of The Social Club married, one by one, Eugene pursued Josephine through frequent separations, due to her travel and his frequent assignments to the Chicago and Los Angeles offices of the railroad. Eugene rapidly moved up in railroad circles, becoming General Traffic Manager of the EP&SW Railroad in El Paso.

Eugene Fox's courtship of Josephine Clardy had many ups and downs. Since her father's death, Josephine was her mother's constant companion. They traveled together to New York for several months each year and lived in California during the summer to escape the El Paso heat. Eugene at that time was working out of the Los Angeles office of the railroad, so the courtship progressed. He was transferred to the Chicago office and his hopes that she would set a wedding date were dashed once again. He remained constant as an admirer and became invaluable to the two women with his business advice.

Josephine's mother, Allie, shocked everyone when in June 1910, she married a young man named J. B. Swinney. Eugene wrote Josephine:

> You can imagine my feelings, darling. I wanted to beat him to death. He has been in charge of the Ready-to-Wear dept. at the Popular. Said he came from Macy's N.Y. . . . He can't be over thirty years old and I am sorry to say it dear but I am sure it can't last always. Of course he is after her money. . . .

Attorneys were consulted, and Josephine and Allie's interests were protected. The marriage was soon dissolved and Allie returned to the name Clardy. The years passed from 1910-1915; finally Eugene broke the engagement, "My one wish and desire for your future is that you may be as happy you have made me miserable. Sincerely, Eugene."

Faced with the real possibility that her daughter had lost Eugene, Allie counseled that Josephine should let him know at once that she loved him and was ready to marry him. On January 20, 1916, Josephine Marsalis Clardy and Eugene Emmett Fox married quietly in the Collegiate Church of St. Nicholas in New York City. It was wartime and a showy wedding did not appeal to Josephine, so the wedding was attended only by Allie Clardy and a friend of Eugene's. After eleven long years, Josephine, at nearly thirty-five, was finally Eugene's wife.

Eugene had promised Josephine that she could return to New York whenever she wished, and as the wife of a railroad executive, Josephine and her mother took full advantage of the free passes until Allie Clardy's health began to fail. Eugene was transferred to El Paso in late 1916, an event that Josephine did not welcome, although her mother's health was declining and Allie needed her daughter nearby. Josephine still imagined her childhood city as a frontier town, with dusty streets. But El Paso had become a thriving city with paved roads, many new buildings under construction, and many civic and cultural organizations established. It was during this time that Josephine reconnected with her old school friends who would later become the original members of *Las Comadres.*

Josephine and Eugene bought a large house at 1119 Montana Street, and Allie moved upstairs to a separate apartment. When Eugene was promoted to vice president in charge of traf-

Many of the original members of *Las Comadres* and their guests; seated on bottom steps: Mabel Falvey, Bella Ainsa Flato. On steps, Lea White Osburn, Jo Marr Fable, Lula McAfee, Lena Falvey Lynch, Eliza Berrien Loomis. Standing at foot of stairs, left to right, Ora Davis, Carmelita Ainsa Pomeroy, Mrs. Edgar Fewel, Nina Neff Searls, Louise Austin Marr, Anne Kemp White, Nell Pollard, Dell Fewel Coles, Anna Shelton Kemp, and Myra Newman Maple.
Courtesy of Las Comadres *records.*

fic for the Southern Pacific Railroad after it bought the EP&SW, Eugene and Josephine moved to San Francisco and left Allie behind in their home in El Paso. For three years they lived in the Palace Hotel in San Francisco. Josephine feared motherhood and Eugene adored children, but she built a life of arts and culture, and his life was his job.

The year 1931 was difficult for the couple and for the country. Eugene's father died, and his mother was debilitated by a stroke. He accepted a position at another railroad that planned expansion, but the Interstate Commerce Commission denied the expansion. Allie was very ill, so Josephine returned to El Paso to help manage her mother's business affairs. The Fox house was burglarized and many of their treasured possessions were stolen. The Depression hit El Paso, and the First National Bank failed. The commercial property owned by Allie and Josephine was managed by the State National Bank, but many of their tenants suffered from the closing of First National. Allie and Josephine derived their income from these rental properties.

Railroads suffered from reduced revenue and Eugene lost his job. He rapidly went through his personal resources but finally found a job as traffic manager in St. Louis, at only a third of his former income. Eugene was deeply in debt and had to leave his trunks behind at a hotel in Washington to satisfy an unpaid bill. After many years of being his own boss, he found it difficult to accept orders and account for his time hourly. During this time, Josephine remained in El Paso. Eugene did come home for Christmas in 1933, but it would be the last time he would ever see Josephine. Eugene Fox died in April 1934 after he suffered a stroke on the train, returning from a visit to his dying mother. Josephine was recovering from a serious car accident when she learned of her husband's death.

Bedridden from her accident, Josephine struggled with Eugene's estate, which was nearly bankrupt. She was able to get his effects returned from his St. Louis hotel residence after satisfying the bill. She and her mother struggled to pay the taxes on their commercial properties, sometimes relying on the generosity of friends to prevent losing the source of their income. Their appearance also suffered as the Depression continued. Once known for their impeccable attire, they began to look shabby. They would go to the Popular Dry Goods Company and stay for hours without making purchases or sit in the lobby of the Paso de Norte Hotel, without eating lunch there, unable to afford that pleasure.

With President Roosevelt's New Deal, Josephine and Allie's finances began to improve and they were able to repay the bank loans that kept them afloat. But six years after Eugene's death, Allie Davis Clardy died on March 23, 1940. Now aged fifty-nine, Josephine Fox, widowed, childless, and without the constant companionship of her mother, was truly alone. It was during this time that she became dependent on her childhood friends, many of them members of *Las Comadres.* It was also during this time that Josephine became very active as a benefactress of the arts in El Paso. Unfortunately, she was deceived by a Count Vladimir Podgousky, whose real name was William Lapko. He sold her many art reproductions that he claimed were the originals. The deception came to light after her death when Parke-Benet Auction house appraised the collection.

In 1959, while visiting in Dallas for the Neiman-Marcus Fall Fortnight, Josephine fell on the stairs at the Statler-Hilton Hotel and broke her hip. She spent the next fourteen months in Providence Hospital in El Paso and decided to sue the Hilton Hotels Corporation for her ordeal, but settled for a nominal sum out of court. Josephine became reclusive and rarely ventured outside her home. Her friends would visit and bring her meals and provide companionship.

During this time, she donated land to the El Paso Public Library, which named a new branch after her, and she continued to sponsor the arts in El Paso. Her health began to fail, and cataracts rendered her completely blind. After yet another fall on her previously broken hip, she went to Providence Hospital where she died on May 11, 1970. Her name was widely known throughout El Paso because of her gifts to the community. Her entire estate was bequeathed to The University of Texas at El Paso, and the Fox Fine Arts Center was made possible by her bequest.

Another original member whose photograph was included in the *Las Comadres* scrapbook was Carmelita Ainsa Pomeroy. The youngest daughter of Manuel Ainsa and Eloisa Serana Ainsa, Carmelita was born in El Paso in 1884. Manuel came to the United States from Spain as a young child. His mother was a great-granddaughter of Don Juan Bautista de Anza, founder of San Francisco. Eloisa Serana was born in Sonora, Mexico. The Ainsa family came to El Paso in 1882 from Umatilla, Oregon, where Manuel was involved in the dry goods and grocery trade.

When he came to El Paso, Manuel opened up M. Ainsa & Sons, a wholesale grocery business. The family settled at 509 North Mesa Street, and Carmelita attended grade school and high school with friends who would join her as original members of *Las Comadres*.

Carmelita married Charles L. Pomeroy around 1908, and they lived at 501 Montana Street. Although Charles's father established Pomeroy's El Paso Transfer Company in 1879, Charles instead went into the grocery business with Carmelita's brother-in-law. By 1920, the Pomeroys, with their two daughters Alice and Eloisa, lived at 501 Randolph Street in Sunset Heights. When Charles died in 1935, Carmelita, now fifty-one, continued her involvement in El Paso's social and cultural activities, serving as the head of *Las Comadres* in 1945 and as one of the founders of El Paso's chapter of the National Society of Arts and Letters in 1946. She was also a member of the Pan American Round Table. For many years, Carmelita wrote columns and letters to the editor of the El Paso newspapers. In the *El Paso Herald-Post* "Thinking Out Loud" column of April 14, 1943, she encouraged her fellow El Pasoans to welcome the soldiers stationed in El Paso during World War II:

> We who love El Paso and feel definitely that it is a friendly place in which to live are hurt at the accusation made against its hospitality. The friendliness of most of its citizens and their willingness to cooperate in every good cause was graphically demonstrated in the last wonderful drive of the Community Chest. Actually, to have had a part in it to collect money for the support of our Human Building Institutions was the greatest privilege that one could experience. It was inspiring to every one who took part. And to old timers, it seemed like a return to our former big family attitude, which El Pasoans used to love.
>
> As a hostess at USO activities, I have had the opportunity to hear the soldier talk about El Paso and its impressions on him. They unhesitatingly tell me the good and the bad of their experiences here. The persistent charge of lots of the soldiers is that they have found El Paso unfriendly, in many respects, and in many cases gougers of the soldier boy. This charge I personally have heard from many boys. If what they say is the truth, and there is no reason to doubt them, the practice must be stopped. For after all these boys are giving their all for the very men who are guilty of this gouging. Most of these boys buy bonds and send money home, I am told. Consequently they have little left to spend . . . especially, as one boy told me, to buy polish to use on his boots, and that means some polish. Those men who make a practice of this gouging are leeches, and the Chamber of Commerce should take them in hand. They should make their names known so that the soldier should be warned to avoid them in the future. This would be a just punishment for the guilty.
>
> The other frequent charge is that in no other city where they have been stationed, have people been so hard hearted in not picking up soldiers to carry them on a little further to their destination. Many times soldiers have stood for as long as an hour while crowded busses pass them by . . . and private cars going in the same direction also pass them by. They might at least have

Above: Carmelita Ainsa Pomeroy on her Hawaiian Honeymoon, 1908.
Right: Portrait of Carmelita Ainsa Pomeroy, no date.
Courtesy of Las Comadres *records.*

given the boys a lift as far as the motorist was going, for the expense is no more for an extra passenger. These boys are giving us a lift into safety, then why can we not give them a lift?

These two charges are made the most frequent. Then others tell us that they love El Paso and have been treated swell. They tell us that after the war they intend to bring their families to live here. In order to regain our fine reputation of friendliness, it is up to each and every one of us to treat the soldier boys like we want our own boys to be treated. When we come in contact with them we immediately fall in love with their boyishness and their loneliness hurts to our deepest hearts. They are our future American hope. We surely do not desire to hurt them. Possibly we are thoughtless. Let's treat these boys fairly and kindly. They show their appreciation immediately. Any hostess will tell you how they love being mothered. They put you and me in the place of their parents and tell us the little, inconsequential homely things of their lives at home. Men and women . . . do your part and you will not be disappointed in them.

Carmelita Ainsa Pomeroy died on June 3, 1963, at the age of seventy-nine in El Paso and is buried in Evergreen Cemetery. The legacy of El

Paso pioneers Manuel and Eloisa Serna lives on, however, as several subsequent generations of Ainsa women have been, and continue to be, members of *Las Comadres.*

The names of the fifteen women who attended that original meeting at Maude Crouse's house, all of whom were members of early El Paso families and had grown up in El Paso, were found in the scrapbook. Anne Kemp White was out of town and couldn't attend the meeting. However, when she returned from her vacation in Virginia, she was told that she was a member. She reminisced in a letter written to a fellow *Comadre* in December 1967:

> I have several times been asked to write a history of this organization and have done so twice only to have it disappear into nowhere later. It is not easy to write because there were no notes, no dates nor dues kept at any time, and in fact, "no nothing"—only a get together, a few times a year, of old friends of the same vintage, just a "fun event" and no trouble to anybody. A group of old friends, realizing that they were growing older, got together at Maud Crouse's home on Mesa Avenue and made the decision to form the organization.

Las Comadres did not keep records about their meetings until 1954, but their activities were written up in the *El Paso Times* with such articles titled: "El Paso Women Friends Since Their Teens to Meet Dec. 7 For First Time This Season" from December 1938; "Longtime El Pasoans find friendship in the Comadre Club" in the *El Paso Herald-Post,* December 12, 1983, and in an undated clipping from the *El Paso Herald-Post,* "Comadre Club Recalls Old Time Diversions: Hayrides and Club Dances are Numbered Among Pastimes." In addition to a list of members, the article quotes Mrs. Woodworth: "Picnics were held in the beautiful cottonwood graves below the Five Mile bridge. It took a whole day to get out to Fort Bliss, so we rarely went that far away from town."

For many years, the group met for luncheons four times a year at the Paso del Norte Hotel in downtown El Paso, owned by El Paso pioneer Zach White. His daughter, Mary White Boykin, made the arrangements for the luncheons. The meetings were usually announced in the *El Paso Times.*

As time went by, the membership grew as their daughters or daughters-in-law joined to continue *Las Comadres.* The members decided that their new recruits had to be at least fifty years of age, with preference given to daughters and daughters-in-law before other women who had family ties to El Paso pioneers were selected.

As the club grew, the membership limit was

Las Comadres in 1959. Seated in the front row, Lily Moye and Frances Brown were wearing identical dresses, separately purchased at the Popular Dry Goods Company for this occasion. They sat next to each other deliberately in this photograph. *Courtesy of* Las Comadres *records.*

Las Comadres in 1953. *Courtesy of* Las Comadres *records.*

set at sixty women who had an interest in El Paso history and participated in programs of *Las Comadres.* Soon, luncheon meetings of reminiscence gave way to talks about early El Paso history related to the early pioneer families, as well as issues relevant to the next generation of members. In the 1960s, members began to make presentations at the meetings, and their topics were recorded in the president's notebooks.

In December 1962, the women discussed the selection of the queen of El Paso's Winter Carnival in 1901. In September 1963, members gave an account of the first dancing classes that were held in El Paso and the recitals that Professor Mahler from St. Louis gave at the Myar Opera House. In October 1966, three army wives gave a talk about El Paso girls who married army men and told of their interesting posts.

Other topics focused on the elementary and high schools that many members attended as well as reading clubs and the origins and production of *luminarias.* When a report on Dudley Elementary School concluded, more than half of the women stood up and sang "Dudley, Fair Dudley," the school song. A presentation on El Paso's Jewish pioneers included a slide show of photographs and a discussion of how these pioneers' descendants married each other, making the limbs and branches of the family trees quite convoluted.

Las Comadres members have read from their ancestor's diaries about their journeys across Texas and they have discussed what brought their families to El Paso. Former Sun Queens have spoken about the Sun Carnival and members have shared their Christmas holiday traditions. By sharing the stories of their lives and their ties to El Paso, these women continue the passing down of memories, reinforcing their connections to one another.

At the December and March meetings each year, *Las Comadres* members invite their daughters and daughters-in-law to hear the stories of the past, and this tradition has carried on for at least three generations. At each December meeting, members celebrate the holidays by sharing family traditions, singing Christmas carols, and wishing each other well. In 1977, new members of *Las Comadres* were serenaded with the following song, sung to the tune of "Rudolph the Red-Nosed Reindeer."

> Now we have eight new members, and we welcome every one
> We may be quite old ladies, but we often have some fun
> Genevieve, Frances, Charlotte, Caroline and Marian,
> We think you may enjoy us, Mary Morris, Mildred, Ann.
> You bring us some needed youth, a new point of view
> And though you may learn from us, we may learn from you
> Let's all be gay Comadres, full of friendship's Christmas cheer
> And let this spirit guide us, all throughout the coming year.

Detta Reynaud Owen recalled going to meetings in the 1940s before she was a member of *Las Comadres:*

> . . . I want to say that before I was a member, I was privileged to go to many of the early meetings on Daughters Day in March

Las Comadres in October 1999. *Courtesy of Ron Stathis Photography.*

> and at Christmas time Guest Day. First I went with my mother, then with my aunt, Glen Thompson, then my cousin Anne White and then with my dear friend Queenie Mapel. I loved going and thought there was no more fun than to hear them reminiscing, especially Mary White Boykin telling abut her escapade with the prostitutes when she was little girl and the Mathias girls, Hedwig Mathias Schwartz and Ellie Mathias Mayer, telling about the time they hypnotized one of the friends and could not un-hypnotize her!

This transmission of stories through the generations makes *Las Comadres* a unique organization that not only keeps the early history of El Paso alive but also recognizes the importance of life-long friendships. And nowhere is the tie that binds this group together more apparent than in the invocations that are read at the beginning of each meeting. A few found in the *Las Comadres* records include:

> We gather today as *Comadres,* friends whose ties in some instances go back to school days or before. But in all instances, we descend from those ancestors who uprooted themselves to cross oceans and part of a continent and through accident or by design, settled here at the Pass of the North. They struggled and labored to build homes, schools, businesses, churches and synagogues, hospitals; they established libraries, orchestras, and museums. We have been bequeathed a heritage of a uniquely bi-cultural and multifaceted community.
>
> —Frances Schwartz Blumenthal, May 1991

> For the achievements of our ancestors who helped build El Paso out of the desert; for this group of "*Comadres*" who gather to pay tribute to them, and who, with pride, call

Las Comadres in 2010. *Courtesy of Creative Images Photography.*

El Paso home. May we preserve the past, contribute to the present, and pass down to future "*Comadres*" a challenge—to continue our efforts. —Hilda Flores Kern, December 1993

In the midst of our fearfully changing world, how wonderful it is to be able to pause and be together as *Comadres*—real friends, longtime friends, daughters and granddaughters of a rich heritage of good friends. —Marian Zork Given, October 2001

"Once a *Comadre,* always a *Comadre.*" This slogan clearly explains the bonds of friendship that have continued for eighty years. Established because fifteen women, friends since their childhoods, wanted to see more of each other as adults, *Las Comadres* continues to combine the tradition of storytelling among women with a strong admiration for their home—El Paso. As their pioneer forebears helped build El Paso, members of *Las Comadres* have followed in their footsteps, helping to enrich the community through their good works. And as their daughters and nieces become involved in *Las Comadres,* the stories of those who built El Paso will continue to be told and passed down to the next generation.

Bibliographic Essay

The records of *Las Comadres* were invaluable as primary sources for this chapter. We are indebted to Carlisle Coldwell Navidomskis, 2010-2011 president of *Las Comadres,* who provided us with access to the group's records, which included scrapbooks, photograph albums, presidents' notebooks, membership lists, and copies of some presentations to the group. A review of the "Society Pages" of the *El Paso Herald-Post* and the *El Paso Times* proved helpful, as they included details of the meetings in the 1930s and 1940s. The vertical files of the El Paso Public Library's Border Heritage Center contain information on the Ainsa family, and Ruby Burns's *Josephine Clardy Fox: Traveler, Opera-Goer, Collector of Art, Benefactor* served as source material for Fox's life.

Members of *Las Comadres* shared wonderful stories of their involvement in the organization. We are grateful to Sugar Goodman, Cita Schuster, Nancy Howell, Frances Litt, Hilda Kern, and Ann Schaechner for sharing their thoughts. As a member of *Las Comadres,* Susan remembers attending meetings years ago with her mother and enjoying the camaraderie of the women as they shared their stories of their lives in El Paso. She is proud to belong to such a fabulous group of El Paso women!

Chapter 10

INASMUCH AS YOU HAVE DONE IT UNTO ONE OF THE LEAST

by Lucy Fischer-West

"GO YE INTO ALL THE WORLD, and preach the gospel to every creature," Christ's great commission reads. The women who settled in El Paso to do the work they felt called to do were many. Their dedication was strong; their perseverance great. Some helped alongside their husbands in the churches they'd helped build. Others came alone, living simply, giving their all. They came to share their beliefs, to teach, to feed the hungry, to shelter children, to heal wounded bodies and souls.

Nineteenth-century El Paso history as documented by C. L. Sonnichsen, W. H. Timmons, Leon Metz, and others, depict the town proper as Sin City, with multiple saloons and brothels coloring the downtown landscape. With the arrival of the railroads to El Paso in 1881 came an easier mode of transportation and the population increased many times over in a relatively short period of time. Seemingly overnight, a dusty village of several hundred people became a community of 16,000. Women's refining influence was felt on many fronts as they demanded, and received, schools and churches. By 1896, El Paso had fifteen churches: five Methodist, four Baptist, two Catholic, one each Christian, Congregational, Episcopal, and Evangelical.

Roman Catholicism came to the Southwest with Don Juan de Oñate in 1598, taking root all the way along the Camino Real. In El Paso's Lower Valley, the Socorro, Ysleta, and San Elizario missions, still conducting services after their founding in the 1600s and 1700s, are a testament to the denomination's long-standing importance. Numerous orders of nuns came to settle in the region over the years: The Sisters of Loretto at the Foot of the Cross arrived in San Elizario in 1879 from Kentucky, and in 1892 assumed charge of St. Joseph's Academy in El Paso from the Sisters of Mercy who had been called to Tucson; the Daughters of Charity of St. Vincent de Paul came in 1892 from Maryland and established Hotel Dieu Hospital; the Sisters of Charity of the Incarnate Word settled in El Paso in 1917 and founded St. Margaret's Orphanage; the Sisters of Perpetual Adoration came in 1925 from Guadalajara, Mexico, to escape persecution, followed by the Religious of

Sisters of the Incarnate Word, ca. 1924.
Courtesy of Sandy Rioux.

Jesus and Mary in 1926, and the Sisters of Our Lady of Charity of the Good Shepherd in 1927; the Sisters of St. Joseph came from Indiana and opened St. Joseph's Sanitarium in 1927; the Sisters of Our Lady of Charity of Refuge came to the border in 1929, were refused entry into Mexico, and in 1932 opened the San Juan Orphanage in El Paso, which closed in 1953 when it became San Juan School; Our Lady of Victory Missionary Sisters opened centers in the parishes of Smeltertown and St. Francis Xavier in 1935; the Sisters of Divine Providence opened a school at Holy Family Parish in 1950, and also assumed charge of St. Pius X school in 1954; more recently, the Missionary Sisters of Jesus, Mary, and Joseph arrived in 1960. Hundreds of Roman Catholic women of faith have come to serve the El Paso area.

The mission of the Sisters of the Incarnate Word, with roots in Lyon, France, was to build schools, hospitals, and orphanages. September 1917 saw the arrival of Sister Mary Blase, Sister Mary of the Angels, and Sister Prudentiana, to the outskirts of Ysleta, seeking a site for a local orphanage. At the time, several El Paso children were housed six hundred miles away in Dallas. The Sisters were welcomed by Mrs. Joe Driscoll and Mrs. Joe Morgan, devout Catholics who shared their vision. They imagined a home for children in a valley green with cottonwood trees and a wide variety of farm crops. Jane Driscoll and Margaret Morgan, in their sporty Model T roadster, took the Sisters onto a tree-lined, semicircular road, set back from the street. The house sitting on eleven acres of land belonged to J. D. Ponder. Joe Morgan, an ardent Catholic and owner of a construction firm, ultimately convinced Ponder to sell the land to him and he in turn donated it to the diocese.

With the Right Reverend Bishop Schuler of El Paso approving the concept, the expansion of the eight-room Spanish-style house under the hand of Joe Morgan created a chapel and a playroom. While construction was going on, the Sisters enjoyed the hospitality first of the Driscolls, and then of the Daughters of Charity of St. Vincent de Paul at Hotel Dieu Hospital. Completion of the building, planned for September 19, 1919, was marred by tragedy. Margaret Morgan, who had worked so diligently on the project, succumbed to an undisclosed illness in 1919. The orphanage was named in her honor.

St. Margaret's Orphanage was to house both boys and girls, at Bishop Schuler's insistence. The Sisters solicited donations of furniture and

Above: Sister Mary of the Angels, with the orphanage's Model T Ford Sedan, ca. 1924.
Right: Sisters of the Incarnate Word riding on a float in the First United Fund Parade, 1957.
Courtesy of Sandy Rioux.

Margaret Morgan.
Courtesy of Sandy Rioux.

other goods to equip the children's rooms. On September 21, 1919, the first child—Mary Woolfe—arrived. The Sisters welcomed all who came; most were not orphans, but children who had lost one parent and the surviving parents entrusted their children to the Sisters while they got back on their feet. St. Margaret's was also a school, and local families sent their children for spiritual teachings. The years of the Great Depression were especially hard; children riding the rails with their parents sometimes found their way to the orphanage.

The motherhouse in San Antonio assigned and rotated nuns on a regular basis so none remained for extended periods of time, but both Sister Mary of the Angels and Sister Mary Blase appear in the record books for over two decades.

Story after story quoted in *A Chance for Every Child* tell of the Sisters' spiritual guidance. By the late 1950s, Mother Superior Mary Gabriel instituted services to address the needs of troubled youths; social workers from Catholic Welfare made regular visits, and psychiatrists were called on when necessary.

One summer evening in central El Paso in 1923, as the Reverend William Hogg watched the sun set behind the Franklins, he pondered what mission the Lord had in mind for him next. He had ministered to soldiers in the French trenches in World War I; together, he and his wife Virgie had taken inspiration to country folks in Tennessee. They had raised five children and then accepted the pastorship of Trinity Methodist Church. He'd even established a soup kitchen in 1921. And yet, Rev. Hogg listened for God's will to instruct him further on what he and Virgie were to do for Him. Such was their faith—that God would speak to them. He did. It was not the summer wind he heard outside their home. It was five trembling, abandoned children with tear-stained faces. A note fastened to the door explained that their mother was dead and their father could not take care of them.

Virgie fed the children pancakes and milk, washed their tired bodies and put them to bed under nice crisp sheets. Looking up at the full moon together, they knew what the Lord wanted them to do. "I believe we've just founded an orphanage." Word spread throughout the community, and children appeared on their doorstep. The Hoggs never turned away a single child. Between them, they took care of the children's needs in the crowded space of their home. Wearied by the labor involved, Virgie had a long overdue talk with her husband, suggesting they find a home that would accommodate future growth. Reynolds and Turrill Realty found them the perfect property only six blocks from the church, a house that took up a quarter of a block on the corner of Ange and Arizona Streets, with shade trees and a play area.

"But, how will you pay for it?" asked Virgie. "With a prayer?"

"Yes, Virgie," William replied with confidence. "My love for children and deep faith will pave the way. God will supply all our needs."

Realtor J. F. Reynolds contributed the first $500 toward the $25,000 purchase. At no cost to the church, the El Paso community furnished the house. By September of 1923, the Hogg Orphanage was caring for twenty children, with Virgie as the caretaker, and William, the business manager and fundraiser. Knowing full well that they would need help if they were to prosper and serve the growing needs of the orphanage, a board of directors was recruited. It consisted of prominent El Paso attorneys C. M. Harvey and Victor Moore, and contractor H. T. Ponsford. It was agreed that the board would handle the business affairs while William pursued additional fundraising ventures, and from two friends, he collected $200. One evening at his desk, he was inspired by Scripture: "Cast your bread upon the waters and it will return to thee many days hence buttered." He mailed two hundred letters to friends and acquaintances, enclosing a dollar in each envelope. Donors indeed multiplied the dollar amount, enclosing generous contributions. The board changed the name of the orphanage to the El Paso Children's Home. A year later, the New Mexico District of the Methodist Church South promoted Rev. William Hogg to district evangelist. He hated to leave the home, but knew that he, Virgie, and the board had established a framework for the work to continue. He had to depart to follow God's plan.

To take his place, the Reverend John Rayner and his wife arrived to take over the home, the only Protestant children's residence in the Southwest. With expansion came a need for additional staff and greater financial resources. In 1924, when tuberculosis spread throughout the United States, victims seeking a warm, dry climate came to the Southwest. Those who died left behind orphans needing care. The Rayners were overwhelmed with children from seven states. What initially felt like a home large enough for their ministry was now woefully inadequate. Mrs. Rayner's health was suffering as a result of the long hours and small staff. In the first year at the home, they had cared for 124 children.

Rev. Rayner, concerned for his wife, contacted Rev. Hogg, who was now a popular evangelist in Chicago. He asked for assistance in the search of a matron for the home. Rev. Hogg immediately recommended his distant cousin Kathleen Drury who had stumbled into social work during World War I, nursing the soldiers at Mississippi's Camp Shelby. She was a single, middle-aged mother who had worked for seven years as Director of the Louisiana Society for the Prevention of Cruelty to Children. Rev. Hogg believed that Kathleen's love for children would make her perfect for the job. Rev. Rayner wrote Kathleen Drury, and visited her in Louisiana, convinced at once that it was she the home needed. Correspondence flowed back and forth, but Kathleen was not easily persuaded. Rev. Rayner pursued her relentlessly while receiving letters of reference from her Louisiana church as well as her former employers. All attested to her love of children and Christian character, describing her as capable, honest, reliable, and energetic. It took a year to convince Mrs. Drury to come to the home. She and her daughter Mildred took the train from New Orleans to El Paso in October 1925.

As soon as she arrived, Mrs. Drury could see room for improvement. Clucking her tongue, she declared that the house "needed tidying and organization." She believed in making "each child responsible for chores" and told Rayner that she would "lead with a firm but loving hand." She pinned up her hair in a sensible bun, put on a white apron, and immediately set out to establish order with a meal and prayer schedule, as well as parent visiting hours. As with St. Margaret's Orphanage, children were sometimes looked after temporarily while a parent or parents were unable to care for them. Rayner was delighted. Mrs. Drury gathered the children around her and told them that her bedroom door would remain open at all times for them, but that they would have responsibilities. She said the latter as she stuck a broom in the hands of a toddler and a dustrag in a teen's hands. She expected them to do well in school, particularly in deportment. Low grades in deportment would result in the loss of privileges for six weeks. She did, however, make an exception for anyone who requested a weekly, signed note from a teacher attesting to behavior improvement. Some of the younger children had trouble pronouncing "Mrs. Drury." She told them they could call her "My Dearie." My Dearie she became and would always be.

My Dearie taught them core values steeped in religious belief: "Be honest, brave, and true. Be clean in all you do. Be a man among a few. Now go on, it's up to you." Under her direction, the home came to order. She was an imposing figure with dark, pinned-up hair, round tinted spectacles, and sensible dress. Under her austere demeanor and demure Mona Lisa smile, she had a heart of gold. With the day-to-day operations in capable hands, Rev. Rayner began to focus on fundraising. He commented that "children were being dropped off by relatives like discarded pets." The home needed help in the maintenance of the building, with clothing, food, and schooling. He put it all in a report to the New Mexico Conference of the Methodist Church, requesting that it assume authority over the home. The New Mexico Conference assembled in Clovis and passed a resolution to take over the home, assume its debt, and reappoint Rev. Rayner as superintendent. They also named Victor Moore, a criminal attorney and board member, as the home's manager. All conference churches dedicated each fifth Sunday's collection to the home. The home's name would remain. For an undisclosed reason Rev. Rayner left his position in March 1926.

Victor Moore had recently become a Christian. In church he prayed for guidance, believing he must change his life's course. Victor had once been near death and promised God that if he lived, he would turn his life around and make a difference in the world. Beneath a weeping willow tree at home, he contemplated a life-altering decision: he would close his lucrative criminal law practice to devote himself full time to the El Paso Children's Home. He sighed peacefully, knowing that it was God's will. Forty-six children had been turned away in 1926, but there were still thirty-two children residing at the home by this time—seven over the limit set by the board of health. Victor knew they needed a larger facility, so he proceeded to do the fundraising necessary to expand their mission.

The board recommended that Kathleen Drury be appointed superintendent of the home. She felt honored, and surprised the board by announcing that she wanted to donate her annual salary to the Home. "I will live off my stipend of $50, which adequately meets my needs. However, I want my $200 monthly salary to go toward the building fund, so that we may eventually obtain larger quarters for these precious children." The board members were dumbfounded by her gesture. Victor Moore choked back the rush of emotions—enamored by her selflessness and gentle manner.

My Dearie's dreams for the home and for the children residing therein came to fruition over and over. The children were treated to the Odd Fellow's Camp on Cedar Creek in Ruidoso for two weeks, courtesy of Arthur Berchording, one of the lodge's members. They were invited back the following summer, in appreciation for their impeccable manners. Mrs. Ike Wingfield, another lodge member, told them then that her husband was donating "ten acres for you to build a summer home." Cheers from the children went up, and My Dearie smiled, knowing God smiled back from above. As the news spread through Ruidoso, local businesses rallied, raising money, donating building supplies. Mrs. Alex Janke contributed a thousand-gallon water tank. Beds, benches, and tables were constructed by an El Paso vocational school. The Southern Pacific Railroad provided a car for transporting equipment to Tularosa, and El Paso banker Chris Fox

Top: My Dearie sewing for the children.
Above: My Dearie at the dinner table with her babies.
Courtesy of Victor Moore Jr.

contributed trucks and manpower. By 1928, Wingfield Lodge was completed, and summer stays became a mainstay of the children's experience.

In March 1928, a measles epidemic struck the home. Kathleen Drury nursed forty-four children, along with one case of scarlet fever. Between bathing tiny bodies in cool water, rubbing lotion on skin rashes, and feeding the sick ones chicken broth and hot tea, she barely slept.

My Dearie at Christmas.
Courtesy of Victor Moore Jr.

Her vigils kept her on a cot in the children's dormitory, and her health was deteriorating as a result of her dedication. Victor worried about her and tried to get her to rest, but she would not leave her babies. Soon thereafter, Mrs. Drury suffered a mental and physical collapse. Emotionally distraught, she also knew that her growing feelings for Victor Moore were a factor in her distress. Alone for twenty years, her mission from God was to care for children, and she didn't want anyone impeding her goals. She resigned, even though Moore reasoned with her that she shouldn't make such an important decision while in such an exhausted state, but no one could convince her to stay.

She and her daughter Mildred went to New Orleans to be with her sister. Mrs. Drury took a Bible to bed with her and prayed to God for the children and for a new sense of direction. Victor Moore wrote her letters that she refused to open. One month later, as she slept, "God spoke to her, quoting a passage from Jeremiah. 'For I know the plans I have for you. Plans to prosper you and not harm you, plans to give you home and a future.' Kathleen's eyes opened wide as she listened. 'Go in peace, my child,' He said. 'You have rested and now it is time to continue my work.'"

She found work at an Albuquerque girls' reform school. Victor visited her and she finally understood that perhaps they could accomplish the Lord's work together because they had a common purpose. It took until 1930 for Victor to convince Kathleen to be his wife. Victor and My Dearie continued God's work at the El Paso Children's Home for decades, raising countless children besides their three sons—Taylor, Brunson, and Victor Jr. My Dearie slipped quietly into the arms of her Lord in July 1979, with her son Victor Jr. by her side.

Miss Mary Tripp, as a staff of one, began working in the *Segundo Barrio,* the Second Ward, with Mexican girls in 1893. When Mrs. Rose Gregory Houchen, a schoolteacher from Pontiac, Michigan, met Mary Tripp, she became interested in the work and recognized the need for a home or institution to serve the community. Her donation of $1,000 became the seed money for a permanent building. The Women's Home Missionary Society of the Methodist Church added what was needed to purchase a piece of land at the corner of Fifth and Tays Streets. By 1912, the Rose Gregory Houchen Settlement House served as a home for young Mexican women who had no decent place to stay at the end of a workday. The staff of one grew to four as more programs were added. Several additions to the building ultimately resulted in seventeen bedrooms on the top floor for nurses and settlement workers, kindergarten on the main floor, and children's clubrooms and a craft shop in the basement. Out of the settlement house grew the Methodist block known as Friendship Square that included a clinic, a hospital, a church, and a day care.

Miss Tripp was succeeded by Miss Elizabeth Rowe, who was director from 1912 to 1914. The next director, Miss Emma Brandeberry, a deaconess of the Methodist Church, remained for thirty-one years, until 1945.

Her vision for expanding the ministry took the direction of health work. She secured the services of Miss Effie Stoltz, a registered nurse, in 1920. The bathroom on the first floor of the settlement house became the infirmary. Seriously ill children were turned away for lack of facilities and of a doctor to prescribe medicines and treatment. Dr. G. N. Thomas stepped in, and as a team, the two began to treat diseases. In 1921, the clinic was moved to the opposite end of the block, to an adobe tenement house on the corner of Fifth and Hill Streets. That building housed the first hospital in which twenty-eight babies were born the first year. Nurse Stoltz and Dr. Thomas concluded that the neighborhood children were coming to them too late, that children's good health began in the womb.

Miss Emma Brandeberry, on the porch of the Houchen Settlement House. *Courtesy of Katherine Talbot.*

Miss Millie Rickford, a farm girl from Kansas, became a registered nurse at Colorado General Hospital in Denver. A Methodist deaconess nurse, she opened the door for maternity work in 1930. By 1937, a new brick building financed and promoted by the Newark Conference of Methodist Women was dedicated on the same corner. It was divided into distinct medical units. Named for Mrs. Freeman, then treasurer of the Woman's Home Missionary Society, the Freeman Clinic opened for eye, ear, nose, and throat, pediatrics, and obstetrical care; Newark Hospital, named for the Newark Conference of Methodist Women, specialized in obstetric delivery and confinement care. Miss Rickford stayed for thirty years, acting as the superintendent for both Newark Hospital and the Freeman Clinic. Miss Brandeberry had started the tradition of a Baby Christmas Party for children born during the year. Miss Rickford's Hospital Guild Birthday Party was held in

October and celebrated the children born at Newark when they turned ten. Those two celebrations brought the community together. It was not unusual for two generations to be present for these get-togethers. In 1940, there were ten sets of twins born. Miss Rickford kept saying that she'd retire as soon as they had a set of triplets. While that didn't happen during her tenure, through her lectures, films, home visits, and prenatal clinic care, the infant mortality rate was lower at Newark than at other hospitals in El Paso.

In an *El Paso Herald-Post* article dated May 12, 1961, Miss Rickford was named the Woman of the Week. She quoted the verse that reads: "Blessed are they who sing in the morning and blessed are they who bestow love on others throughout the day." She had little time for travel or activities outside the hospital. However, true to her calling, she had "no inkling of regret, no self pity at missing any of the alleged 'funtimes' of pleasure seekers. Her triumphs have come in the shape of life for others, the basic and fundamental things as simple as the air we breathe." She was "An Angel In White of South El Paso." Browsing through the archived albums, there are dozens of pictures of Miss Rickford doing what she did best: using her healing hands and her faith to help women bring healthy babies into the world.

According to one unsigned board report of the early years, "This hospital was built with prayers, and consecration of hands, hearts, and tithes." Oh, and by the way, "we should have another nurse so that our night nurse doesn't have to work 72 hours a week." The board did find a recent young graduate from nursing school, who accepted a position without thinking of asking what the salary was until two months after she was hired. Such was her desire to serve. In 1950, in a twenty-two-bed hospital, there were 578 babies born and 238 tonsilectomies performed. The doctors and nurses working at what came to be known as Newark Methodist Hospital in the *Segundo Barrio* brought babies into the world until December of 1986 when its doors closed.

Miss Millie Rickford. *Courtesy of Katherine Talbot.*

While the clinic and hospital workers were ministering to the physical health of the neighborhood, Houchen Settlement House grew into a community center where Boy Scouts, Girl Scouts, Brownies, and Cubs met; Bible, sewing, carpentry, and music classes were offered, and a

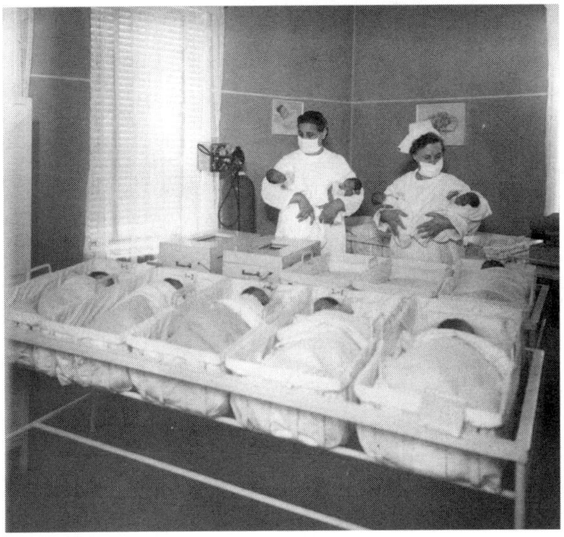

Above: Newark Methodist Hospital Nursery.
Above right: Boys posing with their artwork after a Bible class.
Right: Kindergarten children at Houchen.
Courtesy of Katherine Talbot.

library was made available. A kindergarten prepared children with both math and English language skills for entry into first grade.

In 1950, the monthly activities at Houchen recorded an attendance of 3,000 multi-generational participants. In 1959, Miss Dorothy Little celebrated twenty-five years of missionary work, serving as a kindergarten teacher from 1934 until 1945, and as Houchen superintendent from then until 1968. A brochure from that time boasted that as a result of the "influence of the settlement that there is less juvenile delinquency in the section where Houchen is located than in any other part of the city." The original Houchen Settlement House, an impressive two-story building, was renovated and added to several times in its history. When it was torn down in the 1980s, the Women's Division of the Methodist Church approved a grant to build a youth center with a full-size gym and a weightlifting room, bathroom, and shower facilities. Houchen Community Center was dedicated in 1988 and continues the Methodist Church's mission to this day.

Springing from the early work done at Houchen Settlement House, the next addition to Friendship Square was the Good Shepherd Methodist Church, or more accurately, *Iglesia Metodista El Buen Pastor.* Sunday school may date as far back as 1915 and records show an attendance of up to 200 people, with classes held in the settlement house. In 1932, a small Presbyterian Church on Fourth Street was purchased in which to hold worship services. In 1945, a new stone church was built and dedicated for its growing congregation. The church became self-sufficient and offered church school, Sunday worship services, mid-week prayer services, special services for young adults, and monthly meetings of the Women's Society of Christian Service.

As time progressed and an increasing number of women entered the workforce, the workers at the hospital and clinic became concerned that small children were being left alone while their parents worked. In 1947, the Houchen Day Nursery was founded. Its stated purpose was "to provide wholesome Christian living for small children whose parents are employed." While children had always been the focus of many activities in Friendship Square, this was a further expansion of service to the neighborhood. Children from two to six could be enrolled for seventy-five cents per day or fifteen dollars per month. The day nursery had complete kitchen facilities that also served children attending nearby public schools. Throughout the years, the day care, now known as the Houchen Child Development Center, has continued to be a strong presence in the *Segundo Barrio.* With its present enrollment of ninety-two children, the center's impact on the community is significant.

La Primera Iglesia Bautista Mexicana, First Mexican Baptist Church, was founded in 1892. It all started with a five-year-old girl, Jesusita Ortegón, who loved the hymns coming from the Methodist Episcopal church near where she lived. She would sneak in to listen, without her Catholic parents' permission, to the music and the sermons delivered by the Reverend Alejandro Marchand, a former Catholic priest who had come to Mexico with Napoleon III's troops. Jesusita's father took to hiding her shoes to keep her from going, but in the end, her devotion was contagious, and her father joined her. Soon after, Rev. Marchand developed a close friendship with Elder Viney of the Second Baptist Church. Viney's confidence in his Baptist faith led the way for Rev. Marchand to embrace the doctrine. On July 9, 1892, Marchand and twenty-eight followers were baptized in the Rio Grande, recognized as Baptists by the all-black Second Baptist Church congregation led by Viney. *La Primera's* first meeting place was a small adobe room at the corner of Fifth and Stanton Streets, built on a lot provided by Jesusita's father Cipriano Ortegón.

Ofelia Rivas Machado was born on June 17, 1900, in Lerdo, Durango. As a Protestant growing up in Catholic town, she was frequently ostracized by her schoolmates—boys would tie her long braids to her desk so she couldn't stand up when called upon by the teacher. She came to El Paso with her mother and grandmother in her teens at a time when Mexican Revolution skir-

Ofelia Reyes on her wedding day, 1923. *Courtesy of Olga Reyes.*

mishes were still occurring. They boarded a train in Torreón heading for Juárez, encountering a burning bridge along the way. Amidst a barrage of bullets, with the passengers crouched on the floor, the engineer took the bridge at full speed and they crossed safely, avoiding bandits poised to pounce on the train. When relating the story of that incident, Ofelia would always say that their faith saved them. She said the same when she became deathly ill during the Spanish influenza pandemic of 1917-1918. While people in the El Paso tenements were dying around her, she survived.

In 1923, she married Arturo Reyes in *La Primera,* believing that God had brought them together. Several years later, when the *Misión Val Verde* was entrusted to him as a deacon of *La Primera,* she prayed for a way to spread the gospel, one in which she could involve her three children, Olga, Israel, and Romeo. She opened her home to the children of the neighborhood once a week. Some were children of the budding mission's members, others were drawn by the piano music played by Esther Moreno, another mission worker. They gathered at her house on Tuesday—ironing day—and while she ironed, she taught the children Bible verses and praise hymns, some of which were borrowed from the Salvation Army mission books. The Salvation Army band gathered every Sunday evening at six

La VOZ BAUTISTA

"......Yo soy la luz del Mundo, el que me sigue no andará en tinieblas mas tendrá la luz de la vida. Juan 8:12

SEMANARIO EVANGELICO

Tomo I — El Paso, Texas, Abril 10 de 1938 — Numero 35

LOS PEQUEÑOS OBREROS BAUTISTAS DE LA U. B. DE J. DE EL PASO, TEXAS.

Primera Fila:—David Rojas, Eliseo López, Lidia López, Benito Acevedo, Berta Alicia Ramírez, Viola Téllez, Magdalena Merino, Hortencia García, Alma Acevedo, Rodolfo Téllez y Fausto Montes.

Segunda Fila:—Ascención Rojas Jr., Consuelo Durán, Sarita Morales, Ruth Rojas, Martín López, Estela Rojas, Noemí Sánchez, Edna Durán, Beatríz Téllez, Romeo Reyes, Cecília Merino y Alfonzo Benítez.

Tercera Fila: —A la derecha. Noemí de la Cruz, Elísa Navarro. A la izquierda. Clga Reyes, Israel Reyes y Ernestína Cárdenas.

Cuarta Fila:—Capitanes del Grupo Infantil: Sra Esther R. Moreno, Srita. Prof. L. M. Weatherford, Sra. Ofelia R. Reyes.

En el último programa que presentó el Grupo Infantil de la U. B. de J. de El Paso, Texas, hubo una asistencia de 95 personas que salieron muy complacidas de los bellos números que presenciaron y de los adelantos que nuestros niños bautistas han hecho bajo la dirección de sus padres y de sus eficientes capitanes que también aparecen en esta Fotografía.

Children of the Misión Val Verde.
Courtesy of Olga Reyes.

to march from South El Paso Street to San Jacinto Plaza.

Ofelia not only taught Bible verses and praise hymns, she also taught poetry declamation and drama through skits. A skit about taking the gospel to China used red paper bag lanterns on broomsticks; the same broomsticks served to carry the banners of the wee soldiers of Jesus on parade through the neighborhood. Ofelia used the brown paper in which the laundry was delivered from El Paso Laundry to make props and banners for her ministry, "as directed by God," according to her daughter Olga. Ofelia did such a great job with her ministry that the nuns working in the San Juan neighborhood wanted to recruit her to teach Catholic doctrine. It was a prevalent practice in the 1960s for Catholic homes in the Second Ward, where *La Primera* was located, to post placards on their front doors announcing that theirs was a Catholic home and Protestant literature was not accepted.

The *Misión Val Verde* became a church, and Ofelia's work was continued by the children she had taught; her influence was also felt in the dozens of church programs throughout the year and the Christmas pageants she directed at *La Primera*. For decades, her daughter Olga was the director of the Girl's Auxiliary at *La Primera,* influencing several generations of young women as her mother had. Beyond the mission work that she did with her husband Arturo in several locations, including Ciudad Juárez, Ofelia's children's ministry spanned forty-two years at the First Mexican Baptist Church. She died in 1997,

Certificate created by a church member to celebrate Ofelia Reyes' forty-two years of service. *Courtesy of Olga Reyes.*

having lived by Philippians 4, verse 8: "Finally, brethren, whatsoever things are true, whatsoever things are honest, whatsoever things are pure, whatsoever things are lovely, whatsoever things are of good report; if there be any virtue and if there be any praise, think on these things."

Westminster Presbyterian Church began its ministry in a tent on the corner of Oregon and Franklin Streets on July 12, 1903, with the Reverend Mr. Oliver Jones, a Fort Worth evangelist, preaching every night. On July 21, he was joined by the Reverend Mr. Charles Hyde, pastor of the First Presbyterian Church of Fort Worth. After the services on July 22, they founded a church with fourteen charter members. Officers were elected, ordained, and installed, a Sabbath school was organized, and, most importantly, the Ladies' Aid Society was formed. A lot was purchased on Rio Grande and Florence Streets, and the tent was moved to the lot. Within the week, they met in one of the church members' homes, elected a Session Clerk, as well as officers and teachers of the Sabbath school, and formally chose Westminster as the name of their church.

During their first year, they reported having two elders, two deacons, thirty-one communicants, eight teachers, and forty scholars enrolled in Sabbath school. By 1910, they had doubled their membership and the architectural firm of Trost & Trost was drawing up plans for the building of a church. Plans were completed in 1911 and featured a Spanish Renaissance style with an open bell tower, red tile roofs, arched windows, and stucco-covered walls of pressed brick. The Ladies' Aid Society of Westminster played an active role in "growing the church." Faithful families attended regularly; children were nurtured by Sabbath school teachers, most of whom were women held to a high standard. At the session meeting of November 4, 1913, "amusements as related to Sabbath school teachers" were discussed and a protest was made by one member of the session against electing teachers "who danced, played cards, and attended theaters."

When the United States entered World War I in April 1917, it was the women who mobilized members within the church to help with the war effort. It was they who knitted socks, sweaters, and scarves, made bandages, baked pastries, and saw to it that soldiers both from the church and outside were not forgotten. Proceeds from their baked goods and crafts went to the French and Belgian Relief Fund. Thirty-one members of the church enlisted in the army and navy. It was during the war that interest developed in a mission to minister to the Mexican population living "north of the railroad tracks." Miss Cornelia Taylor arrived in August 1918 and organized a Mission Sunday School on La Luz Street. Four lots on Clifton Street were purchased, and a building was completed in 1920 for La Luz Mission Sunday School. The Westminster Session formally commended Miss Taylor for her dedication and work.

Manhattan Presbyterian Church was organized in 1921, with a membership of 127, most of whom had been members of Westminster and were dismissed to become Manhattan's charter members. The history of Westminster related by the Women's Auxiliary says that the Home Mission Committee of the General Assembly had erected a building on the corner of Grant and Piedras Streets and when it was completed, the city was divided into two districts, with Cotton Avenue as the dividing line. An announcement was made from the Westminster pulpit that all who lived east of Cotton Avenue would be expected to attend Manhattan, frequently referred to as "Westminster's daughter."

The Banks twins need no introduction to anyone who has lived in El Paso any length of time. They were part of the Christian community of the Texas-New Mexico region. If Manhattan Presbyterian Church was known beyond our area, it was because of Mary Ella and Mary Etta Banks. The twins grew up in a deeply Christian household where the family knelt together every evening for prayers, and the children began to tithe at age eight. The twins' father was a Presbyterian minister, as was his father before him, and his grandfather before them. However, if you asked them, they would've told you that the greatest Christian example and influence in their lives was their mother. "Mama" was described as a "beaming Christian" by her daughters. During her last five years, when she was bedridden and often in pain, people would come to cheer her up after church on Sunday and would go away cheered themselves.

Mary Ella and Mary Etta were the youngest of six children born to Reverend and Mrs. Fitzhugh Lee Banks. Three of the Banks babies had died in infancy, and the twins' parents were in their forties when the girls were born. Their only surviving sibling was Fitzhugh Jr., who was seven years old when the twins were born in the cute little town of Star City, Arkansas. Rev. Banks' health broke down in 1914, and he was unable to continue at the pulpit. The family settled in El Paso, encouraged by the reported curative effects of the dry, high desert air. His ill health prevented him from full-time preaching, but he did some supply preaching and lived another thirty years after he arrived.

The family first attended Westminster when the twins were three, but were in their pews on the day that Manhattan Presbyterian Church opened. Mary Etta and Mary Ella were not charter members because they were too young for membership. They sang in the choir for sixty-five years, and taught Sunday school for forty-five, with Mary Ella serving as superintendent of the junior level classes for twenty years. Mary Etta also served as chair of the businesswomen's circle for several years; Mary Ella served as an elder. Aside from their steadfast work at Manhattan, the twins were well known around town as beloved teachers. They knew they wanted to be teachers when they were eight years old, building a rough shed out of scrap metal and opening a backyard school where they supplemented the education of their playmates with academic subjects as well as art and music. Mary Ella said that "the Lord had it planned." They began teaching Sunday school at age fifteen, and took teacher's training at Texas College of Mines after their graduation from El Paso High. Two years of training qualified them to teach in the public schools, but times were tough in the midst of the Depression and jobs were hard to find.

The Depression years were the only period in their lives when they were apart. Mary Etta took a job out of town, teaching the three children of a ranching family, who loved her because she could play baseball and ride horses! Mary Ella taught in El Paso at a Works Progress Administration night school that offered classes in English, citizenship, and other subjects. At the age of twenty-six, she became principal of the school. She also worked for Assistant Superintendent of Schools R. R. Jones, running the mimeograph machine for fifty dollars a month. Eventually the girls were able to return to college and earn their diplomas, Mary Etta in 1938 and Mary Ella in 1939. Their first four years in the El Paso Independent School District, they taught in separate schools. However, when Roosevelt Elementary School was being built, they were asked to be among the teachers to open the new school.

They wrote the Roosevelt school song and taught fourth grade in adjoining classrooms for thirty-four years, as well as teaching upper grade music. "We were old-maid school teachers you know," said Mary Ella, "and that was how God planned it. It gave us lots of energy to give to our students. We loved every one of those kids, even the bad ones!" The year that Roosevelt Elementary celebrated its fiftieth anniversary, the Banks twins were there for all the festivities, dressed in identical outfits, as they always were. They tried briefly to wear different outfits, but their friends didn't like it and convinced them to go back to dressing as they had all their lives.

Mary Etta and Mary Ella Banks in 1960 when they received their Life Membership Certificates and Pins from the Manhattan Presbyterian's Women of the Church. *Courtesy of Manhattan Presbyterian Church.*

The Banks twins' musical contributions to Manhattan and beyond were legendary. Mary Ella and Mary Etta began taking piano lessons when they were ten years old, from their cousin Gladys Ray who was the organist at Westminster. When they were fourteen, they learned to play "Church in the Wildwood" which would become, along with their own arrangement of "Amazing Grace," their signature hymns. The twins played and sang for countless church camps and services, for the Nogal Camp Meeting near Ruidoso, and attended the Bloys Camp in the Davis Mountains every summer for forty-one years. Sunset Nursing Home patients in Ysleta got their loving attention for seventeen years. They were active in senior citizens groups at various churches: the Jolly Elders at Trinity Methodist Church, Club Friendship at St. Paul's Methodist Church, and the Jolly Seniors at Cielo Vista Baptist Church.

Mary Ella had a serious battle with ovarian cancer that spread throughout her abdomen from 1983 to 1985. Two surgeries, prolonged chemotherapy, and her faith pulled her through. The doctors said it was a "miracle" and she wanted "to try to be a witness to that miracle." Mary Ella stayed healthy and it became her responsibility to nurse Mary Etta, who developed Alzheimer's disease. No one present at Manhattan Presbyterian's evening service in May 1996 will ever forget their final duet performance of "Church in the Wildwood." Although it took a little prompting to get Mary Etta started, she played the hymn through to the end. Shortly thereafter, Mary Etta fell and broke her hip and had to be confined to foster home care. Mary Ella went to Bloys Camp without her. Quite naturally, they asked her to play the old hymns for the camp participants. She didn't have the heart to do piano solos. But after a time, Mary Ella said that "the Lord spoke to her and she played out of respect for tradition and to pay tribute to Mary Etta."

The Banks twins ran into their students everywhere they went. "We loved those children," said Mary Ella, "and they knew it. We didn't just teach the three Rs. We taught character. We'd read the children stories from the Bible and we'd pray with them." As far as reaping what they'd sown, their lunch bills at Luby's Cafeteria were frequently picked up by one of their countless students from Roosevelt Elementary School or Manhattan Presbyterian Church, where they gave so much of themselves for so many decades.

The stories told here are but an infinitesimal example of El Paso women who changed the lives of the people they came into contact with. They took Jesus's words to heart and lived their faith:

> For I was an hungered, and ye gave me meat: I was thirsty and ye gave me drink: I was a stranger, and ye took me in: Naked, and ye clothed me: I was sick, and ye visited me: I was in prison, and ye came unto me. Then shall the righteous answer him, saying, Lord, when saw we *thee* in an hungered, and feed *thee*? or thirsty, and gave *thee* drink? When saw we *thee* a stranger, and took *thee* in? or naked, and clothed *thee*? Or when saw we *thee* sick, or in prison, and came unto *thee*? And the King shall answer and say unto them, Verily I say unto you, Inasmuch as ye have done it unto one of the least of these my brethren, ye have done it unto me. Matthew 25: 35-40 (The King James Version).

Bibliographic Essay

The search for the women mentioned above began in the El Paso County Historical Society archives; I am indebted to Patricia Worthington's kindness and expertise in guiding me through the volumes of *Password*. C. L. Sonnichsen's *Pass of the North* (Texas Western Press, 1968), W. H. Timmons' *El Paso: A Borderlands*

History (Texas Western Press, 1990), and Leon Metz's *El Paso Chronicles* (Mangan Books, 1993) provided the colorful picture of El Paso as it was before churches came on the scene. Histories of early churches were captured in "Early El Paso Churches" by William I. Latham; W. H. Timmons in *A History of University Presbyterian Church* (University Presbyterian Church, 1983); and John O. West in *Looking Back: A Reminiscent History of Westminster and University Presbyterian Church, 1903-1983* (University Presbyterian Church, 1983). In the "Historical Notes" in *Password* volume 17, I found a summary of the Catholic sisters who came to the pass. *A Chance for Every Child: A History of the El Paso Center for Children*, by Donna C. Munch, Shirley Clement Fouts, and Sandy Rioux (Trego-Hill Publications, 2009) is the inspirational story of women who touched the lives of children of many denominations for nearly fifty years; by combining their resources and becoming The El Paso Center for Children in 1982, the groundwork laid by women's faith and steadfastness continues. Katherine Talbot has for decades been the historian for Friendship Square as well as Trinity Methodist Church. Her compilation of scrapbooks and reports enabled me to capture the work done in the *Segundo Barrio*. Women were vital to the work there, in leadership positions as well as in fundraising to keep their mission growing. Interviews with Olga Reyes before her death early this year contributed to first-hand knowledge I already had of Ofelia Reyes, her mother, at *La Primera Iglesia Bautista Mexicana*. Olga worked alongside, giving years of service to her church. According to Helen Emery, member of Manhattan Presbyterian Church since 1944, "If there was anything Christian going on, the Banks twins were there." The church scrapbooks attest to their dedication, especially in one unsigned tribute to them in the 1952-1968 volume, which I used almost in its entirety.

The official church histories that I explored talk a great deal about fundraising and building the structures that house a congregation. Almost as footnotes, if at all, they list the women who cooked the potlucks, tended to the nursery children, put on the pageants, taught Sunday school, and brought in community children through vacation Bible schools. Interviews and scrapbooks tell of women who created the sense of community that kept families coming to church, and it was women who were the nurturers, those who built social consciousness and service into their lessons. For every woman's story here told, there are countless people who have been inspired by their acts of faith to follow in their footsteps.

Chapter 11

WOMEN PENNING REVOLUTIONS GREAT AND SMALL

by Brenda A. Risch and Kirstin J. Perez

El Paso's women journalists have been penning revolutions great and small over the last hundred years. Their work, though often passed over and contested, has made its mark on the wider populace of the borderland. Whether through the unforgettably iconic power of Teresita Urrea, the undisputable verve of Peggy Hull, or the wider vision of a homegrown hero such as Robbie Myrick Villalobos, these women and others chronicled the realities of social change in the history of the borderland.

Less than fifty years after the Texas border took its current shape, women journalists were making significant and lasting contributions, although it may have been assumed that newspapers in Texas were run solely by male editors employing male writers writing for a male audience. One of the many signs that men were not completely dominating the fourth estate was the founding of the Texas Woman's Press Association (TWPA, currently known as Texas Press Women, Inc.) in Dallas on May 10, 1893. Established by a group of women writers and led by Aurelia H. Mohl of Houston, this new association encouraged Texas women writers and illustrators in their literary work. TWPA successfully petitioned The University of Texas Board of Regents to establish a school of journalism at Austin, and by 1916, the TWPA was the first group to provide a scholarship for the new journalism department. Early accomplishments such as these point to an active culture of women journalists throughout the state.

Early women journalists in El Paso were no exception to this reality, as they chronicled the many significant revolutionary campaigns sweeping the nation between the 1890s and 1920s. Nationally, women agitated for female clothing reform and women's suffrage and for such alternative political movements as socialism and communism, which threatened to change the balance of power between men and women and to rewrite gender expectations. Texas women may not have followed suit with clothing reform, which they found too radical, but in 1893 they did form a suffrage organization, the Texas Equal Rights Association (TERA), which was active statewide from 1893 until 1895. In 1903, Houston-based Annette Finnegan resurrected suffrage activism with a Texas chapter of the National American

Women's Suffrage Association (NAWSA) dubbed the Texas Equal Suffrage Association (TESA). One of the major women's revolutions of this era had found fertile ground in Texas.

El Paso women were no strangers to revolutionary activism for their community and themselves. The NAWSA required women to join and pay membership dues through their state organization. State organizations were thus able to control membership access and the delegation of funding generated by this progressive group. One example of such power was TESA's 1918 denial of the El Paso Colored Woman's Union's bid for membership. TESA assumed that the name of the El Paso-based group referred to a majority of African American membership, and used common arguments that African American women's participation would alienate powerful conservative Southern white women and men who supported the suffragist cause. TESA never addressed the possibility that the El Paso-based group may have been a majority of biracial, binational, or Mexican American women, and that such a membership was appropriate to this region. This is worth noting as one of the more problematic aspects of a women's liberal social justice movement of the times. Even so, just months after the United States Senate passed the Nineteenth Amendment, El Paso hosted the Texas Women's Suffrage Association's Annual State Convention.

Ironically, though the suffragist movement is typically thought to represent values of equality between women and men, some women who supported suffrage also felt morally superior to men. They thought the vote was the best tool for cleaning up their communities. Voting would allow them to oust corrupt and inefficient governments that had failed to protect the health and safety of their families. In this belief such women were also drawing on the Victorian dichotomy between men and women. Such beliefs motivated women to take public action to promote food purity, city sanitation, and other public hygiene issues. Even the early days of the El Paso Woman's Club (founded in 1894) were marked by such politics to clean up city government until the club later banned political lobbying in their charter.

The Woman's Christian Temperance Union's (WCTU) use of morality to fight for political change makes it an intriguing and unequivocal element in the local realities about which El Paso's early female journalists wrote. By the time a WCTU chapter was founded in El Paso in 1896, the movement's attitudes had already saturated much of the United States throughout the two prior decades of activism. In seeking to make alcohol illegal, the WCTU banked on an extremely powerful Victorian tradition of women's moral superiority over men, and used rhetoric that constantly reinforced how women felt it necessary to stop men from the errors of drunkenness, dissipation, and the social ills that accompanied them. Weak-willed men could not resist the lures of demon alcohol when presented with public saloons and bawdy houses and often wreaked social havoc. Buying votes with liquor and other similar stunts fostered political corruption and a general lack of moral fortitude. The WCTU was eventually successful in its fight, passing the Prohibition Act on January 11, 1919. El Paso/Ciudad Juárez, as a populated binational border, became a hotbed of bootlegging; despite the closing of El Paso's twenty-five saloons, the area carried on with a tradition of "sinful" dissipation—even up until the repeal of Prohibition on December 5, 1933.

The political climate in the 1890s in the borderland was further flavored by the beginnings of the Mexican Revolution, and this prompted many journalists to take stands against the dictatorship of Porfirio Díaz. Historically referred to as the *Porfiriato,* the three consecutive presidential terms served by Díaz blatantly violated Mexican statutes against political reelections. During his ascendancy, as is the case with the majority of dictatorships, many individual freedoms were criminalized as threats to national control. Perceived as traitorous and subversive, hoards of anti-Díaz activists fled or were exiled from Mexico and many settled in El Paso to carry out their revolutionary journalism. While under the immense constraints of censorship the *Porfiriato* implemented, external journalists from the *Partido Liberal Mexicano (PLM)* groups in New Mexico, California, Arizona, and Texas wrote earnestly with a sense of urgency about their attacks on the Mexican dictatorial regime, according to Clara Lomas. In 1906, El Paso became the *PLM* headquarters, and insurgent publications flourished, including the important female-voiced newspaper *La Voz de la Mujer* in 1907.

The factors of an unjust dictatorship and the suffering of the Mexican people wove the threads of revolution—as well as a widespread acceptance of women as models of moral purity, capable of community decisions and political opinions fueled by Christian love and duty—into the story of religious healings of one of the most important early journalistic icons of El Paso—Teresa or "Teresita" Urrea.

Born in 1872 in Sinaloa, Mexico, Teresita Urrea has been historically referred to by many aliases such as "The Mexican Joan of Arc," "*La Espíritu de Tomochic,*" "Mystic Santa Teresa," and

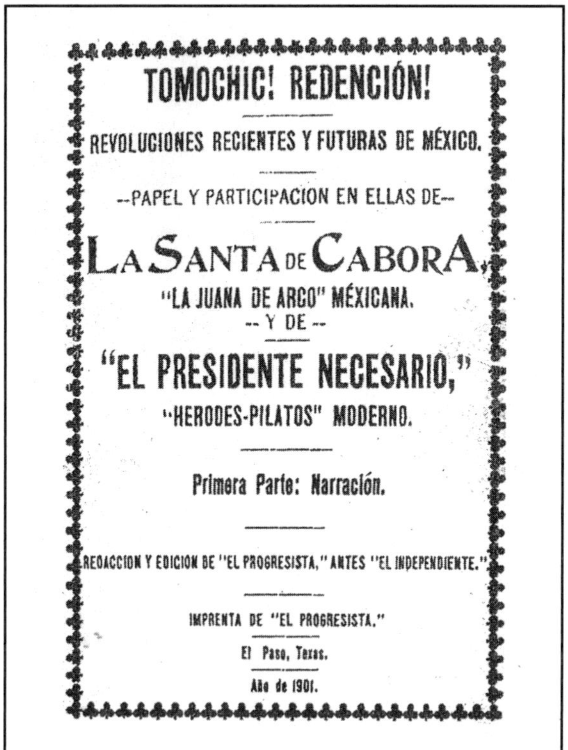
TOMOCHIC! REDENCIÓN!

REVOLUCIONES RECIENTES Y FUTURAS DE MÉXICO.

--PAPEL Y PARTICIPACION EN ELLAS DE--

LA SANTA DE CABORA,

"LA JUANA DE ARCO" MÉXICANA.

-- Y DE --

"EL PRESIDENTE NECESARIO,"

"HERODES-PILATOS" MODERNO.

Primera Parte: Narración.

REDACCION Y EDICION DE "EL PROGRESISTA," ANTES "EL INDEPENDIENTE."

IMPRENTA DE "EL PROGRESISTA."

El Paso, Texas.

Año de 1901.

The book *Tomochic and the Role of the Saint of Cabora* (The Mexican Joan of Arc) was published in serial form by Lauro Aguirre in his newspaper *El Progresista* in 1901. *Courtesy of Southwest Collection, Texas Tech University.*

the "Saint of Cabora." Teresita was the progeny of wealthy Mexican rancher, Tomás Urrea, and an indigenous servant, Cayetana Chávez. Even before she arrived in El Paso in 1896, Teresita was the center of much attention in local anti-Díaz revolutionary newspapers such as *El Independiente* and *El Progresista,* not only for her miraculous healing powers blended with an uncanny strength of will that quickly earned her a reputation as a saint, but for her inspiration in revolutionary activities.

Urrea was specifically considered a threat by the Díaz regime in her perceived influence over the indigenous peoples of the Yaquis, Tomochics, and the Mayo, who believed in combating injustice. Díaz exiled both Urrea and her father Tomás to Nogales, Arizona, in 1892. Lauro Aguirre, a long-time revolutionary and Urrea family friend, moved the headquarters of his incendiary paper *El Independiente* to El Paso in March 1896 in anticipation of Teresita's arrival on June 13, 1896, and hosted her and her father in his home. Three thousand people and Lauro awaited her arrival in El Paso. He immediately made Teresita coeditor of *El Independiente*.

The potential of Teresita's iconic status had not escaped Lauro, and he had some hand in fomenting the Teresita Rebellion of August 12, 1896. According to historian David Romo, El Paso native and author of *Ringside Seat to a Revolution*, before the Teresita rebels attacked the customhouse in Nogales, Sonora, shouting "*¡Viva la Santa Cabora!*" Lauro printed pictures of Teresita with the following statement on the back of the photograph:

> Miss Urrea, during her first year of exile, said nothing against the Mexican government; but she did quietly help prepare for the struggle against it. *El Independiente*, which is written by her and Mr. Lauro Aguirre, has attacked the injustices committed by the Mexican government. Her great moral qualities—her love, unselfish dedication, and the truth of her denunciations against the Mexican government make her the only person who is able to transform the country of Mexico. Only she can topple an oppressive tyranny—that burns villages, exterminates entire races, and murders children. We believe that she will overthrow the actual government and will lead the Mexican people to change their political situation. We see her as the Mexican Joan of Arc. That even the government of Mexico sees her as we do is brought to light by the tenacious manner that it has persecuted her. Miss Urrea has escaped being assassinated or poisoned on various occasions.

One such picture was found on a Teresita rebel killed at Nogales. Another rebel was carrying a lock of her hair, and a third soldier was found carrying a revolutionary letter that was signed Teresita Urrea and John the Baptist (a code name that Lauro Aguirre may have been using). And it was a fitting code name, since Lauro had long heralded Teresita's miraculous healings even before she arrived in El Paso, and she was quickly compared to Jesus Christ by *The El Paso Herald-Post:* "El Paso has the distinction of having a live saint within its borders. . . . Strange as it may seem, dominant religions have never welcomed one that comes to do good in individual lives. The Nazarene had the experience, and Santa Teresa will find that she is no exception to this rule."

Although there is some academic debate over Teresita's exact contributions to *El Independiente* and other revolutionary writings ascribed to her, she had a major journalistic presence as a force in fomenting revolution. In fear for her life, due to several assassination attempts, Teresa Urrea publicly dispelled Díaz's charges of political insurgency and civil disobedience via a statement in the edition of the *El Paso Daily Herald* that appeared on September 10, 1896. Contemporary historians such as José Carlos Chávez and Francisco R. Almada both attest to Teresita Urrea not being in any way guilty of the

Teresita Urrea and her father, Tomás Urrea. *Courtesy of Southwest Collection, Texas Tech University.*

aforementioned charges. However, at the time, her attestation went unheeded due, in part, to the constant attention afforded Teresita by a thankful public. Always travelling, Teresita Urrea repeatedly performed miraculous healings. *The San Francisco Chronicle, The New York Journal,* and *The Los Angeles Times* provide full accounts of Teresita's makeshift clinics erected for disadvantaged minority populations. Regardless of which revolutionary tracts Teresita actually penned, clearly she was iconic to revolutionary and religious factions writing against Porfirio Díaz. One may be left with the conclusion that Teresita's religious significance and the iconic nature of her life as a healer erased her legacy as an articulate political author. At the border, Teresita's impact was—and is—bigger than life.

David Romo reports that *El Independiente* was one of at least sixty anti-Díaz insurrectionist and revolutionary periodicals being published in El Paso at the turn of the nineteenth century. *La Voz de la Mujer,* which was founded by Isidra T. Cárdenas in 1907 (just a year after the *Partido Liberal Mexicano* established El Paso as its headquarters) and continued publishing through 1919, is significant both politically and socially. Characteristics of *La Voz de la Mujer*—meaning "The Voice of the Woman"—including tone, organization, and strategy mimicked *Véspers,* a Mexican publication founded in 1901 that was written and edited by Juana Belén Gutiérrez de Mendoza and Elisa Acuña y Rossetti. According to historian Clara Lomas, *Véspers,* though penned by women, was characterized by "manly" language and a virile style. Both *Véspers* and *La Voz* employed extremely metaphoric language and a sarcastic tone. Although Isidra Cárdenas' *La Voz* did not include a thorough analysis of the social position of women, the paper encouraged women's participation on behalf of a nationalistic cause, adopted a communal identity, and assumed a collective female voice. In the issue of July 28, 1907, *La Voz* declaimed to its readers: "Today the dilemma is another; to take what is needed, liberty! Liberty can be conquered only through rebellion. It is up to us, mothers and wives, sisters and daughters, to confront this dilemma." (trans.)

The newspaper listed a majority of women as the chief officers: Isidra Cárdenas (director); María Sánchez (chief editor); and María Gutiérrez (manager). However, edition secretary León Cárdenas alleged in a letter to Antonio Villareal that he was himself the main author of the publication. Clara Lomas underscores this assertion as unproven, and it may be a product of threatened machismo or clever reinterpretation. However, questions of the true authorship of *La Voz* do not undermine the publication's impact in terms of how it stimulated debate and reconsideration of gender roles in service of a nationalist cause.

Indeed we have some first-hand testimony demonstrating that this call for action was effective. Witness the story of Señora Flores de Andrade, a committed Mexican idealist who moved to El Paso in 1906 not only to seek a fresh economic start, but to "take part in the Liberal propaganda work." Prior to her move across the border, she organized a semi-secret organization in the city of Chihuahua, Daughters of Cuauhtémoc, which worked directly with the Liberal Party of the Flores Magón brothers fighting the Díaz dictatorship. In ". . . 1909 a group of comrades founded in El Paso a Liberal women's club. They made me president of that group, and soon afterwards I began to carry on the propaganda work in El Paso and in Ciudad Juárez. My house turned into a conspiracy center against the dictatorship." Andrade took charge of collecting money, clothes, medicines, arms, and ammunition to prepare for the revolution. In addition, she hid and fed insurgent Francisco Madero during his time in El Paso in 1911, and helped him escape across the border to Mexico. Andrade was captured by a group of Díaz's soldiers who nearly executed her for aiding Madero in his escape. Defiant in the face of death, Andrade grabbed the colonel's gun, and the soldiers broke and ran. She lived, and it was Madero's democratic insurgency that finally toppled the *Porfiriato.* Assuming the presidency in 1911, Madero brought about a fresh sociopolitical perspective. Señora Flores de Andrade produced Liberal propaganda during the time *La Voz de la Mujer* published in support of the insurrection; women worked together as they penned realities of the Mexican Revolution and its consequences for El Pasoans in the early twentieth century.

These El Paso women were not alone. Throughout this time period in the region, there are many examples of women who told their stories of revolutionary activism and wrote calls for social change. Jovita Idar (1885-1946) penned and published *La Crónica* in Laredo; in extant issues from 1911 she addressed the equality of working-class women, called for bilingual bicultural education, and produced scathing critiques of the Catholic Church's oppression of women. In San Antonio in 1910, anti-*Porfiriato* activist Teresa Villareal (who had previously lived in El Paso) used *El Obrero: Periódico Independiente* to assert that working-class women are the equals of working-class men. Thus, the social and political revolutions being penned in El Paso are echoed in other regions of the borderland at this time, paralleling the national movements for suffrage and other reforms.

While the authorship of El Paso's Mexican ex-patriot and Mexican American revolutionary women journalists throughout the period of 1890-1919 has been called into question, interest in patriotic causes was not limited to those of Mexican descent. We have evidence of the published writings of Henrietta Eleanor Goodnough Deuell Skidmore, née Hull, pen name Peggy Hull, from 1916 to 1967. Born December 30, 1889, Hull was sixteen when she was first published. She is a singular figure during the early history of El Paso women journalists, not only in that she was married three times, but she also served as a World War I field correspondent. She became a journalistic icon in much the same way that Teresita Urrea became a religious figure of importance. Her significance as a journalistic authority was such that she signed her columns in cursive simply as "Peggy," and she enjoyed access to interviews with city officials of any rank.

She held the equally high esteem of famous military commanders, local politicians, and high society. During her work in the field during World War I, Peggy Hull had the dubious honor of inciting the jealousy and ire of male war correspondents who used her sex against her as a factor to end her competition with their reports. Peggy was subsequently invited to report on World War II from the field, but declined for personal reasons outlined later.

Peggy Hull defied the proscribed roles for the "fairer" sex in United States society before, during, and after World War I. As the first woman from the *El Paso Morning Times* to be a war correspondent, she was automatically faced with naysayers who thoroughly denigrated her abilities with attacks such as, "you are too young," and most obvious, "you are a woman." According to Bogart and Smith's *The Wars of Peggy Hull,* the political climate of El Paso was such that the majority believed "women had no business going to battle fronts unless they were nurses or Red Cross workers of some kind." Her drive to serve her country in its time of need became the catalyst to overcome such criticism. Peggy Hull testifies as to why she did not settle for staying home and writing society columns: "I did not go to war because I liked the excitement or what my colleagues sometimes erroneously referred to as glamour. I went because I was not a man and could not carry a gun and do something for my country."

Before the assignment in World War I however, Hull ventured into Mexico alongside General Pershing for the Punitive Expedition, which Pershing organized in order to disassemble Pancho Villa's armies beginning in 1916. Other invited journalists included Robert Rhodes of the *New York Tribune* and Bill Griffin of the *Hearst Service.* It is from this mission that she is said to have learned about camp life, the psychology of soldiers, and military mentality, and to have developed her war-reporting skills. A front-page article in the *El Paso Morning Times* for February 6, 1917, reported her triumphant return: "Pershing's Ten Thousand Back from Mexico Desert Silent, Swarthy and Strong."

Upon securing her position as a war correspondent for the "War to End All Wars," Hull was ordered in 1917 to report from Paris, France. Her articles served a larger purpose for the war effort: resistance writing became an outlet to help the troops adjust to being in an alien environment. She served as a two-way conduit of information between Europe and the United States, often writing specific El Paso-related stories, which provided servicemen connections to a home that often seemed unimaginable. Some of her published articles include: October 16, 1917, "Peggy Takes Motor Trip Through France; Finds American Soliders, But Heartless Censor Won't Let Her Tell About Them"; and August 30, 1917, "Peggy Visits American Training Camp Somewhere in France and Finds General Pershing in Mood to Brook no Slacking."

Hull's success was such that many of her male colleagues felt threatened, and they convinced Major Frederick Palmer, who oversaw American war correspondents in Paris, to write a letter to General Pershing protesting her continued correspondence. In part, Palmer's letter accused Hull of using her access to compete unfairly with accredited news correspondents. Palmer directly voiced the threat felt by other correspondents and attacks her based on the fact that she is not "accredited" as a journalist. If accreditation were the sole marker of legitimate journalism, there would be no reason to make such an accusation. Palmer continues leveraging gendered privilege to discredit Peggy Hull with the following statements:

> *The Chicago Tribune,* Paris edition, has not wanted for representation, if it would make use of its privileges. It has a regularly accredited correspondent, Mr. Floyd Gibbons. . . . The complaints against Mrs. Hull on the part of the accredited corre-

Peggy Rides at Head of Cavalcade of Distinguished United States Army Officers

February 16, 1917, *El Paso Morning Times.*

> spondents are unanimous. They add . . . that the work she is doing is undignified.

Palmer escalates his gendered attack by asserting that Hull is consorting with numerous men—including the highest generals—to gain their favor:

> . . . Mrs. Hull says that she was present at a luncheon given by Generals Pershing and March, when both Generals invited her personally to be their guest with the Army. The fact of her having received such an invitation has been widely advertised in her own paper.

Forced by such threats of impropriety she returned to El Paso on November 21, 1917, and began a column for the *El Paso Morning Times* on February 3, 1918, that principally addressed business issues. Paralleling these writings are other more culturally-conscious society columns that drew many French comparisons. Peggy Hull was known for an impeccable fashion sense amplified by her European assignment, from which she supposedly took three chests of Parisian clothes back home to El Paso. She often asserted that the French could always take the most "discouraging ingredients and make a palatable dish out of them." She also reviewed films; in writing about *The German Curse in Russia,* which centers on the war photographer Donald Thompson, Hull again is adamant about contributing to the war effort with her journalistic gifts.

For years, Hull retained a chief desire to report on issues concerning the war. When she mentioned her desire to write a book about World War I and her experiences, the same Floyd Gibbons, who had attacked her integrity in Europe, joked that she should name it *I Slept with a Million Men.* Peggy, however, never let such paternalistic jibes stop her career, and she continued to cover important issues linked to regional and world events: "YMCA Conference in Abandoned Oasis Saloon Plans New War Activities" and "Electric R.R. Increases Trainmen's Pay: $15,000 Clubhouse for Employees: Peggy has Talk With an Old Timer." She was much admired by her El Paso readership, as is evidenced by the article dated January 26, 1918, entitled: "Miss Peggy Hull, Mythical in Past, Becomes Realistic Character for High School: Hundreds of Students in Institution Who Have Heard Much of the *Times* Correspondent Personally Introduced at Auditorium."

PASO MORNING TIMES.

The Popular Shows Smart Spring Apparel

Peggy Finds Sol I. Berg Coat in France

One of the smart satin sport suits which The Popular is making a specialty of in the ready-to-wear department of the fifth floor. The skirt is fashioned of white satin and the blue velvet coat is piped with the same material.

Peggy

CLARENCE EDDY

Peggy Hull's columns exhibit characteristic flair.
El Paso Morning Times February 17, 1918.

Although a second chance to venture overseas to report from France at the start of World War II presented itself, funding was lacking from the *Morning Times.* Later, Hull was invited by General Robert L. Eichelberger to serve as a roving reporter after the war to cover topics and locations in the Pacific. However, Hull chose to remain in El Paso to care for her then-husband Hobert Skidmore, who became severely depressed when his twin, Hubert, burned to death in 1946. Interestingly enough, a reporting position located in Siberia later emerged, which she accepted, ending her El Paso career with a "Farewell El Paso" column in the *El Paso Times.*

Peggy Hull died of breast cancer on June 19, 1967. One of her final statements summed up her long and varied career: ". . . you don't choose a life—Life does the choosing for you—you don't really make a decision with a capital D—Life is a series of pressures—influences exerting pressures from various directions. You ultimately succumb to the greatest pressure." However, Hull's immense strength of will and integrity were clear to others; one acquaintance summed up her golden character in a simple phrase, Peggy Hull, ". . . was an opportunist that made her own opportunities."

Other women who published in newspapers between the late 1890s and 1920 were often focused on more stereotypically feminine subjects such as relationships, society events, and domestic arts. When political, such writers took an active stance against the trend of middle-class and upper-middle-class modern women to educate themselves and aspire to participation in the professions. This reflected the national trend of resistance to changing ideas about women's social roles, which were exhibited in the women's suffrage movement as well as changes in laws, such as the 1848 Married Women's Property Act, which afforded women of means the contractual right to own property separate from their husbands. Often such sentiments were expressed in ironic poetry as the two examples below demonstrate.

El Paso Herald-Post
Friday, September 18, 1896 [reprinted from the *Chicago Post* by male editors]
The "New" Couple

She was "new" and was constructed on the latest modern plan,
But she lost her heart, like others, sad of course 'twas lost to man,
So at last the two were married, and they started married life,
As they thought, equipped and read, well prepared for any strife.

She was posted on his business quest as thoroughly as he.
She had studied all the details, and, as any one else could see.
She could run the shop or office, and it also seemed quite clear.
She could act as his bookkeeper or could serve as his cashier.

She could sell goods on commission or could buy on thirty days.
She was sharper than most merchants in all proper business ways.
She could "take" from his dictation, and his dictate to others too.
There was nothing round the office that she really couldn't do.

So they thought they were well armored for a life of great success,
But the outcome of their trial was a failure, more or less.
They are doomed to boarding houses, and regretfully they roam.
For while both can run the office neither can make a home.

September 7, 1916
The El Paso Herald-Post, Verse Libre by Julie Lee Brown
Love vs. Ambition

Fairer than a summer's day was she, and sweeter than the lilacs. But she did not care for her fairness and sweetness. She had forgotten herself in her great overwhelming ambition. She had just come home from college. Medicine was her vocation. In the best medical laboratories in the world. Then came a fair-haired boy. And for some reason the girl had forgotten medicine. Ambition seemed to lag. Not that she became listless. For otherwise it seemed she had just begun to live. Just as everygirl, every Sleeping Beauty is awakened by the prince.

His poem: "If you were April's lady and I were lord in May, We'd throw with leaves for hours And draw for days w/flowers." The he leaned over and kissed her upon the mouth.

O how bitter medicine would be after that!

Julie Lee Brown's intimations that a focus on love and relationships is mutually exclusive from involvement in a profession is typical of the anxieties of the era about middle- and upper-class women's increasing participation in education and work outside of the home. Similarly the former piece, reprinted in the women's section from the *Chicago Post,* expresses anxiety that a dual career couple is doomed to a life of boardinghouses and transience, because the female has neglected to learn housewifely arts, representing a strategic manipulation of the woman's section by male editors. The long rhyming poem overlooks the fact that such a couple could easily have afforded at least a modicum of hired domestic help, thus erasing class realities and inequities in a generalized fear of changing gender roles. Moreover, such items placed in the women's pages of the newspaper ostensibly ensured that a maximum number of middle- and upper-class women read them and would consequently guide their own actions as well as their daughters' based on such sentiments.

An additional example is extant in Laura Jean Libbey's *El Paso Herald-Post* column "Daily Talks on Heart Topics." A typical day pulled from this column is one from March 16, 1917, in which Libbey advises a "girl of twenty" to consider with suspicion a suitor who presents himself as "jack-of-all-trades," and prompts her reader to require this suitor to have a steady job for at least one year at the same place of employment before consenting to marry him. Her other suitor, Libbey advises, who is a steady worker as a journeyman mechanic, is a much better prospect as a stable economic provider. Another tidbit of advice concerns a reader who wishes to know whether to present her twenty-seven-year-old single daughter or her widowed forty-two-year-old sister to a well-to-do widower friend as a possible wife. Libbey wisely solves this man-woe puzzle by advising that the reader invite the rich widowed friend to a family dinner including both ladies and "let affairs thereafter take their natural course."

Other El Paso journalists publishing at the same time as Libbey differed greatly from these stereotypical attitudes toward marriage and family. Born in Sidney, Ohio, in 1871, Elsie McElroy Slater had quite a prolific journalistic career spanning almost fifty years. Elsie married Hughes Decourcy Slater in 1899 and moved to El Paso, where she bore two children. Prior to their marriage, H. D. Slater had purchased the *El Paso Herald-Post* and then in 1925 purchased the *El Paso Times.* He led these papers to astronomical growth until 1929 when Slater retired and sold them. Although the spouse of a local journalistic force, Elsie McElroy Slater was by no means living in H. D.'s shadow. Noted in John William Leonard's *Women's Who's Who of America: A Biographical Dictionary of Contemporary Women of the United States and Canada (1914-1915)*, Slater's great breadth of works emphasizes her love of the desert Southwest. She kept her research emphasis on both local issues and those that transcend any sort of gendered prescriptions. This journalistic dexterity began while she was publishing various columns for the *El Paso Herald-Post* beginning in 1899, entitled with quirky banners such as, "My Better Half," "An Open Window at Sunny Top," and "Diary of a Spankable Cherub." With such disparate names, it is interesting to note the similarities among the content, all of which emerged as an entertaining hodgepodge of informative quips, book reviews, social commentary, and varying perspectives on the ever-present topic of marriage. Her candidness about equity in relationships clearly differentiated her from the more typical society pages, commonly referred to as the woman's page.

Just for some basis of comparison, the Dear Abby type column for the 1950s *El Paso Herald-Post* was penned by a Mrs. Ann Carroll, and her advice to the anonymous wife "Cane" had been to remain in a relationship that was emotionally and physically abusive and to "not try so hard and accept the present state of affairs gratefully and be a good sport." (May 23, 1951).

Although Slater published in the late 1890s and into the early twentieth century, it is important to note exactly how progressive her take on marriage was. In particular, "My Better Half" offered a model of balanced partnership. For example, on April 25, 1899, Slater includes a literary critique of a book that encourages mutuality and respect in marriage. She endorses the book and quotes the rules it presents for equity in relationships. Offered below is a selection of these rules:

> 4. Never both be cross at the same time. Wait your turn.
>
> 6. You were gentleman and lady before you were husband and wife. Don't forget it.
>
> 10. Permanent mutual respect is necessary for permanent mutual love.
>
> 12. If you take liberties, be prepared to give them.
>
> 18. The man who respects his wife does not turn her into a mendicant. Give her a purse of her own.

Considering this excerpt is from 1899, predating the passage of women's suffrage by twenty-one years, Slater's choice in presenting them is quite progressive. Her belief in social justice was not limited to her writing. Slater was heavily involved in community organizations, such as the Woman's Charity Association and the Community Chest. Elsie McElroy Slater was an endearing figure who had the El Paso community at heart.

Her later years proved to be quite eventful and the natural sciences became her muse. Slater became known as an academically accredited naturalist, using science to explain the surrounding world. This aspect of her career evolved out of her passion for cataloging and dispersing the fruits of her laborious botany studies to the more general, non-scientific El Paso reading audience. Her contributions to natural science could be considered a model of pedagogy if a researcher intends to reach wide audiences, but she also contributed to renowned collections at the Smithsonian. Penning many articles in publications such as the *American Fern Journal,* "Trailing Bommerias in Texas," she begins rhetorically with the jocular simplicity by stating, "We know where to find brommeria—after a rain." The "we" is a useful tool in engaging the reader into a personal relationship that includes all who engage with her texts.

This welcoming tone can be found throughout all her texts, including her major books *Thirteen Ferns of the Mexican Border* (1939) and *El Paso Birds* (1945), which fully affirm Slater as having democratic ideals that knowledge should be made available to all who seek it, even if they are of a lower socioeconomic status or outside of academia. *The Thirteen Ferns of the Mexican Border* does not exclude the seemingly intimidating scientific terms such as *Notholaena standleyi* (Star Cloak Fern), *Phanerophlebia* (veinfern), or three *Cheilanthes* (lipfern). However, Slater makes sure to inform her readership of basic information and admonishes them, "Ferns are not flowering plants, they are leaves, and leaves only. They have no flowers, no fruits, no sex" or, the "lark deserves every protection . . . to shoot one Meadow Lark is quite deliberately to invite in 10,000 cutting worms and weevils." She further strengthens her democratic appeal to make reliable scientific knowledge available to as wide a readership as possible. Another aspect apparent throughout her work is the push for all to recognize the need for natural conservation of, and appreciation for, the everyday beauty that is available for every single El Pasoan.

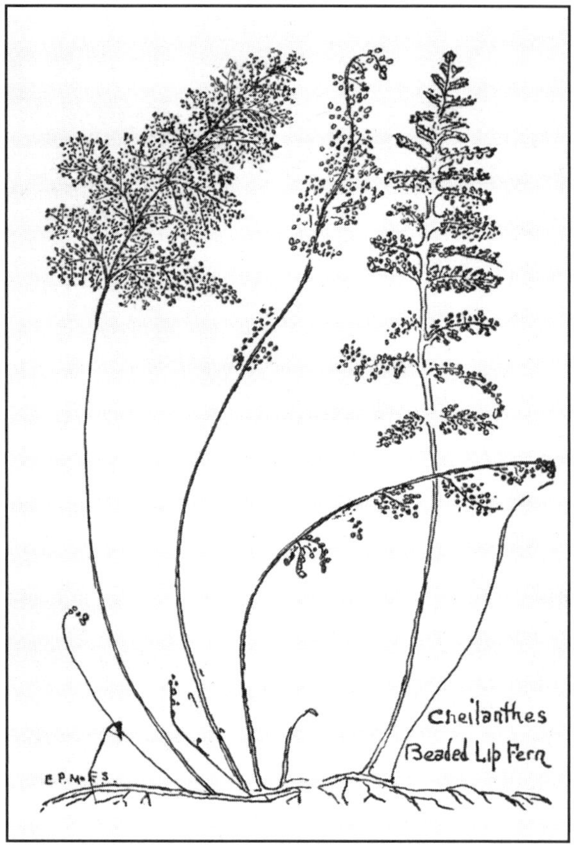

Illustration from Elsie McElroy Slater's *Thirteen Ferns of the Mexican Border.*

Slater's texts sparkle with lyrical beauty throughout; they are poetic science for the masses. The detailed illustrations contained in both *Thirteen Ferns* and *El Paso Birds* accompany the words effectively and give a lasting impression of living organisms from her environment. Her lyricism is exhibited especially through her observations on the characteristic desert flora of the region. She writes:

> So many of our plants you cannot miss—our golden poppies shine for miles, and heliotropes like a soft old purple shawl can be seen a mile away. Every spring, when it

> rains ever so little, the most indifferent nose whiffs the soft lilac or heliotrope of the multitude of soft verbenas that paint the roadsides and come down the streets into the town.

With all the positive attributes Slater combines into one strand of prose, it is clear that this is not a typical scientific entry, but actually tells a story. Using a similar combination of scholarly artistry in *El Paso Birds,* Slater sums up both major selections with the similar caveat that claims not to have compiled an exhaustive list of the subjects in question, but instead aims to give "an account of the ordinary chances for the study of patterns of life and beauty that present themselves to a semi-scientific and not too wise reporter." She ends her book with one of her own poems, "The Collared Lizard says His Prayers."

Elise McElroy Slater died at the age of eighty-one. The variety and perspective of her body of work leaves a legacy of mini-revolutions—the accumulated contributions of a woman whose life may have seemed traditional, but whose work showed an appreciation of values and pursuits considered quite progressive for her time. She patiently blazed a path for other women journalists to follow.

Virginia Turner is another prolific El Pasoan to have made her presence known in the field of journalism. Born in Salt Lake City, Utah, in 1916, Virginia Turner was then raised in Santa Barbara, Mexico, where her father was a mining engineer. Turner received her secondary education from Ysleta High School in El Paso. It was clear that after publishing her first newspaper article in the *Denver Post* at nineteen, Turner was born to write. Her career with the *El Paso Herald-Post* lasted from 1944 until 1969, and her relentless work ethic catapulted her career with a promotion to the city editor position at the *El Paso Herald-Post* in 1959. This position served as a source of strength and empowerment for women journalists, because it provided Turner with an amount of leadership and supervision of other journalists that was not common for women since the era of the Mexican Revolution. Turner had the authority to cover stories that piqued her own interests. Readers wrote her so often that she was one of the three entities in the city to receive the most mail. Turner covered a wide range of topics spanning from front-page international news, to local city elections, to examples of human kindness great and small. Turner never lost sight of the fact that people underlie every story. For instance, the *El Paso Herald-Post* issue that appeared July 29, 1969, contains a full-page article entitled, "Couple Stranded in Ysleta Deluged by Kindness." Such stories depict Virginia Turner as a figure who focused a humanistic lens onto every situation from which she crafted a byline.

One of Turner's series of articles concerned issues with the Tepehuane and Tarahumara peoples, whom she researched between 1966 and 1970 in the southwestern part of the Mexican state of Chihuahua. The first lines of the article entitled, "Not All Tarahumaras Are Starving!" are "Lo, the poor Indians! When so much is being written about what isn't being done for the Tarahumaras, it seems appropriate to mention a few things that are being done." This series was an example of how Turner endeavored to bring attention to stories and issues that were overlooked since they concerned indigenous peoples.

Her ability to cover such various topics with a sense of urgency, yet compassion, led her to win many awards. Some of the most significant are the Disabled American Veterans (DAV) Commander's Award given to those who "have outstanding coverage of news events of interest to the DAV," and on a national level, the American Osteopathic Association Award for her coverage on DOCARE, a story about a society of physicians who fly to treat isolated tribes of indigenous people in Mexico, which was published in the *El Paso Herald-Post* in July of 1966. Texas state senator Joe Christie commended her for this award and presented the resolution to declare May 15, 1967, as Virginia Turner Day. Her awards are well deserved considering the great personal lengths traveled to provide the most thorough coverage. For example, Turner survived an airplane crash during her trip into Mexico to research the Tarahumaras.

The following titles give a good idea of the diversity of topics Turner covered: "Man's First Steps on Way to Moon were Here," "Freedom in China Lies Across The River," "Everyone Bows in Japan; so Do Deer," "Ysleta Tax Office Opened Dedicated to Alex Gonzales," and "Bliss Gets New Commander; Bids Farewell to Staytons." During the years Virginia Turner wrote for the *El Paso Herald-Post* she laid a solid foundation for future female journalists.

Robbie Farley Myrick-Villalobos, who was born in 1954 during Turner's career at the *Herald-Post*, grew up to be as active as a journalist could possibly be in a relatively short time. A professional publishing career that lasted barely more than twenty years—from 1981 until 2004—included work at *The Prospector*, the *El Paso Times*, the *El Paso Herald-Post*, *El Diario de Juárez*, and *El Paso Inc.*, among other regional publications. In addition, Robbie was included in an anthology of works on civil rights entitled *Pieces of a Dream*, which is a selection of editorials on the subject of race produced by the National Conference of Editorial Writers in 1996. Robbie used two pen names throughout her publishing career: Robbie Farley-Villalobos; and beginning in 2000, Robbie Myrick-Villalobos, which included one of her married names. Her acclaimed published work represents only a fraction of her ventures. She pioneered a locally televised program on KCOS-TV entitled *Accents on the Arts*, a show broadcast four times weekly on which Villalobos interviewed local El Paso artists. Reporter Maribel Villalva of the *El Paso Times* quotes Villalobos as stating its purpose was to be "a forum to discuss local arts issues and upcoming events" (July 30, 2000).

The path leading up to Robbie Farley-Villalobos achieving such heights of recognition began with The University of Texas at El Paso's newspaper, *The Prospector.* It was in 1982 that Robbie and fellow *Prospector* writers ventured to Los Angeles for a conference aptly named, "Society of Professional Journalists Convention." Sparking a journalistic fervor, Villalobos joined the *El Paso Herald-Post* as an arts and entertainment editor in 1988 while simultaneously serving on the editorial board. Until the close of the *Herald-Post's* doors in 1997, she wrote on a wide array of topics that included public concerns, popular culture, and the issue held most dear: the El Paso local art scene.

As a feature-story writer, Villalobos engaged with subjects directly affecting El Paso's local constituents. The heading of the September 10, 1994, *Herald-Post* reads, "Demo Candidate gets 'Hood Nods." The issue expressed concerns about a nineteen-mile gasoline pipeline to be rerouted from Austin to El Paso that would uproot two miles of the Lakeside Neighborhood into Ciudad Juárez, until it reached the PEMEX (Petróleos Mexicanos) plant in Mexico City. Other articles, such as that on September 2, 1997, relate to union efforts to prevent worker exploitation. "Workers Back New Union Effort" and "37-year labor activist is honored" shine a positive light on the accomplishments of a community of workers. A subconscious voice of activism permeates her writing with headlines such as "Federal Law Pushed Banks Into Affordable Housing" (September 8, 1997) and "Border Tobacco Weathers Border's Ups & Downs" (September 20, 1997), which indicated a desire not to lose the voices of the poor.

Apart from the *Herald-Post,* in this same year Villalobos penned articles for the *New Mexico Business Journal* and initiated the El Paso Chapter for the Association of Hispanic Journalists, which is a national program intended to increase the numbers of Latina/os in journalism. Other honors include being inducted into the El Paso Commission for Women Hall of Fame in 1996, which recognized her outstanding dedication "to pursue equal rights and responsibilities for all women." Writing for *El Diario de Juárez,* her topics after 1997 were more business-related. In February 2001, Villalobos joined *El Paso Inc.* to expand on the "Business Bridge" pages previously geared to comment on the US-Mexico commerce relations. She states in the November 2001 edition, "Now as *El Paso Inc.*'s border economics editor, I'm glad to help fill the void that exists when it comes to reporting on the intricacies of conducting business between two cities such as El Paso and Ciudad Juárez, two nations such as the United States and Mexico and the 2,000 miles that join them." Robbie Villalobos was civically engaged through her journalism, but also politically engaged as she ran for public office in 2002, vying for the county clerk position against contenders Waldo Alarcon and Pat Siqueiros. Despite defeat, she remained faithful to El Paso County's Democratic Party and became its first ever Public Information Officer (PIO). A prolific writer reaching the El Paso public for over twenty years, Robbie Farley Myrick-Villalobos's career came to a premature end on February 18, 2004, from cancer-related complications. After Villalobos's death, reporter Maribel Villalva of the *El Paso Times* reflected on her impact:

> I'll never pretend to know as much as Robbie did when it comes to arts in El Paso, but all I can do is look to her work and the way she inspired so many people. Through

Robbie, I've learned that all artists really want is someone to tell their story. I hope one day someone will tell her story, too.

These women have given us a mere glimpse into the history of El Paso's women journalists who have shown us how grace married gumption. We believe that both characteristics are essential to the many revolutions through which our foremothers have shepherded us. We record their accomplishments as an homage to the past, a lesson for the present, and an inspiration to the future. Our vibrant binational borderland will doubtless continue to present both opportunities and challenges that will require bold revolutionaries with skillful pens.

Bibliographic Essay

The Special Collections Department of The University of Texas at El Paso Library, with the outstanding expertise of Claudia Rivers, has provided invaluable assistance. Sources derived from the UTEP library include a transcription of the Oral History of Mr. Chester Chope; an MA Thesis by Lucille Soltner entitled "Early El Paso Newspapers"; *The Thirteen Ferns of the Mexican Border* (The University of Texas Press, 1939) and *El Paso Birds* (The University of Texas Press, 1945) by Elsie McElroy Slater.

Alongside university resources, the main El Paso Public Library has been of the utmost help. Without such, the newspaper archives of the *El Paso Times* (referred to as *The Morning Times* between the years 1908-1920), the *El Paso Herald-Post, El Paso Inc.*, and *El Diario de Juárez* would be impossible. The microfilm and microfiche centers of both locations provided investigative leads and insights into the past.

Photographs and historical context were extracted from a multitude of publications. Books included *Ringside Seat to a Revolution: An Underground Cultural History of El Paso and Juárez: 1893-1923* (Cinco Punto Press, 2005) by David Dorado Romo; "Transborder Discourse: The Articulation of Gender in the Borderlands in the Early Twentieth Century" by Clara Lomas; *The Wars of Peggy Hull: The Life and Times of A War Correspondent* (Texas Western Press, 1991) by Eleanor A. Bogart and Wilda M. Smith; *Teresita* (Stemmer House, 1978) by William Holden; *The Hummingbird's Daughter* (Little Brown & Co., 2005) by Luis Alberto Urrea; *A History of the Woman's Club of El Paso 1894-1945* (El Paso, 1945) by Mary S. Cunningham; *U.S. Mexico Borderlands: Historical and Contemporary Perspectives* (Scholarly Resources, 1996) a collection of essays edited by Oscar J. Martinez. Journals referenced include the *American Fern Journal* and *Church History.*

Invaluable research for this chapter was provided by the eagle eyes of Carliene S. Quist and the calming influence of the "Voice of Reason"—Kathryn.

Chapter 12

FROM NUNS TO SUFFRAGETTES: WOMEN PIONEERS IN MEDICINE

by Evelyn Posey

KNOWN AS THE Six Shooter Capital and Sin City, El Paso in the late 1800s was a town where the main street was lined with dance halls, brothels, and saloons, and every saloon had a roulette wheel surrounded by stacks of silver dollars and piles of gold. A horse and buggy boomtown of about ten thousand, El Paso was reputed to be a very drunken place.

An unlikely place for respectable women, El Paso drew women who followed their husbands and others who came alone to this small border town believing that El Paso would soon shed its lawless, frontier reputation and become a town where they could make a difference.

Not only was El Paso an unlikely place, but the late 1800s were an unlikely time for any woman to be working outside the home. Women were not welcome in the workforce unless they were schoolteachers, and if they chose this one upright profession, they couldn't marry, smoke, or drink and couldn't be seen on the streets after sunset. At the turn of the twentieth century, women were considered incompetent in science, technology, and math. Yet, against these odds, a few women chose to work as medical caregivers even while overcoming the hostility of men who didn't believe they were capable and the reality that patients—both men and women—wouldn't always trust their judgment.

In the movie *Butch Cassidy and the Sundance Kid,* Butch says about the guys who are tracking them, "I couldn't do that. Could you do that? Why can they do it? Who are those guys?" The same can be asked about women who pioneered western medicine in El Paso, Texas. Who were these women?

In the late 1800s, Dr. Robert Koch, a German physician, isolated the tuberculosis bacteria and discovered that it would die if exposed to heat and sunshine. This knowledge quickly spread worldwide, sending tuberculosis patients and their families in search of hot, sunny towns like El Paso. With the arrival of the railroads in 1881, so many patients flooded the city in search of a cure for consumption that they were forced to camp in makeshift tents and shacks in the Highland Park area on the east side of the Franklins.

As this squalid tent city grew, a group of concerned El Paso citizens asked Reverend Charles Ferrari, pastor of St. Mary's Chapel, to help bring doctors and nurses to the city to tend to these highly infectious patients. After some research, Ferrari sought the help of a group of nuns known as the Daughters of Charity of St. Vincent de Paul (sometimes referred to as Sisters of Charity) who specialized in nursing and healthcare. Founded in Paris, France, in 1633, these sisters not only took vows of poverty, chastity, and obedience, but a vow of service to the poor. St. Vincent de Paul wanted the Daughters of Charity to be out in the streets helping the poor rather than cloistered behind convent walls. In the early 1800s, when Napoleon refused to allow the Paris nuns to travel to the United States to establish a home, Mother Elizabeth Ann Seton used guidelines sent to her by the Paris archbishop to found her own community in Emmitsburg, Maryland.

These American Daughters of Charity traveled from city to city, performing healthcare services and building hospitals and clinics. When El Paso's Rev. Ferrari asked them to open and staff a hospital in El Paso similar to Charity Hospital that they built in New Orleans, Mother Marianna Flynn sent a small delegation of sisters to El Paso. In February 1892, Sisters Stella Dempsey, Dolores Eggert, and Vincent Lee stepped off the train. Sister Genevieve Hennessy joined them a short time later.

As the train pulled into the El Paso station, the nuns would get their first glimpse of a town described by a New York doctor who visited El Paso as a place where, "The monotony of the ever-present sunshine, the dust, and the high winds make the sick and the well long for a drop of rain; add to this poor food and unsatisfactory accommodations and it requires some courage on the part of the patient to remain here."

As bleak as this small western town may have looked to the nuns, the local residents, waiting to meet the train, must have been fascinated by the nuns' appearance. Each one stepped off the train in her traditional long grey habit, with wooden rosary beads hanging from her belt, and a conspicuous starched white *cornette* or headpiece, made famous seventy years later in the television show *The Flying Nun*.

The sisters, weary from the train ride, moved into a temporary home on the corner of East Overland and Ochoa Streets and immediately began treating patients. Because the nuns were simple, cordial women, with a great deal of interest in the people of El Paso, it wasn't long before the local women rallied behind them. These supporters cleaned hospital rooms and often brought "dainties," small boxes filled with pies, cakes, lemon crackers, oranges, apples, books, magazines, and even underwear to the hospital. Soon, El Paso women helped organize fundraising for a new hospital, seeking donations of money, furniture, bedding, and medical supplies.

Between 1890 and 1920, an estimated twenty-five thousand people came to El Paso to find a cure for tuberculosis. Called "lungers" by local residents, these consumptives often walked to the downtown plaza, sat on the benches, and hoped the sunshine would work its magic. It wasn't unusual to see a person collapse and die while basking in the sun. With the increasing number of patients seeking care, the small hospital was quickly overrun with the sick and dying. Within a few short months of their arrival, the Daughters of Charity bought the second location (named Saint Mary's Hospital) from the Dieter

Above: El Paso, Texas 1890-1900.
Below: Highland Park Tent City. *Courtesy of Otis A. Aultman Collection, El Paso Public Library.*

El Paso train station, 1880-1890. *Courtesy of The University of Texas at El Paso Library Special Collections Department.*

family. However, the sisters practiced at this home for only a short time before realizing that it, too, was inadequate. By August 1892, the sisters borrowed over $5,000 from local banks to purchase land and $60,000 from their motherhouse in Maryland to build a full-fledged hospital in El Paso.

While reviewing the architectural plans for their new El Paso hospital, the nuns decided to model it after the famed Hôtel-Dieu in Paris, a French symbol of charity, renowned for its progressive medical treatment. Opened on January 25, 1894, El Paso's own Hotel Dieu, located on the corner of Stanton and Rio Grande, was an eighty-bed hospital, described in a local paper as "a model of luxury and convenience for the invalid . . ." According to hospital records, in 1897 Hotel Dieu served 387 patients, fifty free of charge. By 1901, the number of patients doubled to 740 and by 1902, the hospital served 1,095. In this final location, the sisters provided excellent, personalized care to patients from all over the US and northern Mexico.

A few years after opening Hotel Dieu, the four nurses could no longer tend to all of the patients themselves, so they opened a nursing school. The Hotel Dieu Training School opened in 1898 with the first training described as "two months of probation for students, no entrance fee, free board and laundry, and a five dollar per month salary for those who remained three years."

Through the years, Hotel Dieu hospital provided patients with a broad range of healthcare and surgical services, including an impressive list of Southwest firsts: first clinical laboratory, first X-ray equipment, first appendectomy, and later, first artificial kidney machine, and specifically for women, first cesarean section, first pediatric department, and first hospital women's auxiliary. The nursing school trained almost all El Paso nurses for the next seventy-seven years.

In 1894, the same year that Hotel Dieu hospital opened at its final location, the Schuster family arrived in El Paso. Dr. Michael P. Schuster was born in Hungary and attended medical

Hotel Dieu, El Paso, ca. 1913. *Courtesy of the El Paso Photographic History Collection, El Paso Public Library.*

school in Vienna, Austria. Eugenia Mananyi Schuster (1865-1946), the daughter of a baron, was also born in Hungary and educated in Vienna. Austrian Emperor Franz Joseph often invited medical students as well as daughters of prominent nobility to his grand balls. Eugenia Mananyi, who spoke five languages and studied piano with Franz Liszt, was a regular on the guest list. It was at one of these grand balls that Eugenia met her lifelong partner, Michael, who would take her a long way from the cultural centers of Europe to a remote frontier of the United States.

One of Dr. Schuster's medical school professors had asked him to come with him to Kansas City, Missouri, to conduct research. Once in the United States, Dr. Schuster accepted a position as chief surgeon for the Towne Smelter in El Paso. A young entrepreneur, Henry Safford Towne, had established this smelter to process the ore from Towne's many Mexican mines. Mr. Towne wanted a doctor for his employees and asked Dr. Schuster if he would be interested in the job. Dr. Schuster said he would come only if Mr. Towne built a small hospital on the site. Mr. Towne agreed and also hired his own nephew, Dr. Henry Towne Safford, to work with Dr. Schuster. Mr. Towne later formed the Kansas City Smelting and Refining Company, which eventually became the American Smelting and Refining Company, ASARCO.

By 1901, Dr. Schuster decided to leave the smelter to open a private practice, and he and his wife, Eugenia Schuster, in conjunction with a small group of other local physicians, opened their own hospital. In 1902, they founded Providence Hospital, the first non-denominational hospital in El Paso, in the Sunset Heights area.

A prominent eye, ear, nose, and throat specialist, Michael tended to people from all over the Americas, including several presidents of Mexico. In addition to his regular practice, which included contracts to provide health care to the employees of the smelter, the border patrol, and customs, he drove his horse and

Providence Hospital, ca. 1910. *Courtesy of the Otis A. Aultman Collection, El Paso Public Library.*

buggy into the poorer neighborhoods of El Paso, including Chihuahuita and Chinatown, to tend to the sick and expected no pay in return for his much-needed services. Because of this dedication to the practice of medicine, he had little time for the business side of the hospital, leaving the bookkeeping and management to the very capable Eugenia. Within a few years, partly because of Eugenia's determination and resilience, the Schuster family bought out their partners and became the sole owners of Providence Hospital.

From all reports, Eugenia Schuster was an excellent administrator who spent countless hours coordinating medical staff efforts and ensuring that all her responsibilities were carried out to perfection. She was always prepared, actively engaged, and willing to take on any assignments required. Providence simply wouldn't have been successful without her leadership. Her daughter Regina Schuster Rabb said, "Mother ran the hospital like a home. That is why people liked to come to Providence when they were sick. She used her own linen during those early days. She did everything from cooking to firing the boilers. She was a combination bookkeeper, receptionist, nurse, housekeeper, cook, and janitor."

Eugenia may have run the hospital like a home because she and her family actually lived in the hospital. Dr. and Mrs. Schuster had four children: Margaret, Frank, Regina, and Stephen. Her daughter, Margaret Schuster Meyer, remembered her mother as a formidable person with a straight back, curly dark hair, and patrician nose, and as a firm disciplinarian who spoke in Hungarian when she didn't want the children to understand what she was saying. Mrs. Schuster believed that children should be seen, not heard. Dinner was a formal affair where the children were expected to sit properly, clean their plates, and ask permission to be excused when they wished to leave the table. Eugenia, who insisted that all of their children attend private schools, had no interest in accompanying her husband and the children in frivolous pursuits such as going to the Barnum and Bailey Circus when it was in town.

Instead of the circus, Eugenia wanted to introduce her children, as well as fellow El Pasoans, to European culture, so after they arrived, she started the Shakespeare Club and began inviting opera singers to perform in the Myar Opera House, a popular stage in El Paso. Later, she helped found the Pan American Round Table, whose local membership was composed of women from both Ciudad Juárez and El Paso. Its purpose was to promote mutual understanding and friendship among women of the Western Hemisphere. She also helped found the Woman's Club of El Paso, whose women regularly met with the male members of the Providence Hospital board to advise them on hospital matters. It wasn't unusual to see Eugenia, dressed in riding habits made in Vienna, sitting sidesaddle on her white horse Daisy, riding to her club meetings, or wearing gorgeous new gowns from Vienna to El Paso balls organized by the Pan American Round Table or Woman's Club.

In the early 1900s, Eugenia, then president of the Woman's Club, teamed with the Citizens League to encourage El Paso citizens to clean up Main Street by passing laws prohibiting gambling and prostitution. She and many other locals hoped to see El Paso shed its "Sin City" reputation. El Paso, where Spanish was spoken more often than English, soon became two cities—one known for its breweries and saloons and one known as the center of trade in the Americas, with four railroads connecting it to San Antonio, Los Angeles, Santa Fe, and Ciudad Juárez, Mexico. A fast-growing young city with no real border separating it from Ciudad Juárez, El Paso was the center of the Americas.

Eugenia Schuster.
Courtesy of The University of Texas at El Paso Library Special Collections Department.

This proximity to Mexico ensured that El Paso would not only be a crossroads, but that it would be drawn into Mexico's troubles. With the 1911 Battle of Juárez, the Mexican Revolution reached El Paso's city limits, threatening the

Downtown El Paso, ca. 1910-1920. *Courtesy of Otis A. Aultman Collection, El Paso Public Library.*

newly developing prosperity of the border boomtown. The Mexican Revolution brought with it another medical caregiver, a Mexican woman by the name of Teresita Urrea, accused of inciting Mexicans to fight the revolution. Even as the Daughters of Charity and Eugenia Schuster were putting their European stamp on the city, Teresita, a local *curandera,* or healer, was dedicating her life to healing the poor. All of these women, of European and Mexican ancestry, worked tirelessly to care for El Pasoans as well as Mexican refugees who fled to El Paso to escape the revolutionary fighting.

The Schusters had an unusual relationship with Pancho Villa, one of the Mexican Revolutionary generals. After the Battle of Juárez in 1911, one of Pancho Villa's emissaries asked Dr. Schuster to tend to his boss, who was ill just across the border in Ciudad Juárez. When Dr. Schuster arrived, Villa was sitting behind a desk. Pointing to a stack of gold, Villa said, "Now doctor, this is what you get if you cure me." Then pointing to a pistol, he said, "And this is what you get if you don't." Dr. Schuster, also pointing to the gold and pistol, replied, "General Villa, I want to cure you and I don't want either one of them."

Dr. Schuster's relationship with Pancho Villa may have helped when Eugenia Schuster and Mrs. Albert Madero formed a group called the

Pancho Villa. *Courtesy of the Otis A. Aultman Collection, El Paso Public Library.*

Amigo Listo in 1915 to help feed, clothe, and provide healthcare to the over 60,000 refugees who came to El Paso from Mexico. Eugenia, with a group from *Amigo Listo,* approached General Villa to ask his help to feed the refugees fleeing the war. As a result of her visit, General Villa agreed to send a cart full of beans to El Paso each day.

After Michael's death in 1918, Eugenia continued to run the hospital until just before her own death in 1946. Eugenia Schuster led by example. She was responsive, thoughtful, and attentive to everyone's needs. She gave a great deal of thought to the well-being of El Paso as a whole and through her efforts, Eugenia brought great visibility to Providence Hospital, the El Paso community, and to herself. When asked how she felt about giving up her life as a noble in Vienna for a life as a caregiver in El Paso, she replied that she found it very interesting and rewarding to shape a town from its infancy.

The El Paso County Medical Society, founded in 1898, had few standards and fewer requirements for admission. All that was needed was a letter from a medical school, a twenty-five dollar filing fee, and that the applicant be a white male. According to Barbara Dent, El Paso medical historian, women physicians, as well as male physicians of other races, could not join. More significant, if you were not a member of the El Paso County Medical Society, you could not join the Texas Medical Association, and if you weren't a member of the state association, owners and board members of local hospitals, who decided who could be on their hospital staffs, often would not grant hospital privileges.

The stated purpose of the El Paso County Medical Society was to promote "fraternity,

Mexican Revolution Refugees. *Courtesy of the Otis A. Aultman Collection, El Paso Public Library.*

mutual improvement, and public weal" with an emphasis on much needed mutual improvement. Western medicine in the late 1800s was quite primitive. Regular or mainstream physicians still used leeches and twelve-blade scarifiers to perform bloodletting and prescribed mercury and other chemical compounds to force patients to regurgitate the impurities that might be causing their illness. Mainstream doctors believed that disease was caused by an overstimulation of nerves and blood and that these heroic therapies would restore the natural balance of fluid in the body. Doctors created their own prescriptions by mixing ingredients with a bit of sugar and forming pills or suppositories. They used newly invented instruments, including the stethoscope, created so that they would not embarrass a woman patient by putting an ear to her chest.

It was in this environment that Dr. Alice Blackadder Merchant (1860-1940), a Canadian by birth, came to El Paso to practice medicine. She graduated from New York College of Eclectic Medicine in 1891 and married Judge W. B. Merchant the same year. She practiced medicine in Fort Worth from 1891-1893 before moving to El Paso. A degree in eclectic medicine meant that she was an "irregular" physician trained in alternative therapies. She, along with others in her field, launched an effective attack on mainstream medicine by pointing out that it simply was not working. Mainstream physicians sometimes used the term "quack" to discredit such alternative physicians. With regular and irregular physicians trading charges, the general public, unfortunately, had no idea whom to believe.

Physicians trained in eclectic medicine believed that doctors should work in tune with the body and use herbal remedies and natural treatments rather than the techniques of bleeding and chemical purging common at the time. In some ways, Dr. Merchant's practice had more in common with *curandera* Teresita Urrea than with her male contemporaries. Dr. Merchant was quick to realize that in El Paso, as well as the rest of Texas, men and women were partners in adversity, but not in other ways. When she first started practicing in El Paso, she was not admitted to the El Paso County Medical Society because she was not viewed as an equal in business or politics. In the late 1800s, no US women had the right to vote. It's not hard to imagine, then, that women like Dr. Merchant had difficulty earning respect as professionals. Like most Southerners, many Texas men and women opposed women's suffrage. The prevailing notion at the time was that women didn't need to vote because men were supposed to take care of them and protect them from such unseemly work as politics. Participation in business and politics would only make women crude and unpolished and would result in their neglecting their primary duties as wives and mothers. To many Texans, women's suffrage was a dangerous affront to the well-established social order.

Suffragists like Alice Merchant, who advocated giving women the right to vote, pointed out that women were citizens, too, and so should be entitled to vote. They encouraged other women to see the right to vote as the opportunity to use their feminine perspective to improve their communities for themselves and their families. As the result of the work of Alice Merchant and others, bills to allow women to vote were introduced in the Texas House of Representatives numerous times between 1895 and 1919, but were never passed. Discouraged by the lack of action, a women's suffrage club was formed in Austin in 1908. By April 1913, more than 100 people from seven Texas cities met in San Antonio to form the Texas Woman Suffrage Association. Men were allowed to join the organization, but blacks were not. When the El Paso Colored Woman's Club applied in 1918, the state leadership refused to act upon its request, in effect denying the group access to state and national membership. The leadership feared that inclusion of blacks would alienate voters both inside and out of the organization.

By June 1918, there were ninety-eight suffragist organizations in Texas, part of a growing national suffragist movement. They sponsored lectures, conducted debates, marched in parades, and distributed thousands of pamphlets. In June 1919, the federal women's suffrage amendment was passed and submitted to the states for ratification. Under pressure from the federal government, the Texas House and Senate finally passed the bill, and Texas became the ninth state to ratify the Nineteenth Amendment, prohibiting states from denying the right to vote to any citizen because of sex.

The League of Women Voters of Texas, a nonpartisan political organization, formed in 1919. Dr. Merchant was an officer in this state organization and remained active until her death in 1940 in this consortium that lobbied for legislation in support of women's issues: minimum wage, maternity care, infant care, improved rural education, and equal representation at national party conventions.

Another female physician, Dr. Ida Shope Bishop (1856-1934), reportedly followed her physician husband to El Paso, where they both established medical practices. She was born in Lacell County, Illinois, and attended homeo-

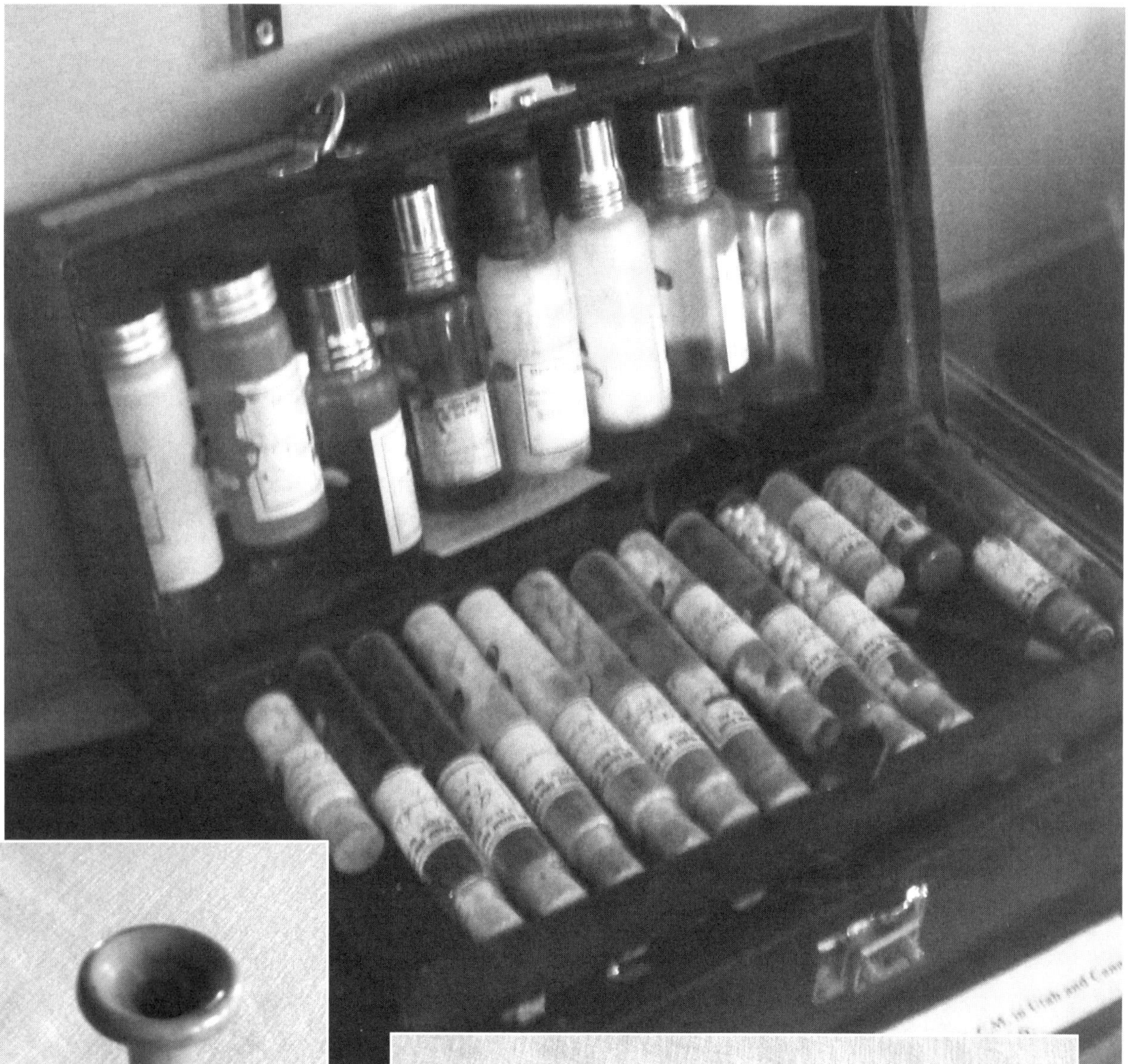

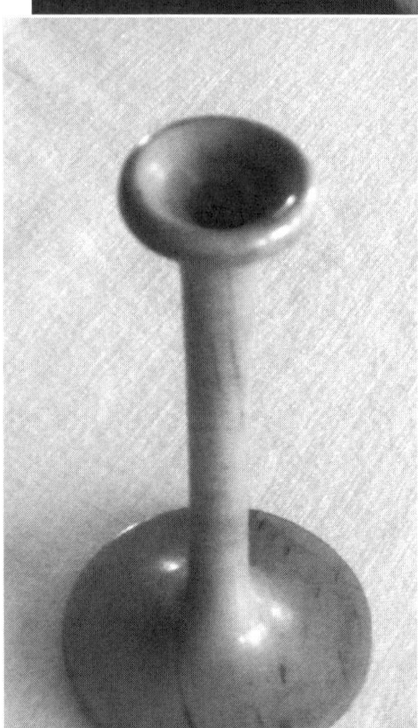

Photo collage of doctor's bag (top), stethoscope (left), and scarifiers (right).
Courtesy of the El Paso County Medical Society.

pathic medical school at Woman's Medical College in Atlanta, Georgia, completing her training in 1892. Homeopathy, much like a degree in eclectic medicine, ensured that Dr. Bishop used a holistic approach to treating her patients. She would conduct a long interview with each patient and gather information on all of the symptoms before providing a simple remedy. Dr. Bishop, who practiced medicine from 1898 until 1931, first in Galveston and then El Paso, was the first woman admitted to the El Paso County Medical Society and the State Medical Association of Texas in 1907, the first year women were allowed to join. She was president of the El Paso Pioneer Women's Association and served on the local committee for the State Medical Association of Texas convention held in El Paso in 1922. Soon after, she moved to Winslow, Arizona, where she died in 1934.

Dr. Mattie Foster Hill (1871-1937), a short, petite woman, was granted a Texas medical license at the age of thirty-eight in 1908. She was born in Weiland County, Province of Ontario, Canada, and practiced medicine from 1903 until 1935. Dr. Hill's El Paso practice was located in the First National Bank Building, with hospital privileges at the Masonic Hospital. Like most doctors of her time, she did a little of everything, including delivering babies. Nancy Miller Hamilton, El Paso author and historian, was delivered by Dr. Hill and went to her as a child. She remembers Dr. Hill as very capable, but somewhat rough when handling her patients. Dr. Hill, who had one son, was very active in local bridge circles until her death in 1937.

It wasn't long after women were able to vote that they came into their own as leaders in the medical profession. While Dr. Merchant was busy working at the state level on women's suffrage, Doctors Bishop and Hill were making their mark in the State Medical Association of Texas. In 1922, they are both listed on the local planning committee for the state convention held in El Paso. This was an extremely prestigious event for El Paso and a testament to the reputation of local physicians, including women, in Texas medicine. It was almost as though the right to vote also granted women full acceptance into the medical profession.

Membership in the state association was in the thousands, and those who traveled to El Paso for the convention stayed at fifteen different hotels, paying up to three dollars per night. Mayor R. E. Thomason welcomed the delegates. Over half of the presentations, with titles such as "The Value of Sunshine," were on the topic of tuberculosis. Texas doctors were impressed when the Mexican Army Band of Ciudad Juárez performed for them and the international bridges remained open late into the night, giving them the opportunity to visit Ciudad Juárez.

Two years after Providence Hospital opened in 1902, El Paso's first woman dentist arrived in town. Isabel Welsh Hoenes (1878-1975) was tall, with dark, wavy hair. A large-boned womanwith a square jaw, bright eyes, quick wit, and a no nonsense manner, she was a member of an ambitious Iowa family. While Isabel attended dental school, her sister, Ernestine, also attended medical school.

At her 1903 graduation from Northwestern University Dental School in Evanston, Illinois, Isabel listened to the president of the university, Edmund James, give an address in which he called for respect for this relatively new field, asking his audience to consider dentistry a

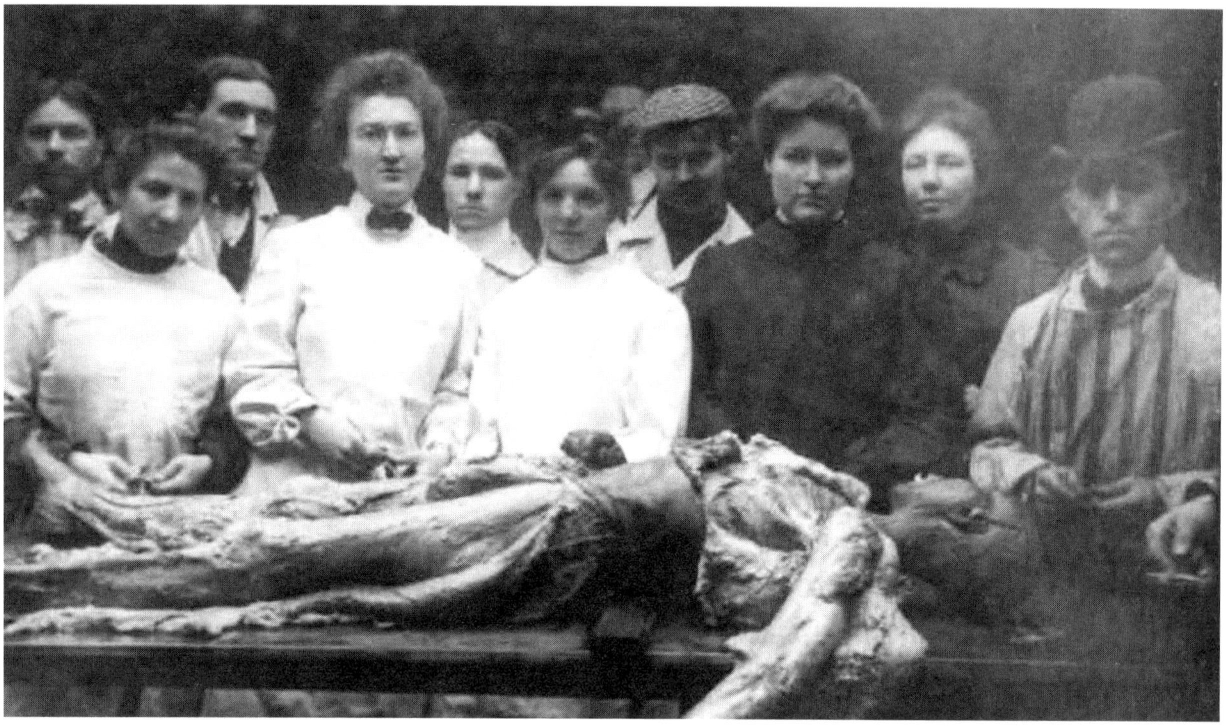

Isabel Welch Hoenes (dark dress) in an anatomy class, Northwestern University Dental School, ca. 1900.
Courtesy of John Gnauck.

learned profession, as was "law, medicine, theology, and teaching." Because the school had just opened in 1894, he felt it necessary to convince the audience that dentistry was a profession not to be practiced by just anyone, such as barbers who would sometimes remove teeth as well as cut hair. Instead, dentistry was an organized, ethical profession that required years of education and training.

Upon completion of her education, Isabel was handed a list of towns that needed a trained dentist. She chose to relocate to El Paso, a town that few people had heard of, but was as free-spirited and independent as she was. Shortly after arriving, she met and married Gustavo Hoenes, a German immigrant who fought in the Spanish-American war. Early in their marriage, they lived a pastoral life in the lush, green agricultural Lower Valley, a place that may have reminded Isabel of her Midwestern roots. Soon after, she and Gus built a house on Altura Street. It wasn't long, though, before Gus wanted to move on to California. Still independent, Isabel decided to live alone in the small El Paso home until 1939, when she moved to an old apartment house behind the Scottish Rite Hall. After Gus left, Isabel devoted herself to her true love: dentistry.

Dr. Hoenes opened her dental practice in the Blumenthal Building and then later moved to the fifth floor of the larger First National Bank Building, on Texas and Oregon Streets.

Her office windows afforded a birds-eye view of early 1900s downtown. When the automobile

North Oregon Street, El Paso, Texas, ca. 1919.
Courtesy of the Otis A. Aultman Collection, El Paso Public Library.

replaced the horse and buggy, Isabel watched as the men on the street tipped their hats to Josephine Clardy Fox, a wealthy socialite, as she drove down Texas Street in her open car.

Smelling of iodine with a touch of cloves, Dr. Hoenes' offices consisted of a waiting room, procedure room, and a personal office. The beautiful dark varnished wood walls and small white hexagon tile floors created a home-like atmosphere in stark contrast to the dental equipment housed within the procedure room. Most conspicuous, of course, was the chair placed near the window to take advantage of the light. Next to the dental chair was the milk-colored glass bowl with swirling water, a hinged tool cabinet, and, looming over the patient, the dreaded belt-driven arm-shaped drill that cut so slowly you could see actual smoke coming out of the

Cloudcroft, New Mexico, ca. 1910–1920.
Courtesy of the Otis A. Aultman Collection, El Paso Public Library.

patient's mouth. Practicing dentistry before the widespread use of anesthesia, Dr. Hoenes reportedly asked her male patients to hang up their guns on the coat pegs next to the door before sitting in the chair and, according to her great-niece, Gretchen Frasier, asked some of her young patients to, "Sit still! Don't be a baby about it. It will be over before you know it."

In spite of her stern disposition and even though she had no children of her own, Dr. Hoenes loved children and was the first El Paso dentist to offer school dental exams. She often provided dental services free of charge or for barter. A founding member and early president of the El Paso District Dental Society, Dr. Hoenes loved her practice, calling it both her profession and her hobby. She recommended that any dentist who didn't enjoy the work, "do something else." She also loved music and flowers, attending the El Paso symphony and, when time permitted, slipping away to a rented Cloudcroft cabin in the summers to enjoy the abundant wildflowers.

Dr. Hoenes practiced dentistry in El Paso

until 1970. Active in the Texas Dental Association, American Dental Association, American Association of Women Dentists, and the American Association of University Women, she received the Texas Dental Association's highest award, the Order of the Good Fellows. In spite of all of her career accomplishments, Dr. Hoenes never forgot one facet of her early El Paso dental career. Her great-nephew, John Gnauck, describes a time in the 1960s when he picked up his then wheelchair-bound Aunt Bell at an El Paso Dental Society meeting to take her back to her apartment. As he was transferring her from the chair to the car, she mentioned that although the association had honored her that evening, she still remembered the time when some of the men in the association felt that she should not be a member of the El Paso Dental Society. Aunt Bell explained matter-of-factly, "They wanted me to join the auxiliary because I was a woman."

Dr. Hoenes' philosophy of life, "Just take it and like it," was as down to earth as she was. Her fondest wish was to die with her boots on in her adopted Southwestern home and to be buried in the family plot of her beloved Iowa prairieland.

European, Canadian, Mexican, and US Midwestern women all converged on El Paso at the turn of the twentieth century to make a new home for themselves and their families. Some were devout, others were stern, but they were all smart, with amazing work ethics. Although some were wives, they didn't really belong to their husbands. At a time when most women were content to be wives and mothers, the Daughters of Charity, Eugenia Schuster, and Drs. Merchant, Hill, Bishop, and Hoenes chose their own direction. All of these women's success as medical caregivers derived from the fact that they seemed never to forget that the purpose of their efforts was not to bring visibility or praise to anyone, but to ensure that El Paso, their newly adopted home, continued to grow and prosper. Because of these efforts, they deserve both visibility and praise from generations to follow.

Bibliographic Essay

Whenever possible, I interviewed people who knew the women in this chapter. Mardee de Wetter was especially helpful with details on the lives of Eugenia and Michael Schuster, Nancy Miller Hamilton on Dr. Mattie Hill, and John Gnauck and his family on Dr. Elizabeth Hoenes. John Gnauck even set up a family Wiki to gather information on his great-aunt. Another valuable source on Eugenia Schuster was an oral history interview of Eugenia's daughter, Margaret Schuster Meyer, recorded in the 1980s by Carol Viescas for The University of Texas at El Paso Oral History Institute.

For the other women in the chapter, I relied solely on secondary research. As a result, the details of their lives are limited to "Just the facts, ma'am." Most helpful with finding these facts were UTEP librarians Laura Hollingsed and Abbie Weiser of the C. L. Sonnichsen Special Collections Department and UTEP student Judith Rivera. Daniel Gonzalez of the El Paso Public Library was extremely helpful and efficient, scanning photos of early El Paso on very short notice. Medical historian Barbara Dent was extraordinarily supportive, providing a tour of the El Paso County Medical Society museum, describing the medical profession in the late 1800s and early 1900s, locating information on

Doctors Merchant, Bishop, and Hill, and fact-checking the final version of the chapter. Bruce King and Michelle Edwards were especially understanding as they listened to me tell these women's stories again and again. Our editor, Marcia Hatfield Daudistel, and my colleagues who also authored chapters provided invaluable counsel throughout the entire process. Mardee de Wetter, John Gnauck, and Carol Clark also provided suggestions for improving the final version of the chapter.

In addition to newspaper articles in the *El Paso Times,* medical records, dental journals, and newsletters, I found the following secondary sources to be especially helpful: Barbara Funkhouser, *The Caregivers: El Paso's Medical History, 1898-1998* (El Paso, TX: Sundance Press, 1999) and Geneva Fulgham and Elizabeth Silverthorne, *Women Pioneers in Texas Medicine* (College Station, TX: Texas A&M University Press, 1997).

To learn more about El Paso's medical history between 1880 and 1920, I relied on the *El Paso County Historical Society,* http://www.elpasohistory.com, El Paso Community College *Borderlands,* http://dnn.epcc.edu/nwlibrary/borderlands, and David D. Romo, *Ringside Seat to a Revolution: An Underground Cultural History of El Paso and Juarez, 1893-1923* (El Paso, TX: Cinco Puntos Press, 2005). For information on the Texas suffragette movement, I depended upon the *Handbook of Texas Online*, http://www.tshaonline.org/handbook/online.

The striking photograph of Isabel Welch Hoenes is from the Gnauck family collection and the photographs of the medical equipment were taken at the El Paso County Medical Society museum. Most of the other photographs are from two online El Paso Public Library collections: The Otis A. Aultman Collection and the El Paso Photographic History Collection.

Chapter 13

MINDING THEIR BUSINESS: FROM DAIRIES TO BALLGOWNS

by Susan Goodman Novick

WITH THE ARRIVAL of the railroads in 1881 and into the twentieth century, El Paso changed from a small town on the Rio Grande to a city full of opportunity. The *El Paso, Texas and Paso del Norte, Mexico Business Directory for 1885* heralded its qualities:

> The City of El Paso is no longer a mere suburb. It is the great converging point for the railroads of the Southwest. It has grown from a small adobe hamlet to the dimensions of a city, lit with gas and electricity, provided with the only international street car line in the world, and claiming a population of enterprising and progressive people whose achievements in the past are an able and trustworthy guarantee for the future.

Further along, the *Directory* describes El Paso's citizens:

> Composed of and directed by an aggregation of people, at an earlier and later period, from the best circles of distant society, the influences have always been toward elevation, and as a result there is today a well-governed community upon the highest plane of moral worth, intelligence, hospitality, and refinement. This is a new community to each other largely and to the locality in a great degree, yet the useful unity now existing is an incontrovertible that goodness reigned and does reign supreme. Come from where you may, you will always find yourself at home when seeking the best society.

Although the railroads brought other types to El Paso—gunslingers, gamblers, and prostitutes—the city's promoters highlighted those assets that would encourage newcomers to move to El Paso and start businesses. By 1905, the *City Directory* reiterated this boastful attitude:

> As a smelting, mining, trading, cattle, and railroad center, El Paso is unexcelled in the West, and with the perfection of irrigation

> methods she is already becoming of importance as the chief city of a surrounding agricultural community. Cattlemen, miners, prospectors, railroad builders, and hundreds of other classes make their headquarters at El Paso, where they buy their supplies and equip themselves for expeditions into the surrounding mountains and plains, and trade is brisk the year around.
>
> A great number of details could be given that would interest anyone seeking for homes, business, or investments, but in line with our purpose of condensation, we leave the details to be investigated by the thousands who are constantly figuring on making El Paso their home, and thus verify the strength of our assertions herein made.

Among the people who made El Paso their home in the twentieth century, and who blazed trails in its business and professional community were four women who were instrumental in the success of their family businesses, were entrepreneurial with their talents, and were major forces in the El Paso community. As cofounders with their husbands of small family businesses that grew to major companies as a result of El Paso's growth in the twentieth century, Mary Smith Price and Hana Farah both faced the challenge of their husbands' deaths and took on the leadership of their businesses. Effie Day, orphaned in her teens, traveled from Colorado to Paris and New York to learn the art of dressmaking and design, and plied her trade at the Popular Dry Goods Company for thirty-seven years, designing and making dresses for El Paso's leading young women. Having faced employment discrimination as a newly-minted lawyer in El Paso in 1946, Ruth Kern spent her career fighting for civil rights as well as women's political and reproductive rights.

These women share several qualities that speak to the uniqueness of El Paso and their talents as businesswomen. They moved to El Paso from the Northeast and Midwest, seeking better economic opportunities or a healthier climate. Their businesses provided products that were in demand as El Paso continued to expand, leading to their commercial success. They were mothers who raised children, who later worked in the business, and instilled within them their values and entrepreneurial spirit. And they involved themselves in El Paso's non-profit community, volunteering for and supporting their places of worship as well as other important community organizations.

The journey of Mary Smith Price to El Paso began in 1866 in her hometown of Ashton, West Virginia. The daughter of an Irish father and an English mother, Mary Smith grew up on a farm on the Ohio River, receiving the religious training and education befitting her family's role in the community. She ventured 130 miles north from her home to attend and graduate from Denison University in Granville, Ohio, a liberal arts institution founded by frontier Baptists. It was there that she met Mark E. Price of nearby Newark, Ohio, and they married in March of 1890.

They lived their early married life on a farm in the Welsh Hills, the area where the Price family had farmed since the 1780s. Mary soon became the mother of seven children, two of whom died in infancy. For fifteen years, Mark and Mary Price labored at the farm, harvesting fruit, farm products, and livestock. In 1905, however, Mark Price decided to move to the Southwest in search of a better and healthier life.

Mary Price in the 1920s.
Courtesy of the Price/Curlin family.

At that time, Mary's brother, Dr. Robert Bruce Smith, served as pastor of the First Baptist Church of El Paso, and he suggested that the family make its new home there.

For one year after their arrival in January 1905, they leased the Coffin Ranch in Clint, where they grew fruits and other produce. Desiring to be closer to El Paso and Dr. Smith, the family moved to a house at 1616 Wyoming Street. It was there that Mark and Mary Price purchased their first cow, a crossbred Jersey-Durham, and their second a month later. Their two older sons, Russell and Bob, barely in their teens, delivered the milk to their neighbors in a hand-drawn wagon. This was the beginning of Price's Dairy.

With increased demand for milk in a growing city, the business began to expand, and the Prices moved the dairy to Alameda and Piedras Streets and then to a newly acquired and equipped facility nearby. Horse and wagon replaced humans, enabling milk to be delivered throughout the city that grew every day. With so much growth in just two years, the Price family enjoyed its early success.

Unfortunately, Mark Price had been suffering from a stomach ailment for many years, and his health began to fail in 1907. Less than a year after having an appendectomy in 1908, Mark died, leaving the business in the hands of his wife and sons. A family friend wrote of the challenge that Mary faced after her husband's death:

> With but a few cows for her small beginning of a dairy, she drove ahead, and with vast stores of pluck and energy and good, common sense, the five boys and their mother worked, worked with zeal, through the days and weeks and years, early and late, and knew no such word as failure, and never entertained a thought of giving up. The children must go to school, and yet the cows must be fed and the milk delivered. Up bright and early in the morning, the family faithfully performed all duties before school time and after school hours in the afternoon. How all the work was accomplished and how the youngsters were kept in school at the same time, no one knew but Mary Smith Price.

For the next ten years, Mary Price served as the active head of Price's Dairy. While her sons were in college at the University of California at Berkeley and the University of Arizona, as well as serving in the military during World War I, she oversaw the company's expansion and ensured

Mary Price and her sons among the herd at the Price's Dairy on Alameda Street in 1909.
Courtesy of the Price/Curlin family.

its reputation for wholesome milk. Continued growth, however, necessitated the separation of the production and distribution parts of the dairy. In 1918, Mary Price moved her herd of over one hundred milking cows to a farm near Canutillo, Texas; when her sons returned from their military service in 1919, they recognized that their mother had made the right decision.

At the farm in the Upper Valley of El Paso, Mary Price imported and developed the finest herd of milk cows in Texas, including the famous Beth de Kol Segis, a champion who later produced more milk and butterfat over a period of six years than any other cow of her class in the entire United States. Price's was known to have the best cows and the highest bred stock in the Southwest. A contemporary wrote of Mary Price:

> In short, from a modest beginning, and with hard competition and all kinds of obstacles to overcome, the transcendent business genius of this quiet, reserved, and modest woman, steadily but surely led upward and onward the enterprise in which she was most interested.

In 1921, the Prices built a modern pasteurizing and distribution plant on North Piedras Street, and they bought a 250-acre farm near Vinton, Texas. And the next year, Mary Price and her sons formed Price's Dairy Company, Inc.

Left: Mary Price surrounded by her sons in 1929. From left to right: David Price, Russell A. Price, Mary Price, Robert B. Price, Paul W. Price. At that time, three of her sons were involved in the dairy. *Courtesy of the Price/Curlin family.*

Below: An advertisement for Price's Milk in the *El Paso Herald* on November 9, 1928. *Courtesy of the* El Paso Herald.

and elected Mary Price, its founder, as president. At this time, Mary Price turned most of the responsibility of running the business to her sons, and although she retired from active management, she continued to provide advice and counsel to her sons.

In 1929, the milk distribution of Price's Dairy merged with other leading dairy product companies to form Midwest Dairies, Inc. of El Paso, which later became a subsidiary company of Creameries of America, Inc. Mary Price continued her involvement with the company into the 1930s. In 1932, she assisted with the organization of Valley Gold Dairies in Albuquerque, later buying the plant property for the company.

For the last years of her life, Mary Price lived in her home on Silver Street, enjoying her family and grandchildren until her death at the age of seventy-one on August 8, 1937. Some highlights of her achievements were written in a Memorial Book produced by the dairy:

She had built and managed a growing business organization, while at the same time she looked after the comfort of her home and family. Men who worked for her listened willingly to both her praise and her reproof. They undoubtedly felt that they

> stood before a woman, just but firm, exacting, too, perhaps, but they respected her.

A condolence letter sent to her family by the head of the International Association of Milk Dealers conveyed similar sentiments:

> Her service to our industry should command the admiration of all those connected with it. What an interesting and delightful character she must have been, founder, president, and active in a business which is a decided success—this is the stuff that makes America.

From that one cow, Mary Price and her husband started a dairy that today provides El Paso, Southern New Mexico, and Mexico with 152 quality dairy products and sponsors community education activities through its "Give 'Em Five" program. Through her dedication, perseverance, courage, and strength, Mary Price raised a family and a business, both of which have made countless contributions to El Paso for over a century.

Hana Farah stood by her husband and sons as together they developed a company that became an El Paso success. Her story begins in Baskinta, Lebanon, where she was born in 1896 and lived with her parents and ten siblings. The second eldest daughter of Aftimous Abihider, an Eastern Orthodox priest, Hana Abihider moved with her family to Lawrence, Massachusetts, in 1910 so that her father could serve a congregation there. At the age of fourteen, young Hana enjoyed life in a new country.

About the same time, a young man named Mansour Farah left the same town in Lebanon bound for a new life in the United States. He and his brother Androus stayed with cousins in Santa Fe before they moved to Las Cruces, New Mexico, to open a dry goods business. While on a trip to New York to buy merchandise in 1915, Mansour Farah mentioned to friends that he was looking for a wife. These friends knew that Reverend Abihider had eligible daughters to court, so Farah took a train to Massachusetts and left three weeks later with Hana Abihider as his bride.

The couple returned to Las Cruces in June 1915 and began their life together. Their son James (Jimmy) was born in 1916, followed by William (Willie) three years later in 1919. At that point, Mansour and Androus Farah had developed their business interests to include a dry goods store and a hay brokerage business, and they opened the first movie house in Las Cruces. Seeing how El Paso was growing, Mansour felt he had an opportunity to venture into the manufacturing business. He moved his family to New York in August 1920 for a brief time so that he could study shirt-making design and production at an industrial design school.

When the family returned to the Southwest in the fall of 1920, Hana and her sons stayed with relatives in Rincon, New Mexico while her husband looked for a home in El Paso. He found a home on Yandell Avenue and rented a 1,250 square-foot room on San Francisco Street to make shirts. There Hana and Mansour Farah founded the Farah Shirt Manufacturing Company. In this small place, five employees worked on six sewing machines to produce blue cotton chambray work shirts sold under the Apache (Legion) label for thirty-five cents each.

Hana Farah looked back at those early days in an interview in 1972:

Mansour Farah and workers at the Farah factory on Oregon Street, 1924. *Courtesy of the Farah family.*

> I watched the workmanship and production to make sure every shirt was perfect. Frank [Mansour] was janitor, cutter, bookkeeper, traveling salesman, and yes, he was an inventor too . . . oh, he was EVERYBODY! I came down only half a day. The boys were small. They needed me and I needed them.

As demand for the shirts increased, the Farahs had to find more space. In 1924, they moved to a larger facility on South Oregon Street and moved to a 5,000 square-foot factory on Leon Street two years later. Hana faced the challenges of this growth along with her husband. One day, they opened the factory and noticed that an order of fifty shirts, which had been ready for shipment, had been stolen. She remarked, "Thank God we didn't worry, and we started to work again and made up for it."

As they grew up, Jimmy and Willie Farah worked at the factory after school and Hana Farah supervised the seamstresses. The growing firm was by then employing twelve to fifteen women on the production lines. It was at this time that Mrs. Farah installed a radio in the sewing rooms to provide music for the seamstresses, introducing what may have been the first of the company's program of employee benefits.

During the Depression, the federal government used convict laborers to produce chambray shirts, and, faced with this competition, Mansour and Hana Farah decided to branch out and manufacture blue denim work pants, enabling their company to prosper in lean times. Bib over-

Jimmy and Hana Farah, with framed photograph of Mansour Farah between them.
Courtesy of the Farah family.

alls, khaki shirts and khaki pants were added to this line in 1935, and to accommodate this growth, the Farah Shirt Manufacturing Company bought the old *El Paso Times* building at 208 San Francisco Street in 1939. Sadly, Mansour Farah died in May 1937 at the age of fifty-two, and his wife and sons took over the operation of the company, running it as a partnership. As he had begun his work as a shipper and cutter at the factory in 1932 before his graduation from El Paso High School, Jimmy Farah assumed the role of president at the age of twenty-one.

With the onset of World War II, the company faced the challenges of sustaining growth during wartime. Willie enlisted in the US Air Force in December 1941 and flew in combat missions over Europe throughout the war. On the home front, Hana and Jimmy oversaw the shift of production from civilian to military use and Farah began to produce combat fatigues and military uniforms. The plant production record of 359,000 consecutive pairs of pants without a rejection and five consecutive work weeks without an absence earned Farah Manufacturing the US Army-Navy "E" flag, awarded on November 3, 1944. Farah was the first apparel manufacturing plant west of the Mississippi to earn this award which recognized the company's high production rate per employee, the saving of critical materials, its willingness to meet unexpected demands, and the willingness of employees to put in long hours of overtime in emergencies. In addition, the quality of the Farah garments was described as outstanding in the entire country.

An *El Paso Herald-Post* article on November

Hana Farah accepts the Army-Navy "E" flag award on November 3, 1944. She sits between Brig. Gen. J. A. Porter, commanding general of the San Antonio Army Services Depot and Lieut. Commander Gordon S. Hanson of Houston. *Courtesy of the Farah family.*

3, 1944 detailed the activities of the hundred women whom Hana supervised as they stitched the cuttings:

> The deft fingers of the girls moved so rapidly that a visitor gets the impression they are consciously working for victory. 'These girls know they are helping the war effort,' Mrs. Farah said. 'They deserve a lot of credit. The cutting room employees also deserve much credit.'

The award was presented at the Farah Manufacturing Plant at a colorful ceremony at which US Army and Navy officials, city and county officials, and more than 1,200 El Pasoans gathered to honor the management and employees of the company.

When Willie returned from his service in World War II, the partnership became a corporation when he became the vice president and plant manager. In 1953, the plant moved into a new building on South Cotton Avenue and Third Street, where 650 workers worked in the most modern clothing manufacturing factory in the Southwest. The company continued to prosper, producing 2,000 pairs of private-label boys' jeans and reaching sales of seventeen million dollars in 1957. As Farah Manufacturing grew, it took a unique approach to employee relations, providing free medical care, a subsidized cafeteria program, free bus transportation, and its own profit-sharing and retirement plan.

Just nine months before the company broke ground on its large Gateway West facility in September 1964, Jimmy Farah died, and his

Above: Hana Farah and other company officials on the floor of the New York Stock Exchange on July 14, 1967, when the Farah Manufacturing Company was listed on the exchange.
Inset: A Farah logo from 1952. *Courtesy of the Farah family.*

brother Willie took over as president. On July 14, 1967, the Farah Manufacturing Company sold shares on the New York Stock Exchange, becoming a publicly-held corporation. And Hana was there when it happened. Her experience was recalled in an article in the *El Paso Times* in 1970:

> One of her proudest recollections is her trip to New York when Farah Manufacturing Co. stock was listed on the New York Stock Exchange. The family, officers and directors of the company appeared at the Exchange at the appointed time for the announcement that Exchange officials make when a new stock is admitted for listing. Naturally, Hana started out on the floor with all the officers and directors in the party. A distressed Exchange official told her that no women were ever permitted on the trading floor. But he was overruled when another official pointed out, 'Mrs. Farah is not only a vice president, she is cofounder of the company.' So Hana Farah is possibly the first women ever to set foot in that hallowed area of finance.

Hana Farah served as a director of the Farah Manufacturing Company until 1970, but she continued to visit the plant daily, helping to serve lunch in the plant cafeterias or supporting the staff in one of the company's in-house medical clinics. Her grandson James C. Farah notes, "she was always focused on expressing the Farah family's interest in the well-being of the employees." And her grandson remembers the dinners that she shared with her six grandchildren, a weekly event that she hosted at her home until her death.

In the 1960s, Farah opened plants in Belgium and Hong Kong and continued to operate seven domestic manufacturing plants: five in El Paso, one in San Antonio, and one in Las Cruces. Combined, the plants employed 9,500 employees and produced $150 million in annual sales. The company's growth in this decade begat labor disputes in the 1970s. In May 1972, 4,000 garment workers at four Farah plants in Texas and New Mexico (85 percent of them women) went out on strike over wages, pension benefits, unrealistic production quotas, and union recognition. Continuing until the workers won union representation in March 1974, the strike included a national boycott of Farah products. The twenty-month long strike weakened Farah Manufacturing and caused the termination of 5,000 jobs and the closure of all domestic plants outside of El Paso. Not only did Hana live through this difficult situation, she witnessed her son Willie being ousted from his position as chief executive officer by the board of directors in 1977 and reinstated in that position by court order the following year.

In July 1978, Hana Farah died, and her death was a loss for the family and the community. In the following years, Farah Manufacturing experienced the ups and downs of the apparel manufacturing industry, and was eventually sold to Tropicana Sportswear in 1999, which was bought by Perry Ellis International in 2005. Fifty-eight years after Hana and Mansour Farah started sewing shirts on San Francisco Street, she could rest well knowing that the company she cofounded had provided a living for thousands of El Pasoans and spurred the incredible growth of El Paso's apparel manufacturing sector. Hana's grandson, James C. Farah, comments on her legacy:

> With the help of opportunities Farah offered, many men and women, including first generation immigrants, gained the ability to provide their families with better income, health care, and educational opportunities to advance their futures. The children and grandchildren of these pioneers have become professionals, as well as business and community leaders, excelling beyond their parents' and grandparents' wildest dreams.

A designer of original fashions at the Popular Dry Goods Company for thirty-seven years, Effie Day dressed generations of El Paso women for their high school proms, their college dances, their Sun Carnival coronations, and their walks down the aisle as brides. Even after her retirement and death, she was lauded by an *El Paso Herald-Post* reporter in 1968 for her unique creations:

> A person of near legendary proportions to residents of El Paso and the Southwest, Miss Day gained a wide reputation for her original designs. Young ladies of the community were all well aware of the impor-

> tance of wearing a "Miss Day Original" for an important occasion. She became the greatest name in the Southwest for her original gowns, especially formals, ball gowns, and wedding gowns, and her originals were considered a "must" for an all important coronation.

Remembered as a polite woman eager to please her clients, Effie Day was entrepreneurial in that once she designed a formal dress early in a woman's life, she had a good chance of designing additional garments as the woman matured. And she prospered in El Paso, a growing city whose connections to Fort Bliss and Ciudad Juárez created a unique social environment for elegant entertaining.

Miss Day, as she was known by her clients and her superiors at the Popular Dry Goods Company, El Paso's largest department store, knew that she wanted to be a fashion designer from a young age. She was born in Texas in June 1879 but grew up in Pueblo, Colorado, becoming an orphan in her teens. She finished high school, saved some money from a job, and left at seventeen with her sister to go to Paris, France, to learn everything she could about fine dressmaking and design. After spending three months there, she spent a month in New York learning about fashion design before she returned to Colorado.

Effie Day's journey to El Paso began during the flu epidemic of 1917 when her doctor suggested she go to a dry climate to recuperate. Before she came to El Paso, she worked in Hollywood designing dresses for the movies. Along with Marguerite, her younger sister, Miss Day moved to El Paso and, with her dressmaking skills in hand, she began work at the Popular on January 2, 1923. It was there that she began to design and make wedding dresses for the daughters of El Paso's leading families. She kept scrapbooks of the dresses she had made for countless brides, most likely a marketing tool used to entice other clients.

Effie Day remarked about her bridal gown work in an article in the *El Paso Herald-Post* in 1959:

> I always feel it is a privilege to make a bridal gown. All of a girl's dreams and ideals are incorporated in her ideas for a bridal gown. Some come in with very definite ideas about what they want, while others are dreamy-eyed and vague about it all. I go along with the desires of the girl whose ideas are already firmly fixed, and I help the other type in selecting a style which will be becoming and will fit her personality. The former girl is easier to work with, because she knows what she wants and doesn't change her mind or leave anything to chance.

Miss Day was able to showcase her considerable talents in 1935 when she designed the Queen's gown for the first Sun Carnival coronation in El Paso. The long blue net gowns worn by the children of the court were also designed by Miss Day. The *El Paso Times* on December 29, 1935 provided a detailed description of the Queen's gown, robe and train:

> The elaborate coronation robe of Alençon lace was studded with tiny rhinestones and silver bugle beads. The bodice of the dress

Right: Effie Day in 1959, when she was named "Woman of the Week" in the *El Paso Herald-Post* on November 13, 1959. *Courtesy of the* El Paso Herald-Post.

Above right: During the Depression, Miss Day would consult with clients regarding their fashion concerns and help them find or make suitable clothes. This advertisement was in the *El Paso Herald-Post* on August 24, 1935. *Courtesy of the* El Paso Herald-Post.

Above: Sun Queen Ruth Staten and the children of her court at the coronation in December 1935. From left to right: Laurence Nickey, Betty Ruth Williams, Frances Zork, and Ann Schwartz. Seventy-five years later, the four children of the court still live in El Paso. *Courtesy of Ann Schwartz Schaechner.*

Mary Jo Ponsford Melby in her gown designed by Miss Day.
Courtesy of El Paso Woman's Club Records, MS 576, Special Collections Department, University of Texas at El Paso Library.

> is made with a high neck in front and a deep V décolletage in back. The rever collar, which is draped on each side, falls in points on either side. The dress is posed over white satin, draping the lines of her figure. Wide princess bands extend low over the hip line, to which a full skirt is attached. The fullness of the skirt is obtained by the use of fan-shaped inserts of accordion pleated panels. The skirt is slightly entrain. The full court train, made of silver cloth and metallic lace, is attached to the high Duchess collar, also of silver cloth. The collar is trimmed with silver cloth roses with insets of rhinestones.

Throughout her career, Effie Day designed and supervised the making of gowns for the Sun Carnival Court. Mary Jo Ponsford Melby, a duchess in the 1960 Sun Carnival Court, has kept the chiffon gown and the matching opera coat that she wore in the court fifty years ago. Melby recalls that Miss Day made sketches of twelve different gowns that would be made in the same fabric and visited with each duchess to let her choose the gown that would suit her. "The year I was a duchess Miss Day designed twelve different long dresses in the same pink chiffon to go with long, hot pink opera coats. We were in heaven!" And the gown and coat are in fine shape, even today.

Melby remembers getting her first Miss Day party dress when she was fifteen years old and a student at El Paso High School. She recalled the process by which Day designed the dress:

> I would sit down with her and she would ask, 'What do you see, what are you thinking? Would you like flowers, ribbons, flounces, ruffles?' I told her what I'd like and she would sketch out her ideas. When I saw what she had sketched, I knew that this was a dress made just for me . . . I was getting a Miss Day dress.

Miss Day made four other dresses for Melby, some of which she has packed in their original boxes from the Popular Dry Goods Company. Melby marvels at the construction of the dresses, the attention to detail, and the fact that the dresses have lasted through the years. "All of her designs were timeless. You could wear them today."

Effie Day's reputation extended beyond El Paso and the Southwest. In the 1940s and 1950s, she designed and shipped dresses to women who attended Vassar, Stephens, Smith, Sophie Newcomb, Mills, and other colleges. "Her dresses are to be seen on ballroom floors in college towns from the East to the West," wrote the *El Paso Times* in 1953.

> Scores of beautifully-gowned college girls mingled with their escorts in dress uniforms at the West Point formal ball. Suddenly a girl from El Paso clutched her escort's arm and said, 'Oh, look! There's a Miss Day dress!' 'Well what on earth is a Miss Day dress?' the young man inquired, being one of those unfortunates who never lived in our town. The young lady explained that they were dresses designed and made by Miss Day of El Paso with a style so beautiful and distinctive that a girl who has ever worn one can always recognize a Miss Day dress anywhere.

In that same year, Miss Day spoke of the pride she had in her work:

> It is gratifying to see how happy a girl is with one of my designs . . . to see her eyes glow when she has the final fitting and know that the 'Miss Day' formal has come to life and is really hers. Then it is wonderful to watch her grow up remembering her first formal, the gowns for the various high school and college festivities and finally to create her wedding gown. This is what makes life worth living and memories worth remembering.

In addition to the Sun Carnival, Effie Day designed dresses for the Cotton Style Shows that the Popular sponsored as part of the Maid of Cotton events. Beginning in the late 1920s, when the first Cotton Style Show in the United States was held in El Paso, Effie Day supervised the production of the cotton styles modeled in the show and she worked on the fashion shows throughout her career at the Popular. In fact, she designed the dress that El Pasoan Beverly Pack wore when she was named Maid of Cotton in 1954 in Memphis, Tennessee. During Peck's reign, she served as a goodwill and fashion ambassador of the cotton industry in a five-month, all-expenses-paid tour of more than thirty major American cities from coast to coast.

Effie Day retired from the Popular on June 25, 1960, ending a thirty-seven year career. She passed away in Waurika, Oklahoma, on September 1, 1964 at the age of eighty-five. At her funeral at Restlawn Memorial Park in El Paso, pallbearers included Herbert Schwartz, the president of the Popular, as well as W. R. Dorris, the piece goods buyer who supplied her with the exquisite fabrics and accessories that were part of the elegant dresses she designed throughout her life.

Born on August 22, 1914, in Chicago, Illinois, the daughter of working-class Swedish immigrants, Ruth Kern grew up poor on Chicago's South Side in a small frame house her father built. She excelled in both academics and athletics and worked her way through college and law school as a file clerk and as a legal editor for *Commerce Clearing House,* supervising the work of five assistant editors. She received her law degree at Chicago-Kent College of Law in 1946, the only woman in her graduating class. After six months working in a law office in Chicago and getting a divorce, she was told by her doctor that for her son's health, she should move to a better climate. She chose El Paso as her home in 1946 and lived and worked in El Paso for fifty-six years prior to her death. El Paso is a far better community today because Ruth Kern chose to make it her home. But her many accomplishments did not come without struggle.

Ruth Kern's challenges began immediately upon relocating to El Paso from Chicago. Even though she had a law degree, she encountered sex discrimination in employment. With a wry laugh and a broad smile she often told the story of her interviews with law firms in El Paso in the late 1940s. "They looked at me like I was from Mars when I told them I was an attorney," she said. "They had never heard of a woman attorney before and certainly had never seen one." As a result, Kern was unable to find work as an attorney and had to take work as a legal secretary. She worked for a title company and for County Judge Victor Gilbert. As she used to put

Ruth Kern. *Courtesy of David Kern.*

it with her characteristic grin: "I was one whiz-bang secretary!"

Kern remarried in 1949 and her young son Peter was soon joined by boy and girl twins, David and Suzan. For the next eighteen years her priorities were on raising a family. In an interview in the *El Paso Times* in August 1979, she remarked, "I stayed at home and was a housewife and mother. And when the kids started school, I did volunteer work." During those years she kept active in various civic activities including the McCall Day Nursery, the Jaycee Wives, the Sisterhood of Temple Mount Sinai, and the National Council of Jewish Women, where she was one of the founders of the El Paso County Book Fair.

After raising a family, and at an age (fifty-four) when many people start thinking about retirement, Ruth Kern began a new career. She took some education courses and thought about teaching, but her old love for the law resurfaced. She had been out of practicing law for so many years that she had to study and take the bar exam all over again. One summer, she set up a card table in the living room of her home in Kern Place and piled it high with law books. She spent that summer poring over the texts and refreshing her memory of the law. Then she took and passed the Bar in Texas on her first try and finally achieved her life-long goal of becoming a practicing attorney. She was sworn in as a member of the State Bar of Texas on September 27, 1967, the only female lawyer engaged in full-time practice in El Paso at that time. She first practiced with another lawyer at what she described as "starvation wages" and then struck out on her own as a sole practitioner.

In the early 1970s, Ruth Kern attended the first meeting of the El Paso Women's Political Caucus. "I went to the first meeting and it was a marvelous experience," remembers Kern. "The women who came were all dynamic, interesting, and excited. I hadn't realized there was an organization through which you could work." And she became involved with the National Organization for Women, giving workshops and speaking about women's political and reproductive rights, rape awareness, women and the law, and family law. In 1978, Kern helped identify the need for a shelter for battered women in El Paso, secured funding, and established the shelter (the YWCA Transitional Living Center), which is still in operation today.

Throughout her career, she worked tirelessly to improve the community, further the rights of women, and protect those in unfortunate circumstances. Ruth Kern helped to establish the El Paso County Women's Bar Association (when there were only five female lawyers practicing in El Paso) and served as its first president. She also took and passed a very difficult certification exam and became Board Certified in Family Law by the Texas Board of Legal Specialization, a high distinction earned by only a small fraction of Texas lawyers. Concentrating on divorce, adoptions, child custody suits, and other family-related cases, Kern helped countless clients deal with domestic violence and divorce. "I think the women's movement is responsible . . . for women feeling free to leave a marriage if it's totally unsatisfactory. I had one woman who had been married fifty years. She was just out of the hospital. Her husband had shot her and it was not the only time. She finally had decided not to put up with it. Before the women's movement, I think she would have gone meekly home and felt she had no alternative." Kern helped many divorced women by encouraging them to aspire to more than a clerical position as they looked for employment.

A watershed moment came in Ruth Kern's life in October 1976 when she was raped and beaten by a stranger in her own backyard in broad daylight. In keeping with her life-long philosophy of seeking the greater good from every situation, she gathered her closest friends and advisers around her and made the decision to go public about the rape. In 1976, when rape was still considered a shameful secret, Kern's decision to go public was very controversial. Nevertheless, undaunted by public conventions and stigmas, she spoke out about her ordeal in the hope of inspiring other women who had been raped to not let their shame silence them. "I feel no shame for being raped. I am not afraid to tell my story because I feel it is important that rape is viewed for what it is—a vicious and violent act," she told the *El Paso Times* in 1976. Her courageous act inspired countless other women to come forward and prosecute their attackers and brought greater awareness of what rape is to the entire community.

Kern also believed strongly in achieving social change through non-violent political action. Working with the American Civil Liberties Union, Kern and another attorney filed and won "the long-hair suit" against the El Paso Independent School District on behalf of the civil liberties of students. She specialized in draft counseling during the Vietnam War, which she opposed, and was proud of the fact that she never had a client drafted. She also helped to identify inhumane conditions at the El Paso County Jail and, with two other attorneys, filed a class-action suit on behalf of the prisoners that resulted in a new jail being built. Kern also served on the committee to pass the bond issue for the new jail construction.

Ruth Kern accomplished all that she did despite the fact that she became legally blind in the 1970s as a result of macular degeneration, and could no longer read or write without the aid of high-tech visual equipment. She did not consider herself disabled and never let her visual condition slow her down in her constant quest to achieve justice for her clients and in the community at large. Kern continued in the full-time active practice of law well into her seventies. And, even into her eighties, she continued her community work by teaching law courses to senior citizens at UTEP's Center for Lifelong Learning.

Ruth Kern was tirelessly devoted to the causes she believed in. Without her work, there might not have been a shelter in El Paso for the victims of domestic violence, or an advocacy center for AIDS victims, or a jail with humane conditions for its residents. Without Kern's help, a long list of women's organizations might not have been created, or achieved what they did: the El Paso Women's Bar Association, the El Paso Older Women's League, and the El Paso Women's Political Caucus, among others.

Ruth Kern passed away on January 26, 2002, at the age of eighty-seven, and written on her gravestone is the phrase, ". . . justice, justice, shall you pursue." These words from the book of Deuteronomy sum up Kern's life and have inspired her children to follow her values and her love of teaching and the law. Her son Peter is a college professor, and David and Suzan are both lawyers who have devoted their careers to achieving justice and equality in the workplace as well as defending the rights of immigrants.

The lives of these four women illustrate those qualities important to entrepreneurs and businesswomen today—perseverance under adversity, flexibility, creativity, courage, and family and work balance. These women came to a new place, made it their own, and prospered. The companies they started and worked for became major forces in the El Paso economy in the twentieth century. And their legacy has continued through their children and grandchildren, many of whom remain here, to make El Paso a place of continued opportunity.

Bibliographic Essay

I am grateful to several of the descendants of the women profiled who gave me access to source material and photographs. Tom Curlin, great-grandson of Mary Price, provided me with a memorial article detailing her life as well as relevant correspondence. James C. Farah, Hana Farah's grandson, recalled his memories of Hana Farah and provided an oral history of her from 1975. I based the life of Ruth Kern on a memorial article that David and Suzan Kern wrote about their mother.

A review of the "Society Pages" of the *El Paso Herald-Post* and the *El Paso Times* provided information on Effie Day's creations, as did conversations with women who wore Miss Day originals. Mary Jo Ponsford Melby showed me some of the gowns that were designed for her by Effie Day, and Ann Schwartz Schaechner and Frances Zork Litt told me of their involvement in the 1935 Sun Carnival coronation. I also consulted the Popular Dry Goods Company Records (MS 317) of the Special Collections Department of The University of Texas at El Paso Library for information on Miss Day.

About the Contributors

Meredith E. Abarca earned a PhD in Comparative Literature from the University of California at Davis. She is associate professor of English at The University of Texas at El Paso. Her courses include Chicana/o Literature, Mexican American Folklore, Film and Literature of the Americas, Critical Theory, and Women Philosophers in the Kitchen. Her work has been published in edited anthologies and scholarly food journals. She is the author of *Voices in the Kitchen: Views of Food and the World from Working-Class Mexican and Mexican American Women* published by Texas A&M University Press, 2006. *Voices in the Kitchen* was a finalist for the 2007 Liz Carpenter Book Award. Her latest work appears in *Storied Dishes: What Our Family Recipes Tell Us about Who We Are and Where We've Been.*

Irasema Coronado earned a PhD in political science from the University of Arizona and is professor and associate provost at The University of Texas at El Paso. Her area of specialization is comparative politics. Her research interests include border politics, cross-border cooperation, environmental and gender issues on the US-Mexico border region. She is co-author of the books *Fronteras No Mas: Toward Social Justice at the US-Mexico Border* and *Politicas: Latina Public Officials in Texas.* She is co-chair of the Coalition Against Violence Toward Women and Families on the US-Mexico Border.

Marcia Hatfield Daudistel is the editor, most recently, of *Literary El Paso,* published by TCU Press in 2009 and winner of the 2010 Border Regional Library Association Southwest Book Award. As the former associate director of Texas Western Press, she helped publish over seventy books and established the bilingual imprint Frontera Books. Daudistel is the West Texas/Trans Pecos editor of *Texas Books in Review.* She is on the advisory committee of the Made in Texas: Cultivating Teachers to Engage Mexican American Literature in Middle and High School Classrooms project. She was a presenter at the 2009 Texas Book Festival and was also a member of the first Texas Book Festival on the Road committee. Daudistel is a member of The Friends of the University of Texas at El Paso Library Board and a 2009 Hertzog Award committee judge. She was a presenter at the March 2011 annual meeting of the Texas State Historical Association. She is currently at work on a book with award-winning photographer Bill Wright.

LUCY FISCHER-WEST received her BA from The University of Texas at El Paso. Fischer-West was a finalist for the Mary Jon and J. P. Bryan Leadership in Education Award for the Texas State Historical Association in 2008. Her articles and essays have appeared in *Border-Senses*, *Password*, and *Literary El Paso*, as well as the following Texas Folklore Society Publications: *The Family Saga: A Collection of Texas Family Legends*, *Both Sides of the Border: A Scattering of Texas Folklore*, and *Celebrating 100 Years of the Texas Folklore Society: 1909–2009*. Her book *Child of Many Rivers: Journeys to and from the Rio Grande* won a Southwest Book Award from the Border Regional Library Association, a WILLA Literary Award Finalist Award from Women Writing the West, and a Violet Crown Special Citation from the Writer's League of Texas. She teaches world history at Cathedral High School.

MIMI REISEL GLADSTEIN is the author of five books and coeditor of two, one of which, *The Last Supper of Chicano Heroes: Selected Works of José Antonio Burciaga*, won an American Book Award and a Southwest Book Award. Her books and articles cover a diversity of subjects ranging from Steinbeck, Hemingway, and Faulkner, to Ayn Rand, feminism, and film adaptations. At The University of Texas at El Paso she has chaired the English and Theatre Arts Departments, served as associate dean of liberal arts and was the first director of the Women's Studies Program. Her work on Steinbeck has won national and international awards and she currently serves as president of the John Steinbeck Society of America. The El Paso Commission for Women named her to their hall of fame in 2011.

NANCY MILLER HAMILTON received her BA and MA from The University of Texas at El Paso. She retired in 1990 as associate director of Texas Western Press. Hamilton edited and wrote for the university's magazine *Nova*, and for *Roundup*, the magazine of Western Writers of America. She is the author of *Ben Dowell: El Paso's First Mayor* and *UTEP: A Pictorial History*, as well as many articles for journals and other publications and is a past president of Western Writers of America.

YOLANDA CHÁVEZ LEYVA is a Chicana historian and writer who was born and raised on the border. She is currently chair of the department of history and an associate professor at The University of Texas at El Paso. She has spent her life listening to and now documenting the lives of people who live on *la frontera*. She specializes in border history, public history, and Chicana history. She has directed various public history projects focusing on the US-Mexico border over the past decade. Most recently, she served as Project Developer for "El Paso: The Other Side of the Mexican Revolution," a groundbreaking museum exhibit on El Paso's role in the Revolution. She serves as codirector of Museo Urbano, an indoor-outdoor museum located in El Paso's *Segundo Barrio*. Dr. Leyva is revising a manuscript entitled *Cruzando la Linea: Mexican*

Children on the Texas-Mexico Border, which investigates the ways in which the presence of children has shaped the border historically. She has published numerous articles on Chicana, lesbian, and border history. In addition, she is a published poet.

DEANE MANSFIELD-KELLEY was born in Big Spring, Texas, and comes from many generations of Texas women. She received her BA from Texas Western College, MA from The University of Texas at El Paso, and her PhD from The University of Texas at Austin. Professor of English at The University of Texas at El Paso, Dr. Mansfield-Kelley specializes in southwestern literature, Native American literature, and detective fiction. She and Dr. Lois Marchino are coauthors of *The Longman Anthology of Detective Fiction* (2005), republished as *Death by Pen: The Longman Anthology of Detective Fiction from Poe to Paretsky* (2007). Dr. Mansfield-Kelley also teaches a course on Native American women writers that is used in the Women's Studies Program.

LOIS A. MARCHINO is a long-time professor of English at The University of Texas at El Paso. She received her PhD from The University of New Mexico at Albuquerque. Her literary areas of specialization are detective fiction and women in literature. Dr. Marchino and Dr. Mansfield-Kelley coauthored *The Longman Anthology of Detective Fiction* (2005), republished as *Death by Pen: The Longman Anthology of Detective Fiction from Poe to Paretsky* (2007). Dr. Marchino has written numerous articles on women writers, including one on Texas women who write detective fiction. She is also a former director of the Women's Studies Program at The University of Texas at El Paso.

ADAIR MARGO received her BA in art history from Vanderbilt University, studied Renaissance art in Florence, Italy, with Syracuse University, and earned her MA in art history from New Mexico State University. Margo owns Adair Margo Fine Art. She has recorded and coedited the oral histories of artists Tom Lea and José Cisneros, and writes on El Paso's arts and culture for *El Paso Style* magazine. She chaired the President's Committee on the Arts and the Humanities from 2000 to 2008 and was a member of the United States National Commission for UNESCO from 2003 to 2008. Margo received citations from the governments of Mexico and the United States for strengthening international relationships—the Aguila Azteca from President Felipe Calderón in 2007 and the Presidential Citizens Medal from President George W. Bush in 2008.

SUSAN GOODMAN NOVICK is a certified archivist who works with families, organizations, and businesses to organize and preserve their historical records. A native El Pasoan, she served as an archivist/manuscripts librarian at the Special Collections Department of The University of Texas at El Paso Library prior to starting her archives consulting business. Novick serves on the advisory board of the Museum and Cultural AffairsDepartment of the City of El Paso as well as on the executive committee of the Friends of the Smith College Libraries. She is a member of the Academy of Certified Archivists and the Society of Southwest Archivists. Novick holds a master of science in library science from The Catholic University of America, a master of public affairs from The University of Texas, and an AB in history from Smith College.

Born in 1987, KIRSTIN JACKLYN PEREZ has been a proud resident of El Paso, Texas, since the age of five. As an undergraduate, Perez obtained a four-year dual-degree in English-American literature and history while working and maintaining a 4.0 GPA in both majors. Appointed as a graduate research assistant under the directorship of Dr. Brenda Risch, Perez eagerly anticipates completing the MA Literature Program in the fall of 2011. While in the graduate program, she recognized the importance of civic engagement and giving back to the community. Her internships include the Women's Fund of El Paso, which raised over $200,000 dollars for single mothers and other deserving women in the El Paso-Las Cruces region through the "Power of the Purse" event, and United Way's Young Leader's Society. Board appointments include PFLAG (Parents, Friends of Lesbians and Gays), UTEP's Women's Advisory Board, and Triota Women's Honor Society. For the City of El Paso, Kirstin was a founding member of both political action committees to protect health care benefits (2010) and El Paso For Equality (2011), which sought to amend the city charter to include an anti-discrimination clause. Currently, the upcoming May 2011 election has become a side endeavor. Consulting the campaigns for City Representative candidates Cortney Niland and Lyda Ness-Garcia has ignited the desire to seek public office in the future. She lives daily by the quote, "The service to others is the rent you pay to live here on earth" (Muhammad Ali).

EVELYN POSEY, PhD, is a professor of rhetoric and writing studies in the department of English at The University of Texas at El Paso. With Kate Mangelsdorf, she authored three textbooks: *Choices: A Basic Writing Guide with Readings* (2008), *Discoveries: A Step-by-Step Guide* (2006), and *The World of Writing: A Guide* (2011). She was principal investigator for a $3.4 million National Science Foundation grant for the advancement of women in science and engineering, and now serves as a consultant for improving the recruitment of women faculty. She served UTEP as chair of the department of English, associate dean of Liberal Arts, and associate vice president for Academic Affairs. For her work in the El Paso community, she received the YWCA REACH Award and was inducted into the El Paso Women's Hall of Fame and the El Paso Technology Hall of Fame.

BRENDA RISCH, PhD, is the director of women's studies at The University of Texas at El Paso and assistant professor of women's studies. She earned her master's and doctorate in comparative literature from the University of North Carolina at Chapel Hill and her bachelor's degree from Northwestern University. She was chosen as a Fulbright scholar to study in Augsburg, Germany, and also as one of only twenty-six US women to attend the prestigious 2000 International Women's University held in Hanover, Germany. She studies gender issues with topics such as community organizing, women and technology, the body, feminist film, and German film. Her community efforts in North Carolina and El Paso have included projects as diverse as racial justice activism, organizing conferences, founding a lesbian health resource center, and serving as the president of a community television station.

Index